8.80

Vertical Man/Horizontal World

VERTICAL MAN

Laurence Ricou

HORIZONTAL WORLD

Man and Landscape in Canadian
Prairie Fiction

UNIVERSITY OF BRITISH COLUMBIA PRESS

VERTICAL MAN/HORIZONTAL WORLD
MAN AND LANDSCAPE IN CANADIAN PRAIRIE FICTION

The book has been published with the help of a grant from the Humanities
Research Council of Canada, using funds provided by the Canada Council.

Library of Congress Catalog Card Number: 73-80447
International Standard Book Number 0-7748-0022-4 (cloth)
0-7748-0023-2 (paper)

Printed and bound in Canada
by
T. H. Best Printing Company Limited

For Treva

Contents

Preface

For who are we? We merely are intruders.

PETER STEVENS, "Saskatchewan"

Man on the prairie, as portrayed in Canadian fiction, is defined especially by two things: exposure, and an awareness of the surrounding emptiness. The basic image of a single human figure amidst the vast flatness of the landscape serves to unify and describe Canadian prairie fiction. This is the image—to turn for a moment to poetry—which is so striking in Peter Stevens's "Saskatchewan":

> All skylocked, this enormous flatness holds
> Like a prehistoric beast a long machine
> Angularly unheroic.[1]

While Stevens's immediate reference is to an automobile, it soon becomes clear that the "prehistoric beast" is also man, trapped in a landscape from which "there's no escape or hideout," and confronted with the problem of his own significance: "For who are we? We merely are intruders."

I was born and raised in a small prairie city, so my interest in this image of prairie man as questioning intruder came, I suppose, naturally enough. Yet it was not until I moved to Toronto that I began to read large numbers of western writers, and to sense how distinctive the prairie landscape was. Then the theme began to emerge. Again and again the prairie writer gave unusual prominence to landscape; often it almost became an obsession. The very obvious contrast of man to land, man's dramatic vertical presence in an entirely horizontal world, presented itself in an intriguing variety of contexts and was used for remarkably different artistic purposes. So obvious was the image, it seemed, that, despite the history and persistence of the land as a theme in Canadian criticism, few commentators had even mentioned it, and hardly any had explored it with thoroughness.

Those were the impressions which began to occupy my attention and to lead first to a doctoral thesis for the University of Toronto, and then to the present study. In the process I wished to provide an understanding of a pervasive image

[1] *To Every Thing There Is a Season: Roloff Beny in Canada,* ed. Milton Wilson (Toronto: Longmans, 1967), pp. 118-19.

ix

and a deep-rooted theme which, though they, more than any other, unified a regional literature, have been ignored or taken for granted. This purpose dictated the mention of a number of minor fictions which are of very limited relevance to my further intention of providing, through detailed critical comment from a single perspective, new insight into the meaning and achievement of Canadian prairie writers.

Limiting this study to Canadian fiction is somewhat arbitrary since the prairie does not end abruptly at the United States boundary. But examining only the impact of the physical landscape one would expect similar themes and images to occur in the fiction of the American Middle West; Sinclair Lewis's *Main Street* or Wallace Stegner's *Big Rock Candy Mountain*, for example, lend support to the assumption. My heavy reliance throughout this book on Wallace Stegner's *Wolf Willow* (and Stegner's own comments on his confused identity) is further evidence of the difficulty of drawing national lines in literary study. On the other hand, though I have not attempted a detailed comparative study, it seems that nowhere in American fiction is the image of man as vertical intrusion so prominent, or so insistent as I have found it to be in Canada.[2] Willa Cather's *O! Pioneers* or *My Antonia* provide some parallels; Owen Wister's *The Virginian* juxtaposes giant man and infinite spaces; Walter Van Tilburg Clark's *The Oxbow Incident* shows no awareness of man's relation to landscape. Clearly much of the difference can be attributed to the rich tradition of the Wild West in American popular literature, a tradition in which sensitivity to landscape has little place.

When Edmund Wilson notes the Canadian writer's consciousness of "infinite forbidding spaces,"[3] his implication is that while the United States shares the spaces, those spaces have not been found to be nearly so forbidding. This idea is developed in Marcia Kline's essay, *Beyond the Land Itself*. She notes that the natural world as described in American literature is usually moral and understandable, "a metaphor for that harmonic and superior state, Nature,"[4] while the more typical Canadian nature is so terrifying that man turns away from it. Thus Natty Bumpo continually moves on into the wilderness when threatened by civilization, while the English garrison at Detroit, in Richardson's *Wacousta*, is trapped and terrified by the savage ferocity surrounding it. The myth of the garden, which Leo Marx has shown to be central to the American experience,[5] has only very limited application to a country where the more usual themes are the severity of climate or the unsuitability of the land for

---

[2]Various useful studies of the land in American literature seem to bear out this impression: Henry Nash Smith, *Virgin Land* (Cambridge: Harvard University Press, 1950); Wilson O. Clough, *The Necessary Earth* (Austin: University of Texas Press, 1964); Edwin Fussell, *Frontier* (Princeton: Princeton University Press, 1965); Roy W. Meyer, *The Middle Western Farm Novel in the Twentieth Century* (Lincoln: University of Nebraska Press, 1965).
[3]Edmund Wilson, *O Canada* (New York: Farrar, Straus and Giroux, 1965), p. 96.
[4]Marcia B. Kline, *Beyond the Land Itself* (Cambridge: Harvard University Press, 1970), p. 25.
[5]Leo Marx, *The Machine in the Garden* (New York: Oxford University Press, 1967), *passim*.

cultivation. Applying Kline's distinctions to prairie fiction helps to explain the particularly sharp contrast between man and landscape in the writing of the Canadian prairie. As Henry Kreisel expresses it in the only essay to investigate at any length the meaning of the prairie in Canadian fiction: "Man, the giant-conqueror, and man, the insignificant dwarf always threatened by defeat, form the two polarities of the state of mind produced by the sheer physical fact of the prairie."[6] In its many variations this basic image, man standing out in the prairie, an obvious intruder, appears in most of the fiction set on the Canadian prairies.

Obviously, setting, in itself, does not fundamentally alter the theme of fiction. Man's consideration of his own nature in the universe and his formulation of a personal philosophy to deal with the emptiness—emotional, cultural, intellectual—that is so much a part of his world is, of course, a universal theme. What is noteworthy about Canadian prairie fiction is that the imagination so often starts with the same basic image to explore these questions. The landscape, and man's relation to it, is the concrete situation with which the prairie artist initiates his re-creation of the human experience. Even those writers who do not use this image explicitly can be seen to be utilizing it tangentially.

From this perspective Canadian prairie fiction is the record of the implication of man's exposure, for, as Kreisel's comment suggests, he may be anything from a giant swelled with a sense of his independence and power to a miniscule speck, cowed by his insignificance and mortality. Still more significant, it is the record of man's response to the emptiness, to the hollowness so often found at the core of life, to the void beyond, which is death.

For the earliest prairie writers the emptiness did not exist, or if it existed it was ignored. Some writers made of the emptiness a lush garden, a world of beauty and plenty where human relations ran according to a widely accepted, if simplistic, moral pattern. While Robert Stead represents the culmination of this tendency, his novels also contain the seeds of a new willingness to face the emptiness and to try to understand it. This willingness was given its greatest impetus by Frederick Philip Grove. In his novels we find that the image of man in the level landscape, whatever its metaphorical overtones, is still very literal—his protagonists are mainly farmers, devoted to the day-to-day task of cultivating the land. The image is developed on new planes of experience by Sinclair Ross and W. O. Mitchell.

Finally it is seen to inform the works of the past two decades when the literary imagination has faced, with a new spirit of adventure and courage, the bewildering emptiness of twentieth-century human experience. For the recent writers of Canadian prairie fiction, the totality of the vacuum in the modern age was dramatically mirrored in their own physical landscape. The use and

[6]Henry Kreisel, "The Prairie: A State of Mind," *Contexts of Canadian Criticism*, ed. Eli Mandel (Chicago: University of Chicago Press, 1971), p. 256.

development in fiction of the image of man in the prairie landscape, leading up to the sophistication of these more recent authors, is the subject of the following chapters. Man, in sum, is vertical—and vertical is waking, consciousness, health; land is horizontal—and horizontal is sleeping, unconsciousness, debilitation.

Several new expressions of these themes have appeared since this book has been in press: in the frugal prose of Terrence Heath's *The Truth and Other Stories*, in the frantic journey of Ken Mitchell's *Wandering Rafferty*, in the nostalgia for a prairie boyhood of Harry Boyle's *The Great Canadian Novel*, and in an American graduate student's discovery of the northwest in Robert Kroetsch's *Gone Indian*. Recent criticism, too, has provided new insights, most notably W. H. New's *Articulating West*, and Eli Mandel's "Romance and Realism in Western Canadian Fiction" in *Prairie Perspectives 2*. While it is frustrating that these and other works appeared too late for inclusion, it is a great pleasure to note the vigorous development which they represent.

I would like to thank Professors G. H. Roper (Trent University), F.W. Watt (University of Toronto) and, especially, D.G. Lochhead (Toronto) for their advice and encouragement during the preparation of the first version of this study. Of my many generous colleagues at the University of Lethbridge, Professor W.C. Latta has been particularly helpful. Miss Dorothy Phillips typed the manuscript with patient good sense.

Parts of this book appeared originally in somewhat different form in "Empty as Nightmare: Recent Canadian Prairie Fiction," *Mosaic, A Quarterly Journal for the Comparative Study of Literature and Ideas*, University of Manitoba Press, Vol. VI, No. 2 (Winter 1973), 143-160 and "From King to Interloper: Man on the Prairie in Canadian Fiction 1920-1929," In *The Twenties in Western Canada*, Ed. Susan Trofimenkoff. Ottawa: National Museum of Man, 1972, pp. 5-31.

For permission to quote from the unpublished works of Frederick Philip Grove I am deeply grateful to A. Leonard Grove.

University of Lethbridge   Laurence Ricou
April, 1973

I Trying to Embrace Our World: An Introduction

> A few speculative images
> shyly define our place
> trying to embrace our world
> the necessarily outrageous flats
> pitted against the huge sky.
>
> PETER STEVENS ''Prairie: Time and Place''

Anyone who writes on the fiction of the Canadian West would do well to start with a tribute to the author of the only book-length study of the subject yet attempted. I turn first, though, not to Edward McCourt's *The Canadian West in Fiction*, but to his travel book, *Saskatchewan*, a work filled with sensitive observations about man's life on the prairie.

> The Saskatchewan prairies are a world that enables man to see himself clearly in relation not only to his fellow men but to those values that are inherent not in the Many but in the One. It is a world that persuades him to accept the fact of his own curious duality—that he is at once nothing and everything, at once the dust of the earth and the God that made it; a world that permits him to come to terms, perhaps subconsciously, with that dualism which, in Sir Thomas Browne's mystic previsioning, ''maketh pyramids pillars of snow and all that's past a moment.''[1]

The prairie man, McCourt is suggesting, is subtly distinctive: in his contradictory sense of supreme self-importance and total insignificance, in his understanding of time, particularly in the singularity of his upright position on a ''great empty plain,'' which stimulates these other sensations. McCourt's comment corresponds to what many readers feel about the fiction of the Canadian prairie: that there is a remarkable unity in it, and that the unity derives from the unusual and continuing prominence which writers have given to the landscape. It is no doubt true, in fact, that McCourt's own observations derive almost wholly from his literary experience and scarcely at all from empirical evidence.

Implicit in those observations is the idea that man is an intrusion in this landscape. Basically, to relate man to the prairie landscape is to become conscious of the striking contrast between the vertical and the horizontal. Though the geometric image is always implied, it is explicit often enough that Stephen Scobie can draw on it in a recent story both to make a point, and to burlesque a tradition:

---

[1]Edward McCourt, *Saskatchewan* (Toronto: Macmillan, 1968), p. 224.

He spoke horizontally. I thought, goddamit, I've got to get this horizontal/vertical thing out of my head! There must be other ways of thinking about life. But he did speak horizontally, that was the only word you could use. Long vowels, long pauses between words. Clipped t's and d's sticking up like telegraph poles, along a flat horizon.[2]

Both a broad generalization from an intelligent travelogue, and a specific character description from a contemporary short story, depend, almost unconsciously, on a landscape made distinctive by the dramatic visual impact of a single vertical object in a completely horizontal world. Two random examples do not, of course, make a convincing case, but they do indicate the direction for a fascinating, and I think productive, approach to Canadian prairie fiction. How thoroughly, and in what fashion, one asks, did this vast, level landscape enter into the psychology and the literature of our prairie west?

This is the regional form of a question legitimately asked of all Canadian literature. As early as *The History of Emily Montague* (1769) the physical environment seems to be shaping the national consciousness: "I no longer wonder the elegant arts are unknown here [writes Arabella]; the rigour of the climate suspends the very powers of the understanding: what then must become of those of the imagination? . . . Genius will never mount high, where the faculties of the mind are benumbed half the year."[3]

Arabella's opinion of the influence of land and climate is one which has, in its various ways, shaped Canadian literature from *Wacousta* to *La Guerre, Yes Sir!*, from Albert Lozeau to Al Purdy. What the artists sensed immediately, however, was not so readily accepted by others. Nineteenth-century observers of Canadian culture, preoccupied with British precedents, believed that until a wealthy, leisured class had arisen, no great literature was possible.[4] Sir John George Bourinot seems to have noticed the tendency of Canadian poetry, but only long enough to hope it would soon change: "Descriptions of our meadows, prairies and forests, with their wealth of herbage and foliage, or artistic sketches of pretty bits of lake scenery have their limitations as respects their influence on a people. Great thoughts or deeds are not bred by scenery."[5]

By 1926, however, Lionel Stevenson was finding cause for joy in Canadian literature's concern with nature. He wrote: "In Canada the primordial forces are still dominant. So Canadian art is almost entirely devoted to landscape,

---

[2]Stephen Scobie, "Streak Mosaic," *Stories from Western Canada*, ed. Rudy Wiebe (Toronto: Macmillan, 1972), p. 162.
[3]Frances Brooke, *The History of Emily Montague* (Toronto: McClelland and Stewart, 1961), p. 90.
[4]See, for example, two articles in *The Canadian Monthly and National Review*: James Douglas, "The Intellectual Progress of Canada During the Last Fifty Years and the Present State of its Literature," VII (June 1875), 465-76; and J.E. Wells, "Canadian Culture," VIII (December 1875), 459-67.
[5]Sir John George Bourinot, *Our Intellectual Strength and Weakness* (Montreal: Foster Brown, 1893), p. 24.

Canadian poetry to the presentation of nature. . . . Canadian poetry is
. . . concerned with the apocalyptic. The poetic mind, placed in the midst of
natural grandeur, can scarcely avoid mysticism."[6] Such observations have
become so commonplace that it seemed inarguable when Robert Fulford told
us in 1967 that "we are still governed by the land, because we can see no
way of governing it."[7]

Some scholarly description of this whole phenomenon can be found in a
1966 collection entitled *Nationalism in Canada*. Commenting that weather and
climate have seldom "been exalted as major attributes of nationality," Carl
Berger examines the genesis of "the idea that Canada's unique character derives
from her northern location, her severe winters and her heritage of 'northern
races.' "[8] This concept, which can be conveniently termed the myth of the north,
is complemented by the geographer's view in Cole Harris's essay, "The Myth
of the Land in Canadian Nationalism."[9] Harris's study dwells on the unique
geographic problems of Canadian agriculture, although he concludes that the
idea of Canada as a distinctive northern land faces erosion by exploding urban-
ism and communication.

These two essays represent the first extended examinations of these specific
concepts in Canadian criticism. It is surprising that an aspect of Canada which
so impressed our writers has so seldom been analysed by our critics. Allusions
to the importance of the land have often been made with a casualness implying
that something so obvious needs no further comment. Even an article with
as promising a title as Wilfrid Eggleston's "Canadian Geography and National
Culture" makes only slight reference to the impact of the land.[10]

Recently, however, particularly since the founding of *Canadian Literature*
in 1959, numerous articles have appeared which touch on this theme. Hugo
McPherson recognized it when he wrote: "In looking at the transcontinental
sweep of Canadian fiction, critics from Northrop Frye to Warren Tallman have
seen its development as a struggle against the violence, or the snowy indifference
of nature—as an effort to humanize and give articulate shape to this vast landscape; to encompass it in imaginative terms, and in so doing, to discover the
self."[11]

In what follows I have acknowledged my debt to many of these critics.
Yet it still seems curious that, except for two recent books—Jack Warwick's
The Long Journey, a study of the *pays d'en haut* theme in French Canadian
literature, and D.G. Jones's *Butterfly on Rock*—the land, as theme and image,

[6]Lionel Stevenson, *Appraisals of Canadian Literature* (Toronto: Macmillan, 1926), pp. 11-12.
[7]Robert Fulford, "This Is an Open Country Still," *To Every Thing There is a Season*, p. 251.
[8]Carl Berger, "The True North Strong and Free," *Nationalism in Canada*, ed. Peter Russell (Toronto:
McGraw-Hill, 1966), p. 4.
[9]*Nationalism in Canada*, pp. 27-43.
[10]*Canadian Geographical Journal*, XLIII (December 1951), 254-73.
[11]Hugo McPherson, "Fiction 1940-1960," *Literary History of Canada*, ed. C.F. Klinck (Toronto:
University of Toronto Press, 1965), p. 722.

has never been explored in the sustained way which its persistence in our literature enjoins. The prose fiction of the Canadian prairies provides an ideal place to begin this exploration, illustrating, as it does, both the prevalence of the myth of the land in Canadian writing and the regional qualities which derive from the encounter with a specific distinctive landscape.

This study concentrates on the prose fiction set on the prairies of Western Canada, in that region defined by geographers as the "grassland and park country of the sedimentary plains of southern Manitoba, Saskatchewan and Alberta."[12] Though this landscape is most often characterized by its flatness, "the prairies are very rarely level, except over small areas. They have undulations that often swell to the height of several hundred feet, or for miles the traveller winds among abrupt conical eminences; and it is only the general absence of timber, and the sameness of the scenery, that deceive the eye and give the appearance of flatness."[13] But, since the setting of fiction is an imagined geography, it is vain to decry a lack of factual accuracy based on arbitrary association of specific novels with specific landscapes. Even the identification of places in Hardy's Wessex, one of the most famous literary landscapes, was likely the novelist's reluctant response to a growing public clamour for such identification.[14] The fiction writer attempts a photographic rendering of a particular geography at his peril. As Robert Liddell says, "a love of 'descriptions' comes from not taking fiction seriously enough as an art, from not valuing highly enough work in which 'the most thorough knowledge of human nature, the happiest delineation of its varieties, the liveliest effusions of wit and humour are conveyed to the world in the best chosen language.' "[15]

Setting should combine elements from the writer's observation and memory, fused in his imagination to serve the total design of his work. For all Lawrence's concern with precise detail in nature description, for example, his main interest is in expressing the "vivid relatedness between the man and the living universe that surrounds him."[16] Cleanth Brooks has shown that Faulkner's sensitive contemplation of nature leads to a variety of uses of setting in his fiction, particularly as a manifestation of "the boundless vitality of nature, a vitality that renders death unimportant and meaningless."[17] Such settings, created and utilized by the literary imagination, are the central concern of this study. The prairie, for example, may in many instances not be as flat as it is described,

---

[12] John Warkentin (ed.), *The Western Interior of Canada* (Toronto: McClelland and Stewart, 1964), p. 2.

[13] James Hector, "On the Capabilities for Settlement of the Central Part of British North America," quoted in *Western Interior*, p. 173.

[14] W.J. Keith, "Thomas Hardy and the Literary Pilgrims," *Nineteenth Century Fiction*, XXIV (June 1969), 80-92.

[15] Robert Liddell, *A Treatise on the Novel* (London: Jonathan Cape, 1947), p. 110.

[16] D.H. Lawrence, "Pan in America," *Phoenix*, ed. E.D. McDonald (London: Heineman, 1936), p. 27.

[17] Cleanth Brooks, *William Faulkner: The Yoknapatawpha Country* (New Haven: Yale University Press, 1963), p. 32.

but it is precisely this prairie—that seen by the artist and conceived to be necessary in his design—which is significant.

Similarly, questions about the psychological accuracy of the writer's derivation of certain human characteristics from man's relation to the land are of little importance. Observing that the shapes of Scandinavian roofs are clearly reminiscent of spruce and fir trees, and that thirteenth-century French cathedrals evoke the interior of the hardwood forests, Paul Shepard dismisses the notion of "a simple linear determinism unrelated to the character of the human society and matters of choice and accident."[18] In other words, man and his geography are very complexly interrelated and the impossibility of mathematical equations should not invalidate relationships which are confirmed in the less precise realms of emotion and instinct. Professor Berger's emphasis on the falsehood of the northern myth seems, in the present context, to be beside the point. The myth of the land is imaginatively valid, by virtue of its being shared, often almost intuitively, by a people trying to express their sense of themselves in time and place. The reflection of the collective consciousness, or subconsciousness, in the repeated references to the land in prairie fiction is constant, and convincing.

If I might speculate for a moment, then, on the attitude of the typical prairie writer to the importance of setting in fiction, I am sure he, or she, would disagree with Gerald Brace that setting in fiction "is far less important than it used to be,"[19] and agree with Elizabeth Bowen that "the locale of the happening always colours the happening, and often, to a degree, shapes it."[20] Again, I suspect the prairie writer would deny Robert Liddell's insistence that "the landscape in the background is merely incidental,"[21] and assent to the claim of a "proud partisan . . . of regional writing," that "the impression of place as revealing something is an indelible one."[22] Beyond the fundamental recognition that a setting, "rendered vividly and memorably, tends to increase the credibility of character and action,"[23] the prairie writer will use his setting as reinforcement of the general meaning of the work, and as an index to character. He will seek, in sum, the symbolic settings of Dickens, or the functional settings of Hardy, more often than the spare, strictly utilitarian settings of Jane Austen.

Surrounded by "quiet earth, big sky,"[24] the prairie writer becomes preoccupied with space. He turns naturally to geometric figures, the mathematician's means of defining space, to make sense of his own space: "I feel how the world

---

[18]Paul Shepard, *Man in the Landscape: A Historic View of the Esthetics of Nature* (New York: Alfred A. Knopf, 1967), p. 59.
[19]Gerald Brace, *The Stuff of Fiction* (New York: Norton, 1959), p. 103.
[20]Elizabeth Bowen, "Notes on Writing a Novel," *Myth and Method: Modern Theories of Fiction*, ed. James E. Miller, Jr. (Lincoln: University of Nebraska Press, 1960), p. 39.
[21]Liddell, *Treatise*, p. 111.
[22]Eudora Welty, "How I Write," *Understanding Fiction*, ed. Cleanth Brooks and Robert Penn Warren (New York: Appleton-Century-Crofts, 1959), pp. 547-48.
[23]"Description and Setting," *Understanding Fiction*, p. 647.
[24]Wallace Stegner, *Wolf Willow* (New York: Viking Press, 1966), p. 11.

still reduces me to a point and then measures itself from me. Perhaps the meadowlark... feels the same way. All points on the circumference are equidistant from him; in him all radii begin; all diameters run through him; if he moves, a new geometry creates itself around him'' (p. 19).

Wallace Stegner describes the landscape in geometrical terms, as a giant circle; then the entire image becomes the vehicle of a wider metaphor describing man's situation in the universe. His geometric figure is the elaboration of a still simpler geometry: in a world which is otherwise totally horizontal, man is the sole vertical intrusion. "In its flatness," Stegner observes, "you are a challenging upright thing" (p. 8). This image is basic to man's attempt to discover his significance in the prairie environment for it summarizes, by emphasizing the contrast between man and land, man's shock at the emptiness, at the lack of comfort and companionship in the land. Other metaphors describing the land, such as the most popular analogy of the prairie and the sea, can be seen as variations of this basic image. A man alone on the sea is isolated, distinctive, forced to consider his own uniqueness. Vertical man in a horizontal world is necessarily a solitary figure; the fiction of the Canadian prairies is the record of man conquering his geographical solitude, and, by extension, his other solitudes, not so much physically as through imaginative understanding.

This theme of solitude is the most persistent in Canadian prairie fiction. The individual man, standing erect on the prairie, is without either the physical shelter or the psychological comfort of substantial vegetation or significant contours of landscape. Such exposure, compounded by the rigours of a northern climate, inevitably prompts the theme of man's aloneness in a hostile, or at the least indifferent, universe. There is a good deal of the "evocation of stark terror" which Northrop Frye finds so notable in Canadian poetry. This is "not a coward's terror, of course," Frye goes on to comment, "but a controlled vision of the causes of cowardice. The immediate source of this is obviously the frightening loneliness of a huge and thinly settled country."[25]

The cause of the terror in this specific instance, that is absence of vegetation and substantial contour of the land, is only the most visually immediate symbol of many solitudes—of physical solitude, of course; but also of social and cultural solitude; and ultimately of internal solitude. To many other of his themes as well—the quest for freedom, the bond to the land, the search for religious conviction, the aspiration of the artist—the prairie writer finds that the contrast of vertical man to the horizontal landscape has an application. Joseph Addison anticipated the first of these when he wrote: "The mind of man naturally hates every thing that looks like a restraint upon it, and is apt to fancy itself under a sort of confinement, when the sight is pent up in a narrow compass and shortened on every side by the neighbourhood of walls or mountains. On the contrary, a spacious horizon is an image of liberty, where the eye has room to

---

[25]Northrop Frye, "Canada and Its Poetry," *The Bush Garden* (Toronto: Anansi, 1971), p. 138.

range abroad, to expatiate at large on the immensity of its views."[26]

Addison might have been describing the conception of freedom held by the singular human figure in the prairie vastness. The uninterrupted view to the horizon gives the impression of uninterrupted personal freedom. The yearning of the prairie dweller for such freedom is perhaps, as Jack Warwick sees it, the survival in Canadian literature of the unsatisfied quest of the voyageur.[27] The universal urge, in any case, is given a particularly dramatic visual equivalent in the prairie landscape. Such freedom as is represented in this manner is, of course, quite often discovered to be illusory. The absence of other men, and of laws and of social custom, is a temporary state, lasting only as long as it takes to settle a district. But in prairie fiction the sense of freedom usually persists to be countered more strongly by the dictates of the land itself.

The response to the dictates of the land is a deep sense of bond to the land, which often coexists with the feeling that nature is man's antagonist. In the absence of more congenial surroundings or human fellowship, vertical man looks to the horizontal and readily arable land for company. The bond may vary from a healthy respect for the source of daily bread to an insane devotion to the land, or more often, to the extraneous material goods which the land may provide. The geometric image has another application to this theme, for the man is not only distinct from the land, but also, of necessity, rooted in the land from which he derives his nourishment. The vertical, that is, is always in contact with the horizontal. The bond to the land, unarticulated, emotional, even spiritual, is also, in a sense, religious. It is one of several religious themes which fascinate the prairie writer.

The flourishing of fundamentalism, with its emphasis on a literal and unquestioning belief in the Scriptures, was a natural outgrowth of the rural society, satisfying the need for a simple, readily available, religious belief. Though landscape has little recognizable effect on organized religion, which derives so greatly from inherited tradition, prairie literature does reveal specific uses of the landscape in interpreting a character's personal knowledge of God. Prairie man raised above the surrounding land has an unobstructed view to the horizon. In a contemplative pose, eyes fixed on the distant horizon, he is often portrayed pondering the ultimate question of the nature of man and God. The location of God in nature is intensified by the characteristics of the environment. The vastness of land and sky, both seeming to extend to infinity, the simplicity of an uninterrupted landscape, the ordered pattern of the fields, and the severe demands of a rigorous climate are especially significant. Infinitude, elemental simplicity, order and severity are all attributes which the land shares with the Deity. Man at the centre of the vastness may be awed by the power of this God, or even terrified by it, but he will be aware, at least as Wallace Stegner sees it, of a very personal God. "Puny you may feel there, and vulnerable, but

[26]Number 412, *The Spectator*.
[27]Jack Warwick, *The Long Journey* (Toronto: University of Toronto Press, 1968), *passim*.

not unnoticed. This is a land to mark the sparrow's fall'' (p. 8).

When a character in a prairie fiction is either an artist, or of artistic temperament, the writer's creative responses to the environment are objectified. The absence of feature in the bleak and empty landscape, like the absence of feature in the social and cultural life of the prairie community, leaves the aspiring artist without stimulus, without encouragement, and without the varieties of human intercourse which are his traditional subject. But there is a counter-theme to that of the despairing artist in a spare and unchanging physical and cultural landscape. John Peter sensed it in the winter description which opens his second novel: ''The whole effect was so blank, so bare of living creatures, that it could have represented almost anything: peace, sterility, or cataleptic anguish.''[28] Here the landscape is not discouraging, but a reserve of possibilities. In terms of the upright figure in the midst of flatness the theme becomes art's abhorrence of a vacuum. The physical emptiness is an imaginative vacuum which must be filled, and which offers new freedom to the artist to choose what he may to fill it.

In addition, as Grove remarks in his nature essays, the writer discovers a new sensitivity to the minutest details of life. In the absence of landscape spectacle the artist must sharpen his observation and detect those nuances which are the essence of art. The urge to erect something in the prairie emptiness, of no matter what material—bricks, or paint, or words—is the urge of man to assert his presence in a forbidding land. The building of a vertical equivalent to man, it seems, allows man to take the measure of his achievement, to insist on his determination to endure.

A man's raising of a concrete object to mark his presence is parallel to the artist's attempt to interpret or articulate his sense of the land. The literary process, creating from the new experience something meaningful and familiar, is slow and gradual. The historical encounter with the new environment becomes a part, either consciously or unconsciously, of the national psychology. This encounter, or at least its interpretation in literature, demanded a new language. ''Not only did plain objects have to be identified and named,'' Professor Clough remarks, commenting on the inadequacies of the explorers' vocabularies, ''but new emotions strained old formulas.''[29] Words such as ''spring,'' ''meadow,'' or ''snowfall'' in their British context were inadequate to the Canadian experience. Traditional vocabulary had to establish new connotations and new words had to be discovered.[30] The gradual articulation of the sense of the land begins, then, with the observations of the early explorers. A glance at their descriptions, such as that provided by the judicious selection of excerpts

[28]John Peter, *Take Hands at Winter* (Garden City: Doubleday, 1967), p. 3.
[29]Clough, *The Necessary Earth*, p. 14.
[30]Roy Daniells, ''Poetry and the Novel,'' *The Culture of Contemporary Canada*, ed. Julian Park (Ithaca: Cornell University Press, 1957), p. 13.

in John Warkentin's *The Western Interior of Canada*, is an appropriate prelude to the more conscious concern with a new language in the fiction. The observations of Kelsey, Henday or Keating, for example, anticipate the principal uses of the prairie in the fiction of the twentieth century; others, such as those of Thompson and Hind, represent some characteristic less usual aspects of the description of the prairie.

The first recorded European encounter with what is now the prairie provinces is found in the reports of the Danish navigator, Jens Munck, who wintered at Churchill in 1619-20. Munck describes, of course, the Hudson Bay coast, not the plains region, but his comments anticipate a recurring ambiguity. The exclusively "flat, bare and swampy land"[31] is depressingly bleak. His remarks are reminiscent of Cartier's opinion of the Labrador shore as "the land that God gave Cain." But as Cartier was to discover much that was pleasing in the new land, so Munck notes with satisfaction the abundance of game and the consequent good hunting.

The record of Henry Kelsey's 1690 journey inland from Hudson Bay provides the first slight reference to the European's experience of the plains landscape. Since the journal of the 1690 journey is written in awkward rhyming couplets, Kelsey also has the distinction of being the first English-language prairie poet. Although Kelsey's stated aim was "through God's assistance for to understand/The natives language & to see their land,"[32] his chief concern was with the possibilities of the fur trade and his record of the terrain is slight and generalized. He does refer to the country as "desert" and mentions the hunger, cold and loneliness which faces his expedition. Kelsey's description of the plains area itself is brief, concentrating on his fascination with the buffalo and suggesting that he was little impressed:

> This plain affords nothing but Beast & grass
> And over it in three days time we past
> getting unto ye woods on the other side
> It being about forty six miles wide (pp. 23-24).

The record of Kelsey's second journey inland in 1691 and 1692 is similarly spare in its references to a landscape which he finds heath-like and barren. Kelsey's remarks, scant as they may be, indicate the lengthy fictional history of the attitude that the typical prairie landscape is unremarkable, if it does not, in fact, inhibit verbal expression. The prairie farmer is often as laconic, especially about landscape aesthetics, as Kelsey seems to have been.

The comments of these early explorers reflect their mission; they tend to disregard landscape and the response it elicits in order to discuss the economic

---

[31]*Danish Arctic Expeditions, 1605 to 1620*, quoted in *Western Interior*, p. 12.
[32]*The Kelsey Papers*, quoted in *Western Interior*, p. 22.

potential of the areas involved. To many of the explorers, in fact, still filled with dreams of China or other exotic lands, Canada was "really the wrong country."[33] This attitude was reinforced by the fur traders for whom Canada was "an economic resource to be exploited rather than a country to live in."[34] This economic predilection dictated a general preference for the forest lands over the plains. For the most part there seems to have been plentiful supplies of game, fish, and even berries, but the prairie, it is agreed, because it lacks water and trees, is ill-suited to permanent settlement and the development of agriculture. Anthony Henday, in his journal for August 11, 1774, describes the least favourable of these lands in characteristically terse phrases: "Level lands, short grass; no woods; and no water but what is salt."[35]

Henday's journal is particularly remarkable, as Warkentin observes, for the sense of awe at the immensity of this region conveyed by his repeated, almost disbelieving, comment: "We are still in the Muscuty Plains" (p. 52). Bewilderment at the vastness of the prairie becomes a common response for the explorer and an important psychological factor in the novels of this century. The journals of Pennsylvanian mineralogist and chemist, William Keating, are much more expansive about the prairie vastness. Keating's 1823 account of the Red River Lowland shows a new sensitivity to the uninterrupted view. He uses a suggestion of the geometric image, man at the centre of a circle, to convey his perplexed, yet exhilarated, response:

> A broad expanse of verdant prairie, spreading beyond the utmost extent of vision, is here presented to the view.... There is very little to interrupt the simplicity and uniformity of the scenery; scarcely is there an undulation to variegate the prospect, save what is afforded by an optical illusion that makes the traveller fancy himself in the centre of a basin, and surrounded by an amphitheatre of rising ground at no great distance, which constantly eludes his approach.[36]

This image of man at the centre of an amphitheatre clearly anticipates the solitude, the tremendous personal responsibility, and the feeling of being noticed, which are part of the fictional view of prairie man. The topographer, John Lambert, describes effectively the contrast between the easy encompassing of the vastness with the eye, and the impossibility of encompassing it with the mind or the imagination: "It is difficult to convey an adequate idea of these dreary solitudes. Let it be remembered that a few minutes' reading embraces sections which require tedious weeks to traverse; and that even travelling over and observing

---

[33]Patrick Anderson, "Poem on Canada," *The White Centre* (Toronto: Ryerson, 1946), p. 32.
[34]D.G. Jones, *Butterfly on Rock* (Toronto: University of Toronto Press, 1970), p. 35.
[35]"The Journal of Anthony Henday, 1754-55," quoted in *Western Interior*, p. 52.
[36]W.H. Keating, *Narrative of an Expedition*, quoted in *Western Interior*, pp. 139-40.

them with the patient labor of months, leaves but a *feeling* of their vastness, which baffles the effort to express it."[37] The comments of Keating and Lambert represent a step beyond simple description, for both sense that the uninterrupted landscape has an impact upon man which defies expression, and, by metaphor, or extended comparison, they attempt to provide that expression.

David Thompson's extensive travels in the Canadian West yield comprehensive accounts of the nature of the country. Though he finds the plains south of latitude 44°N bleak and unpromising, Thompson finds in the northern plains the natural order which is the image of a benevolent God. "Who ever calmly views the admirable formation and distribution of the Rivers so wonderfully conducted to their several seas [Thompson wrote]; must confess the whole to have been traced by the finger of the Great Supreme Artificer for the most benevolent purposes, both to his creature Man, and the numerous Animals he has made, none of whom can exist without water."[38]

Although Thompson's observation is not restricted in application to the prairie, it indicates the possibility of finding a benevolent God in an often forbidding landscape. His other accounts are hardly as approving. He writes effectively of the threat to man in a prairie blizzard, and regarding the possibilities of European settlement concludes: "The great Plains appear to be given by Providence to the Red Men for ever, as the wilds and sands of Africa are given to the Arabians" (p. 103).

A totally different outlook, influenced by the rise of a romantic enthusiasm for nature and landscape, characterizes the poet M. Bibaud, who, in revising Gabriel Franchère's 1814 account of the Saskatchewan River country, transformed the prairie into a European garden: "All these champaign beauties reflected and doubled as it were, by the waters of the river; the melodious and varied song of a thousand birds, perched on the tree-tops; the refreshing breath of the zephyrs; the serenity of the sky; the purity and salubrity of the air; all, in a word, pours contentment and joy into the soul of the enchanted spectator."[39]

His bubbling description has many descendants in the fiction of the later nineteenth and early twentieth centuries. Such reliance on conventional literary formulas is clearly inadequate to the evocation of a new land; it stands as a measure of the challenge which the prairie writer faced in articulating his sense of place. At the same time it must be mentioned that the Franchère narrative, despite its excesses, is much more sober when describing the complete absence of natural beauty and man's total devotion to survival in the winter season. The fact of the north, the threat to survival itself, seems inescapable, even in this most romantic of representations.

[37]*United States: Pacific Railroad Reports* (1855), quoted in *Western Interior*, p. 151.
[38]*David Thomson's Narrative*, quoted in *Western Interior*, p. 100.
[39]Gabriel Franchère, *Narrative of a Voyage to the Northwest Coast of America*, quoted in *Western Interior*, p. 110.

From a literary standpoint the reports of the various explorations of the prairie culminate with the Hind-Dawson Explorations in 1857 and 1858. H.Y. Hind's description of the Red River Plain in 1858 is genuinely alert both to the distinctive qualities of the landscape and to the abundant fertility of the land. It merits quoting at some length:

> It [the plain] must be seen at sunrise, when the vast plain suddenly flashes with rose-coloured light, as the first rays of the sun sparkle in the dew of the long rich grass, gently stirred by the unfailing morning breeze. It must be seen at noon-day, when refraction swells into the forms of distant hill ranges the ancient beaches and ridges of Lake Winnipeg, which mark its former extension; when each willow bush is magnified into a grove, each far distant clump of aspens, not seen before, into wide forests, and the outline of wooded river banks, far beyond unassisted vision, rise into view. It must be seen at sunset, when, just as the huge ball of fire is dipping below the horizon, he throws a flood of red light, indescribably magnificent, upon the illimitable waving green, the colours blending and separating with the gentle roll of the long grass, seemingly magnified towards the horizon into the distant heaving swell of a parti-coloured sea. . . .
>
> These are some of the scenes which must be witnessed and felt before the mind forms a true conception of these rich prairie wastes, in the unrelieved immensity which belongs to them, in common with all the ocean, but which, unlike the everchanging and unstable sea, seem to offer a bountiful recompense, in a secure though distant home, to millions of our fellowman.[40]

The features of Hind's ardent description: the use of the diurnal pattern; the emphasis on shifting qualities of light; the sense of limitlessness and consequent optical illusions; the sea metaphor; become typical of prairie fiction. Hind's awareness of the difficulty one has in forming an adequate conception of these spaces is an anticipation of those who would follow him and who would attempt to articulate more fully the spirit of the land and man's place in it.

After Hind the verbal exploration of the Canadian prairie begins to move in two distinct directions. From their earliest incidental mentions of the character and influence of landscape, and their attempts to classify various features of the landscape, the explorers and the scientists become more interested in detailed comment on very defined areas, and, therefore, turn to an increasingly technical vocabulary. The broader description of landscape and the attempt to assess its impact upon the human emotions and imagination becomes the concern of poets, essayists and, particularly, of the prose fiction writers.

---

[40]*Report on . . . the Country Between Lake Superior and the Red River Settlement*, quoted in *Western Interior*, pp. 194-95.

Neglect of landscape in the voyage and exploration literature was due primarily to the commercial preoccupation of the authors. Landscape aesthetics were clearly outside their special interests. Furthermore, it was well into the eighteenth century before landscape description in English literature moved from the generalized account of an ideal and selected nature to something more exact and detailed of the sort that explorers so inclined conceivably could have used.[41] This movement is marked by the interest in the specific features of the rural environment and landscape in the work of Crabbe, Goldsmith, and, particularly, in Thomson's *Seasons* (1730). Interest in the picturesque, "the search for significant art-emotion amidst natural scenes,"[42] is initiated by Thomson's poem and remains, according to Marshall McLuhan, a central factor in English poetry until the changed emphasis to interior landscapes in the early twentieth century. The picturesque treatment of landscape became a feature in the growth of Romanticism, although the stress, in Wordsworth, for example, is not on the strictly pictorial, but on the spirit, or surrounding presence of landscape.

Landscape, which became less obvious in English poetry after the Romantic period, became an important element of nineteenth-century English fiction, from George Eliot's Midlands and Emily Bronte's *Wuthering Heights*, to Hardy's Wessex, and even to the urban landscape of Dickens's London.[43] The increased interest in landscape in fiction was paralleled by the great popularity of landscapes in the visual arts and the success of Constable, Turner and numerous other landscape artists. It was the period, as Kenneth Clark describes it, of "the natural vision" in landscape painting:

> In the course of the century landscapes which at least purported to be close imitations of nature, came to hold a more secure place in popular affection than any other form of art. A peaceful scene, with water in the foreground reflecting a luminous sky and set off by dark trees, was something which everyone agreed was beautiful, just as, in previous ages, they had agreed about a naked athlete or a saint with hands crossed on her bosom.[44]

With these trends in British culture, and the transcendental reverence for natural detail in Thoreau's *Walden*, for example, as background, landscape inevitably, aside from other more immediate reasons, became an essential of the Canadian literature just being born. The problem, illustrated by the

[41]See R.A. Aubin, *Topographical Poetry in XVIII-Century England* (New York: Modern Language Association, 1936), and the excellent summary in John Barrell, *The Idea of Landscape and the Sense of Place 1730-1840* (Cambridge: Cambridge University Press, 1972).

[42]H. Marshall McLuhan, "Tennyson and Picturesque Poetry," *Critical Essays on the Poetry of Tennyson*, ed. John Killham (London: Routledge and Kegan Paul, 1960). p. 69.

[43]Brief, but useful, summaries of the shifting uses of setting in fiction are found in Liddell. *Treastise*, pp. 113-28, and in Dorothy Van Ghent, "On Sons and Lovers," *The English Novel: Form and Function* (New York: Holt, Rinehart and Winston, 1953), pp. 251-52.

[44]Kenneth Clark, *Landscape into Art* (Boston: Beacon Press, 1961), p. 74.

Confederation poets' imitations of Wordsworth and Keats, was to escape the vocabulary and formula appropriate to the English countryside and discover a new language suitable to a new, and what was felt to be a distinctive land. Since the problem could only be resolved, as Carman, Lampman, Roberts and D.C. Scott indeed began to resolve it, through gradual evolution, the Canadian prairie fiction of the late nineteenth and early twentieth centuries, lagging several decades behind English literature in its adaptation of new techniques, tends to be highly derivative in its treatment of landscape.

The first step, then, already illustrated to some extent in the explorers' accounts, was to re-create the region, especially its physical qualities, in language. This basic requirement for the creation of a regional literature is necessarily my primary concern in the early romances, in much of Stead's fiction, and in most of the works which are discussed in chapter IV. Gradually, though, my attention shifts to the writer's use of the prairie to reveal not the local and provincial, but the universal. This aspect of prairie fiction provides the focus for the bulk of the study from Grove onwards, providing one test for the quality of Western Canadian fiction.

The romance, which had its greatest success in England in the early part of the nineteenth century, is the predominant form of prose fiction about the Canadian West until the First World War. Because the principal emphasis of the romance is on action and adventure, character and setting receive little of the writer's attention. When the land and climate become an increasing concern of the writers, as they do for Ralph Connor or Arthur Stringer, the descriptions are romantic, idealized, and excessively enthusiastic. The vocabulary inevitably seems inconsistent with the country being described.

Gilbert Parker's *Pierre and His People* (1892), an attempt to recapture the romance of the days of the voyageur, is typical of the vogue for stories of high adventure involving hardy men with a touch of the strange and unorthodox about them. Parker's references to setting are generally slight and vague, as in the introduction to the final section of the story, "She of the Triple Chevron": "It was a lovely morning. The prairie billowed away endlessly to the south, and heaved away in vastness to the north; and the fresh, sharp air sent the blood beating through the veins. In the bar-room some early traveller was talking to Peter Galbraith."[45] His description, although longer than usual, is typical for its use of undescriptive adjectives like "lovely," its use of the sea image to suggest vastness, the occurrence of the romantic notion that the northern air promotes physical and moral health, and the total lack of any attempt to relate the vastness and invigorating air to the immediate characters and action.

John McLean's stories appeal still more directly to the cult of the primitive, at once idealizing the Indian's culture, and showing the beneficial influence of Christianity upon him. Jake is one of Christ's cowboys, in *The Warden*

---

[45]Gilbert Parker, *Pierre and His People* (London: Methuen, 1892), p. 120.

of the Plains and Other Stories (1896). Typical of his romantic inclinations, he considers the whole prairie to be his church; his sermons, heavy with the jargon of the range, are superficially reminiscent of the nautical turn of Father Mapple's sermon in *Moby Dick*. Yet such use of the setting is rare and incidental. McLean's primitivism is totally cultural, with scarcely any reference to the physical wilderness.

Predictably, Ralph Connor finds Jake's concept of the prairie a congenial one. Connor's west is a land of infinite possibility, offering to even the most downtrodden the hope of a new, rich life. "It was a place," comments F.W. Watt, "where Biblical parables easily merged with actuality."[46] There is just a hint in the opening paragraph of *The Sky Pilot* (1899) that Connor relates the physical vastness of the country to the untramelled opportunity which it provides to both the individual and the Christian church. But landscape is seldom significant in Connor's highly didactic novels, and descriptions of it are characterized by shallow, romantic ecstasy: "How beautiful our world seemed! About us rolled the round-topped, velvet hills, brown and yellow or faintly green, spreading out behind us to the broad prairie."[47]

When parable merges with landscape the prairie becomes a wind-swept, sun-dried plain where the fruits of the Spirit (love, joy, peace, gentleness, meekness and self-control) either do not grow, or do not flourish as they do in the protected canyons (p. 161). Connor is using the dramatic contrast between flat prairie and the deep, jagged canyons, which seem like the prairie's wounds, to point up God's purpose in allowing human suffering in the midst of a world where most live seemingly placid, untroubled lives. The metaphor is forced and excessively ingenious, but it has significance for the developing use of the landscape in the prairie novel. Unlike Parker or MacLean, Ralph Connor made a serious effort to use the scene at hand as a source of metaphor. His effort reveals a considerable awareness of the uniqueness of the western landscape and the distinctive expression which it could provide the writer.

Prairie writers in the early part of this century were beginning to sense the need, which Connor anticipated, of interpreting their own time and place with less slavish adherence to a vocabulary and a formula created to fit circumstances far removed in time and space. They were not to become experimental in a technical sense, but they did begin to look more closely at their own environment for subject matter and setting. The settlement of the country, and the consequent growth of a social context which made more indigenous fiction possible, was almost entirely agricultural in nature, and agriculture did not easily fit itself to the formulas of romantic adventure. The Wild West hero who proved so hardy in American literature had little place where the law and order of the

---

[46]F.W. Watt, "Western Myth, the World of Ralph Connor," *Canadian Literature*, No. 1 (Summer 1959), 34.
[47]Charles William Gordon (Ralph Connor, pseud.), *The Sky Pilot* (Toronto: Westminster, 1905), p. 161.

North West Mounted Police had preceded settlement. Even the apparent anarchists, like W.A. Fraser's Bulldog Carney, were peace-loving at heart. The first efforts to use local materials were likely to seem as gratuitous as E.A.W. Gill's description of a young woman's blush, "like a dewdrop on a prairie rose on a May morning."[48] But this mere addition of an adjective to an otherwise conventional formula seems to have been a necessary stage in the evolution of a more indigenous expression.

As it came increasingly to concentrate on people involved in the agricultural pursuits, Canadian prairie fiction began to move from the romantic to the realistic. If Desmond Pacey is right, "it was prairie writers . . . who began the systematic transformation of Canadian fiction from romance to realism."[49] Pacey adds that one of the reasons for this growing realism was the impossibility of idyllicizing the rigorous conditions of prairie agriculture. In choosing the common man and everyday activity as subject matter, in refusing to idealize the demanding conditions of agriculture in this environment, and in describing setting with an eye toward evoking the actual, these writers moved toward realism. But a strong strain of romanticism persists, particularly in the repeated references to the profound effects on man of his communion with nature. W.O. Mitchell's *Who Has Seen the Wind* is a more recent example of the vitality of this strain. Claude Bissell has distinguished two aspects of realism in the Canadian novel. The work of Ralph Connor, or Mazo de la Roche, represents the decorous realism which gives way to the more comprehensive, contemplative realism of later writers.[50] In the prairie novel Nellie McClung and Arthur Stringer prepared the way for Robert Stead, one of the central figures in the school of decorous realism.

Nellie McClung, although a much less able writer, is a spiritual sister to Ralph Connor, whom she joined occasionally in temperance campaigning. She makes no apology for the didactic nature of her fiction: "I have never worried about my art. I have written as clearly as I could, never idly or dishonestly, and if some of my stories are, as Mr. Eggleston says, sermons in disguise, my earnest hope is that the disguise did not obscure the sermon."[51] Because she is so concerned with her moral message, McClung is not especially concerned with the setting in which her characters operate, nor, indeed, with fiction. She is determined to write of the common people, and to avoid sentimentality by drawing upon her own experience: "When I wrote I would write of the people who do the work of the world and I would write it from their side of the fence."[52] This democratic aim and a stolid Methodist outlook combine to create a decorous realism, which, in McClung's case, usually shows more concern for decorum than for realism.

---

[48]E.A.W. Gill, *Love in Manitoba* (Toronto: Musson, 1912), p. 33.
[49]Desmond Pacey, "Fiction 1920-1940," *Literary History of Canada*, p. 676.
[50]Claude Bissell, "The Novel," *The Arts in Canada*, ed. Malcolm Ross (Toronto: Macmillan, 1958), pp. 92-94.
[51]Nellie McClung, *The Stream Runs Fast* (Toronto: Thomas Allen, 1965), p. 69.
[52]McClung, *Clearing in the West* (Toronto: Thomas Allen, 1935), p. 226.

The novels, short stories, and autobiographies of Nellie McClung evince a strong love for the prairies and particularly for the pioneer vocation. McClung does show considerable awareness of the landscape features, especially of the vegetation which is distinctive to the prairie. The "golden and purple flowers of the fall" which grow along the roadside are specifically named: "wild sunflowers, brown-centred gaillardia, wild sage and goldenrod."[53] She has a sure sense for establishing local colour, but little awareness of the need to integrate her distinctive setting with the other elements of her novels. The image of man in a horizontal world, while present, seldom seems essential to McClung's conception of character: "It was on one of the highest of these banks that Arthur had built his house, and it was a pleasant outlook for anyone who loves the long view that the prairie gives, where only the horizon obstructs the vision" (p. 206). The view to the "pleasant" horizon is there, and McClung apparently feels that the physical environment is important, but she does not reflect upon the possible psychological or imaginative impact of this distinctive situation.

The mixture of agrarian realism and exaggerated melodrama in Nellie McClung's fiction is still more incongruous in the prairie novels of Arthur Stringer. The novels of the prairie trilogy, and *The Mud Lark* (1931), are filled with the natural disasters which threaten agriculture in this environment: hail, prairie fire, violent summer storms and winter blizzards. Though contributing to a cumulative effect of despair, they seem somehow to be mere incidents, less than essential in Stringer's scheme of things. Stringer's central characters are cultured socialites transplanted to the uncultured Canadian West. His situations tempt him to romantic melodrama liberally sprinkled with dilletantish literary allusions. In *The Prairie Wife* (1915), for example, Chaddie, the heroine, is involved with Mr. Red Coat in the capture of a murderer. Such an incident seems a gratuitous intrusion in the rigorous life of the prairie farm. Stringer writes to the pattern of a traditional formula which demands a happy ending or an optimism that things will improve beyond the pages of the novel. Thus valuable shares in a Chilean nitrate mine and abrupt reconciliations are staples of his fiction.

Stringer turns to the figure of man in the prairie to emphasize man's essential loneliness and isolation. "This prairie home," Chaddie writes to her close friend, "must always remain so like an island dotting the lonely wastes of a lonely sea."[54] Yet Stringer's repeated references to the isolation of man in this landscape are not developed. His novels are too shallow to provide a sense of the characters coming to terms with their own selves and with their environment. Stringer's effective scenes are lost in the sentiment and melodrama. When Chaddie climbs the windmill to look down on the farm, she discovers, from this vantage point, the truth of her situation: "As I stared down at the roof of our shack it looked

[53]McClung, *The Second Chance* (New York: Doubleday, 1910), p. 226.
[54]Arthur Stringer, *Prairie Stories* (New York: A.L. Burt, 1936), p. 14.

small and pitiful, tragically meager to house the tangled human destinies it was housing. And the fields where we'd labored and sweated took on a foreign and ghostly coloring, as though they were oblongs in the face of an alien world, a world with mystery and beauty and unfathomable pathos about it'' (pp. 237-38). This impressive image of man in his landscape is inconsistent with the novel as a whole where the mystery is lost in the patness of the resolution, the pathos is submerged in ludicrous sentiment—'' 'O God, but you're lovely!' he said in a half-smothered and shamefaced sort of whisper'' (p. 239)—and the beauty is lost in the excess of such passages as this description of sunset a few paragraphs before: ''A fire of molten gold burned behind the thinnest of mauve and saffron and purple curtains . . . an unearthly and ethereal radiance'' (p. 238).

The fiction of Stringer and McClung, slight as it is, marks a necessary stage in the continuing attempt, in Peter Stevens's phrase, ''to embrace our world.'' Those writers who follow them, and who choose to treat some aspect of prairie life in their fiction, almost invariably sense the need to interpret the physical environment, to describe ''the necessarily outrageous flats,'' and to consider their many possibilities as fictional material. In this respect prairie literature shares with all Canadian literature the theme of the land, and the evolution of the mental capacity to make some sense of the land's vastness and complexity.

Among the ''few speculative images'' by means of which the prairie artist ''define[s] his place,'' the image of the man as vertical intrusion in a horizontal world is primary. The implications of being a solitary figure raised above a flat and uninterrupted landscape are many, and it is by variations on this basic image that the writer can explore his characters and the impact which a distinctive terrain makes upon them. The variations and nuances of this image provide a measure of unity to the fiction of the Canadian prairie, which a more detailed examination of the fiction of Robert Stead, Frederick Philip Grove, Sinclair Ross and W.O. Mitchell will show. The progression in the work of these writers involves an increasing literary sophistication and an increasingly profound intellectual and imaginative study of man in his physical environment. The novels of Edward McCourt, Margaret Laurence, John Peter, to name the representatives who come first to mind, reveal a continuing interest among more contemporary writers, even among those using urban settings, in the distinctiveness of the prairie experience as summarized by the basic image of man's isolation, and his awareness of self, in a world without features.

Stead's prairie is not often particularized, nor does he often mar the impression of an idyllic environment. He occasionally introduces the image of vertical man, and his novels intimate some of the metaphorical implications inherent in the landscape. Grove is both more honest than Stead, and more sensitive to detail in his prairie settings. Man, as Grove repeatedly observes, is an intruder in an environment characterized by unthinking caprice, which ceaselessly works to eliminate all vertical intrusions, to return man and his work to the levelness which is oblivion. In contrast to Stead's almost casual references to his setting, Grove is alive to the prairie's significance as a comprehensive metaphor for his view of human experience. In Grove's novels the reader is repeatedly returned to the basis for the metaphor, the literal relationship of man and land. Sinclair Ross seems to move a step beyond this, particularly in *As For Me and My House*, where the prairie becomes an integral part of both his own and his characters' way of thinking. In the continuing attempt to "embrace our world," the Bentleys' unexciting but quietly meaningful acceptance of the existence of the void, both in the physical and emotional landscape, is an important step. With W.O. Mitchell the reader again becomes aware of the tremendous beauty of the prairie, but the beauty does not detract from the treatment of serious themes. The image of man in this landscape is one of stark simplicity and Mitchell sees it as the ideal departure point for the consideration of the most elemental factors of life: birth, love, death and the nature of God. His novels provide a valuable approach to the enigma which is ultimately at the heart of these realities.

To read much fiction of the Canadian prairie is to become aware of an increasingly profound imaginative study of man in his physical environment. Martha Ostenso's exploration in *Wild Geese*, of the "unmeasurable Alone surrounding each soul" is a major contribution to this development; the works discussed in chapter IV, on the other hand, are undoubtedly minor. They are works selected to illustrate quickly the efforts of some of the lesser writers during the period of the four major writers just mentioned. The final chapter turns to representative fiction of the last two decades to illustrate the increasing concentration on the prairie landscape as a wasteland, more barren and disorienting than anything previously encountered. The final chapter also examines briefly the survival and development of the basic situation of man's abrupt confrontation with the prairie landscape in fiction with an urban setting. Through its re-creation and metamorphosis in fiction the prairie writer is coming to know his land and, more significantly, is presenting a vision of man's encounter with a pervasive emptiness, of which the prairie is only the mirror.

II

The Benign Prairie:
The Novels of Robert Stead

> Up from the soil comes all life, all progress, all development.
>
> ROBERT STEAD, *Dennison Grant*

The benign prairie of Stead's fiction is the image of an ordered and harmonious universe; in such an environment man's stature is grand and heroic. In his poem, "The Prairie," he paints his usual picture of a landscape ordained for man's glory:

> Where wide as the plan of creation
> The Prairies stretch ever away,
> And beckon a broad invitation
> To fly to their bosom and stay;
> The prairie-fire smell in the gloaming—
> The water-wet wind in the spring—
> An empire untrod for the roaming—
> Ah, this is a life for a king![1]

The single stanza is an excellent summary: the prairie, designed by a benevolent Creator, has the qualities of a generous host and ample mother; it is best described in the language of another era and another place; it elevates man to the position of emperor and king.

Unlike Edward McCourt, whose emphasis is quite the opposite,[2] I am inclined to characterize Stead as never escaping the influence of the American Wild West and, consequently, as often disappointing the expectation of a realistic picture of prairie life in an accumulation of maudlin incident and extreme coincidence. Stead's desire to portray the actualities of prairie farming convincingly is contradicted by a desire to cater to the market for mystery and melodrama. Typically disconcerting is *The Homesteaders*, in which he abandons a detailed account of selecting and creating a homestead for an improbable tale of murder and intrigue.

The reflection of major social forces in Stead's novels—the challenge to the market economy in *Dennison Grant*, mechanization and the Great War in *Grain*—indicates that the social novel was supplanting the romance as the dominant fictional mode. In turn, one would expect the greater degree of localization demanded by the novel to reinforce the emphasis on the physical landscape in prairie fiction. The expectation is only partially realized in Stead's fiction.

---

[1] Robert Stead, *The Empire Builders and Other Poems* (Toronto: William Briggs, 1910), pp. 33-34.
[2] Edward McCourt, *The Canadian West in Fiction* (Toronto: Ryerson, 1970), p. 94.

His response to the prairie landscape and climate is most remarkable for its pervasive nostalgia and its neglect of the harsher aspects of prairie life.[3] While Stead frequently refers to the natural environment, he pays scant attention to the integration of setting with character and plot. Often, it seems, Stead uses landscape description merely to conform to a mistaken conception of the conventional literary way to begin a chapter.

Stead, then, remains in the realm of decorous realism. In the earlier novels, where realism in the conduct of human affairs is either defied or pushed to the extremes of possibility, the actualities of the physical environment are also neglected. As Stead moves toward a more realistic treatment of prairie agriculture and of the complexities of human interaction, his descriptions of the setting hardly keep pace. The realism is thus a partial one, not only in the lingering sentimentalism of even the later *Grain*, but also in the insistence on the benign and bountiful prairie, or in the total neglect of the landscape. In some respects Stead initiates the serious treatment of the Canadian prairie in fiction, but there are certain possibilities, man's vulnerability and insignificance in this world, which he is unwilling to encounter.

For Stead, man on the prairie is the honest labourer, toiling in his own soil for his daily bread. The bond between man and soil is fashioned and strengthened by the abundant fertility of the land. The typical prairie homesteader is given voice in another poem:

> Yes, this is my place of probation,
>   Though woefully windy and bare,
> I am lord of my own habitation,
>   I mock at the meaning of care;
> For here, on the edge of creation,
>   Lies, far as the vision can fling,
> A kingdom that's fit for a nation—
>   A kingdom—and I am the king![4]

If the reader ignores, for a moment, the abysmal quality of Stead's verse, he will note that implicit in the homesteader's jubilation is his sense of being the sole vertical thing in a horizontal world. The experience exalts man. He is solitary, but not lonely; barrenness and human cares are of no consequence; the hint of precariousness at "the edge of creation" is safely neglected by a lord and king. Consistently, Stead emphasizes the regality of prairie man in a land appointed to his gratification and aggrandizement.

Tested by a harsh climate and stimulated by magnificent vistas, this king of the soil is living life as it should be truly and vitally lived. He figures

---

[3]This argument is developed in A.T. Elder's "Western Panorama: Settings and Themes in Robert J.C. Stead," *Canadian Literature*, No. 17 (Summer 1963), 44-56.
[4]"The Homesteader," *Empire Builders*, p. 21.

strongly in the theme which more than any other unifies Stead's fiction: the necessity of making a distinction between *life* and mere *existence*. Closer examination of this theme in several novels reveals both the ambiguities in Stead's evocation of the prairie and the dominantly idyllic tone. The desire which many of Stead's characters express to *live* in a new sense, though often roused by books, is fulfilled, curiously, not by movement to traditional centres of culture, but to a region in which one can discover the best of both worlds, where the mind is nourished and the body developed free of crass urban materialism. The influence of Stead's prairie on physical health is clearly positive; its influence on spiritual health is considerably more ambiguous—and interesting. Unfortunately Stead never probes this influence as Ross, for example, does with such marked effect in *As For Me and My House*.

But, though he does not approach Ross's artistry, Stead was a serious enough writer to learn from his mistakes. Except for his last published novel, *The Copper Disc* (1930) (a crime thriller complete with love triangles, shots in the night, and a diabolical professor out to control the world), his novels, in general, reveal a progressively developing and maturing writer. Stead's diction becomes more precise, his characterization less trite, and his examination of social issues more assured.

In his first novel, *The Bail Jumper* (1914), Stead heads each chapter with epigraphs from his own poetry, a sufficient warning to the reader that the exaggeration and melodrama of the story have a specific ancestry in five volumes of trivial verse. Young Raymond Burton has left his father's farm to become a clerk in the Plainville general store managed by Mr. Gardiner. When he falls in love with Myrtle Vane, to whom his boss is also strongly attracted, Raymond finds himself accused of the theft of two thousand dollars from Gardiner's safe. To this plot skeleton Stead adds the flesh of a hard-drinking villain, a beleaguered orphan, two private detectives and a steady progress toward the eleventh-hour courtroom discovery of the true thief.

In a mystery novel with a plot hinging on wild coincidence, the setting will be of minor importance. Though the reader is usually aware of the setting he seldom feels it is essential to the novel. The epigraph to chapter one, a stanza from Stead's poem, "Prairie Born," mentions the winter cold, the blizzard, and the countless dangers that confirm Stead's version of the myth of the north: "Hardy races grow from hardy circumstance." The concluding note of firm affirmation is typical of Stead's view of the prairie's effect on man. Yet the epigraph, and this is true of most in the novel, has only the most indirect application to character and action. There is little evidence to suggest, for example, that whatever resourcefulness and determination Raymond Burton may possess he owes to the struggle with the elements.

In *The Bail Jumper* Stead first urges the distinction between life and existence. The theme is introduced at the dance in chapter one when Burton is asked to entertain and obliges with a recitation of Oliver Wendell Holmes's "The Chambered Nautilus." The recitation immediately distinguishes Burton and

Myrtle Vane from the "stone wall of mental vacuity"[5] which characterizes the audience's poetic sensibilities. The final stanza of the poem, especially the line, "Build thee more stately mansions, O my soul," becomes a motif by means of which Raymond and Myrtle can express their common aspiration and their growing love for one another. The pair's desire to add to their lives the dimension of poetry and music is not, as one might expect, specifically attributed to the monotony or the harshness of this particular natural environment. Though she misses the city's " 'atmosphere of refinement,' " the spareness of the geography does not appear to be a factor in Myrtle's depression. Contemplating a tiger lily prompts her to hymn the importance of beauty, natural as well as artistic, in life: " 'And if God took all the beautiful flowers, and the wonderful clouds, and the glorious sunsets and dawns, and the singing birds, and the weep of the wind as it blows up out of the dark, and—and the beautiful people out of the world, it wouldn't be such a nice place to live in, would it?' " (p. 218).

Flowers, birds and glorious sunsets, the blessings of a generous deity, are as available here as in any other landscape. In Myrtle's opinion the people in this country are too concerned with the physical necessities; they "have not learned that 'the life is more than food, and the body more than raiment' "(p. 219). The undeveloped implication is that the demands of wresting a living from the reluctant prairie leave the individual with neither time nor inclination for his spiritual development. But the prairie, or less specifically, the rural, still seems more hospitable to such development than the urban, as Myrtle affirms in the rhetorical question: " 'What great thing has ever been that could not be traced to the land?' " (p. 74).

Raymond has not advanced to the same state of cultural self-assurance as Myrtle, but he has similar aspirations. Stead makes uncertain use of symbolic bars of sunlight to represent his hero's condition, imprisoned not only by legal and romantic circumstances, but also by a limited experience, which leaves him constantly anxious to enrich the life of the soul. "They circled him, they compassed him, they crowded him. Bars, and stones, and water! They would strip him of the dress of civilization and clothe him in the garb of infamy. They would feed his body with prison fare, but his soul they would leave to shrivel and starve" (p. 159).

Abandoning Myrtle, Raymond attempts to escape conviction as a thief by fleeing from Manitoba to the Alberta foothills. In this new and untouched land Raymond experiences a renewal and rededication which eventually carries him back to Plainville to clear his name or suffer the consequences. His arrival in the ranching country sets the tone for his change of heart: "The two slender threads of steel seemed the only connecting link with modern civilization, and as they strung far into the endless West the very minds of the passengers under-

[5]Stead, *The Bail Jumper* (Toronto: William Briggs, 1914), p. 26.

went an evolution, a broadening, a disassociation with Established Things, and assumed an attitude of receptiveness toward That Which Shall Be" (p. 197). Clearly Stead relates the broad landscape to the open mind, ready and eager to accommodate new ideas. But the parallel he suggests is little more than shallow cliché. If we are to presume, for example, that Raymond has thus been enabled to accept his fate it is merely ludicrous. The only inevitability in the subsequent course of events is that the author will manipulate things so that everything will come out happily.

The peace and beauty of Stead's world are rarely disturbed by such natural hazards as the prairie fire in this novel. Then it is indicative of Stead's inability to accept the realities of prairie life that the fire is scarcely out when the beauties of a star-filled night and the northern lights impart awesome beauty to the scene, prompting from Myrtle a reminiscence which makes of the fire a vast spectacle designed for man's entertainment: " 'These great prairies—how majestic they are, how silent, how awe-inspiring. It is the first time I have seen them in anger—at war with the puny efforts of man. And even in their anger how beautiful they are!' " (p. 260).

In this same scene Stead includes an incident which must be mentioned in passing, for, in a minor way, it makes a connection between the love story in the novel and its setting. In confessing his love to Myrtle Vane, Gardiner argues that love on the prairies is unique because of the imminence of the natural world:

"The love of the prairies is peculiar. How can a soul, hemmed in by the works of man, seeing life in all the seaminess of man's—and woman's—depravity, and knowing that it is but one drop in the ocean of humanity, rise to the sublime heights experienced by the dweller on the prairie, where all the works of nature seem combined to elevate the individual? The greatest organisms come out of the cities, but the greatest individuals will always come out of the country. And love is individual" (p. 261).

Perhaps the villain's declaration is deliberately specious, but it matches so closely Stead's frequent theme of rural superiority that I am sure the strength of the author's conviction lies behind it. Man's elevation in the prairie above all the non-human world gives him a sense of power, distinctiveness and individuality. There are no forests, no buildings to diminish his stature; all nature seems appointed to answer his needs. Ultimately, of course, Gardiner himself is left to wallow in the seaminess of man's depravity, while Raymond and Myrtle rise to the sublime heights, secure in a world of harmony and moral certitude.

In the character of Raymond and the account of his attempt to escape the prison of circumstance and build more stately mansions for his soul, Stead has the potential for a powerful story. But slowly, yet certainly, the cliché of

Raymond's surprise appearance in court, the mechanical discovery of the thief by two unlikely private detectives, and the excessively sentimental resolution to the love story destroy that potential.

Similar criticisms, as I have already hinted, can be made of Stead's second novel, *The Homesteaders* (1916). In this novel Stead comes closest to using his own family's experiences as source material—the arrival of John and Mary Harris in southern Manitoba in the spring of 1882 coincides with the date of the Stead family's settlement near Cartwright. The first five chapters of the novel are absorbing in their detailed account of homesteading: the procession of the carefully provisioned sleighs west from Emerson; the intimate knowledge of soil, climate and topography which the wise choice of a homestead demands; and the construction of a sod hut.

Stead's disconcerting mixture of documentary detail and the melodrama of the western romance is exacerbated here by the twenty-five-year gap between chapters five and six. The transition from the birth of the first Harris child to the problems of the grown family is abrupt and disturbing, leaving the struggles of a rising prairie farm just as they had become interesting. Although the characterization is slight in the early chapters and becomes more definite after the twenty-five-year interval, the gap hinders our understanding of the new John Harris, who is suddenly presented as selfishly materialistic. Though this particular change in character is common in prairie fiction, in the absence of any account of the stages of transition, the presentation of Harris in the latter part of the novel becomes didactic and stereotyped. In a broader sense, Stead fails to integrate his social criticism, in particular his criticism of the rise of materialism in the Plainville area, with the narrative. Intrusive moralizing, such as his comment that Harris "was now sweeping along with the turbulent tide of Mammonism,"[6] is a poor substitute for the revelation of character and society through the flow of events in the novel.

The shift in values comes, Stead indicates, when the farmer's inarticulate, almost religious, bond to the land is broken by a gradual awareness that his land represents a financial asset, potential wealth beyond the mere means to a livelihood. The religion of the soil is expressed in a memorable passage early in the novel:

> Then there was more land to plough, and Harris's soul never dulled to the delight of driving the ploughshare through the virgin sod. There was something almost sacred in the bringing of his will to bear upon soil which had come down to him through all the ages fresh from the hand of the Creator. The blackbirds that followed at his heel in long, respectful rows, solemnly seeking the trophies of their chase, might have been incarnations from the unrecorded ages that had known these broad fields

---

[6]Stead, *The Homesteaders* (London: Unwin, 1916), p. 100.

for chase and slaughter, but never for growth and production. The era of the near vision, demanding its immediate reward, had passed away, and in its place was the day of faith, for without faith there can be neither seed-time nor harvest (p. 71).

Here prairie soil becomes a metaphor for certain values: the joy of individual accomplishment, a reverence for God, the love of peace, and a confidence in the future. Notably, the Darwinian world of ''chase and slaughter'' is replaced by a world of bountiful fertility. But the growing consciousness of the land as a financial asset leads to the diminishing influence of this metaphor on the farmer. Most significant, however, is Stead's continuing belief in the validity of the metaphor, as marked by Allan Harris's later recognition that they had ''really given expression to their lives as best they could in the black, earth-smelling furrows'' (p. 71).

The attempt by Harris's daughter, Beulah, to redefine her life provides the stimulus in the novel for the eventual confirmation of the moral power of the land. Beulah, inarticulate in the expression of her desires as she might be, is Stead's foremost exponent of his dominant theme:

> She had not yet reached the philosophic age, but she was old enough to value life, and to know that what she called the real things were escaping her. At night, as she looked up at the myriad stars spangling the heavens, the girl's heart was filled with an unutterable yearning; a sense of restriction, of limitation, of loss—a sense that somewhere lay a Purpose and a Plan, and that only by becoming part of that Plan could life be lived to the fullest (p. 111).

Though she is greatly disturbed by her academic ignorance and believes so strongly in the merits of flight to the Alberta foothills, the fulfillment of Beulah's aspirations lies ultimately neither in books nor in a new geography, but in the discovery of a new life-style where the freedom that comes with simplicity and love is more important than the acquisition of material goods.

As in *The Bail Jumper* the movement to the farther west brings with it a restoration of the spirit, but Stead is not so pessimistic as to present this pattern as the ultimate solution. In both novels the final movement is a return to the area of Plainville, there to resume the old life with a new attitude. That this is a reaffirmation of the validity of the land as the source of contented accomplishment and quiet faith is clear from Allan's memory of the farm: ''How those old smells beat up from the mysterious chambers of memory and intoxicated his nostrils with fondness and a great sense of having, in some few hallowed moments, dovetailed his own career into the greater purpose of creation!'' (p. 260). This revelation, and John's eventual conviction that his daughter was right, confirm that man comes closest to Beulah's ideal of becoming part of ''the Plan'' of life by intimacy with the land. The smells of fresh-turned furrows and ripening wheat are the distillation of true vitality. The farmer's task is sacred for he is intimately involved with the natural rhythms of seedtime and harvest, the rhythms which are basic to all creation. He is the instrument, it seems, of God's purpose, and therefore especially blessed.

Such optimism is sustained through the resolution of the novel in which Stead again relies upon courtroom melodrama to ensure that virtue is rewarded, crime punished, and love's vicissitudes overcome. So barren is Stead's imagination for mystery thrillers that he must make the villains of *The Bail Jumper*, Riles and Gardiner, serve the same function in this novel. In his next novels, however, Stead does begin to move away from reliance on the conventions of the Wild West romance.

Strictly speaking neither *The Cowpuncher* (1918) nor *Dennison Grant* (1920) are prairie novels since both are set in the Alberta foothills where the flat plains are on one side and the towering mountains on the other. But the prairie continues to make its presence felt; in *The Cowpuncher* the world is almost wholly pastoral—"an Arcadia where one might well return to the simple life; ... sheltered ... by the warm brown prairies and the white-bosomed mountains."[7] The distinction between existence and life is again inherent in the contrasting experience of the Hardys in eastern social circles, and the life which is stimulated by the western environment.

Stead's usual idyllic landscape is conceived much more definitely in this novel as the symbol of a life of freedom and possibility. This symbol is a key element in the characterization of Irene Hardy, daughter of an eastern doctor, who falls in love with the prairie and with the cowpuncher, Dave Elden. An artist of modest accomplishment, Irene responds excitedly to the light and colour of the prairie landscape; more importantly she conceives of it as both fostering and embodying an especially attractive life-style. Contrasting sharply to her mother, who finds the prairie "so much desolation and ugliness," Irene is stirred by the sight as she returns for her second western visit: "For her the boundlessness, the vastness, the immeasurable sweep of the eye, suggested an environment out of which should grow a manhood and womanhood that should weigh mightily in the scales of destiny of a great nation; a manhood and womanhood defiant of the things that are, eager for the adventure of life untrammeled by traditions" (p. 198).

From Irene's artistic perspective the uninterrupted flatness expresses the absence of traditional obstacles to the free determination of one's selfhood. The man standing on the prairie sees that he can move off easily in whatever direction he chooses. His naïve but persuasive conclusion is that similar freedom is possible in all phases of his life. Irene goes on to paint, in her mind, a brilliantly coloured prairiescape, and then, as evening comes, realizes the absence of an essential element: "The settlers' lights began to blink across the prairie, and

---

[7]Stead, *The Cowpuncher* (New York: Harper, 1918), p. 34.

Irene's eyes were wet with an emotion she could not define; but she knew her painting had missed something; it had been all outline and no soul, and the prairies in the night are all soul and no outline; all softness and vagueness and yearning unutterable . . ." (p. 199). The freedom of limitless spaces and the spiritual nourishment of a quiet and uninterrupted land are, for Irene, the essence of the prairie environment. That Mrs. Hardy, a withered socialite, cannot respond to the prairie's beauty only reinforces the validity of this landscape symbol in the lives of those who are receptive to it. But Mrs. Hardy, too, comes slowly to sympathize in some measure with the enthusiasm and freedom of the new land.

Irene finds that the foothills country has a peculiar symbolic quality of its own:

> It was beautiful, not with the majesty of the great mountains, nor the solemnity of the great plains, but with that nearer, more intimate relationship which is the peculiar property of the foothill country. Here was neither the flatness that, with a change of mood, could become in a moment desolation, nor the aloofness of eternal rocks towering into cold space, but the friendship of hills that could be climbed and trees that lisped in the light wind, and water that babbled playfully over gravel ridges gleaming in the August sunshine (p. 15).

The landscape is pastoral, soothing to man, and subservient to his will. The possibilities of desolation or terror are fleeting and easily neglected. Throughout the novel both Irene and Dave have memories of the ranch and often look to the foothills outside the city with yearning. Their memories are, of course, not exclusively of a physical landscape, but of the youthful love, the natural companionship, and the sense of freedom with which they automatically associate it. These associations provide the idealized moral background for the development of a story which is largely urban in its setting.

The Cowpuncher begins with a familiar pattern—the innocent Dave Elden moves to town where he becomes enmeshed in a net of gambling, drink and evil women. The expectation is that Dave will be eventually rescued from decadence by the sudden appearance of the beautiful Irene, under whose influence he had fallen briefly in the opening chapters. While the stereotyped plot is followed for a time, it is the variations from it that are interesting and that mark Stead's slight movement away from the sentimental and romantic. Dave's descent to decadence, for example, is short-lived, and he matures through jobs as a coal-hauler, a warehouse man, and a reporter. Before his reunion with Irene, Dave has acquired a fair measure of material wealth and has maintained an only slightly weakened hold on his deep-seated instinct for honesty. The resolution of the novel is sentimental, certainly, but much less so than that of *The Bail Jumper* or *The Homesteaders*. Unlike those novels *The Cowpuncher* ends with the death of the hero and the quiet disappointment of his two lovers,

Irene and Edith. The mawkish hope expressed at the novel's close that the valleys of hate will all be flooded over is nevertheless quiet and resolute, rather than exuberant and unquestioning. That Dave shared Irene's vision of the potential inherent in the western landscape is emphasized at his death by his final imaginative glimpse of the foothills ranch and the final description of the ranch home where Irene continues to live. The return to this setting, physically by Irene, and spiritually by Dave at his death, serves to affirm the values with which it has been associated. The values of individual freedom, embodied ironically in Dave's death; of love, sustained by Irene's memories and her son's quiet pride; and of spiritual calm are reinforced in the novel by their having, beyond mere abstract presentation, symbolic existence in the landscape.

The provocative and sustained social comment in *Dennison Grant* (1920) marks a further step in Stead's development as a novelist. Grant, despite his antecedents among the captains of industry, is a passionate social reformer. When he expounds his doctrines to Zen Transley in the moonlight, McCourt throws up his hands and dismisses the novel as an impossible mixture of romance and economic theory.[8] But as A.T. Elder notes, Grant's attempted reforms provide the novel with an intellectual texture which marks it as something superior to popular romance.[9]

In presenting the genesis and first realizations of Grant's utopian dream Stead introduces the most pronounced tension of any of his novels between Eastern and Western Canada. Grant himself conceives of the clash between east and west as a deep-seated thing: "The East says because things are so, and have always been so, they are in all probability wrong."[10] Curiously, perhaps, this regional distinctiveness is not attributed in any special way to geography. The difference is one between social environments—one settled and secure, one empty and only beginning to grow. The foothills and plains setting is described in Stead's usually idyllic terms, but with little of the sense, detected in *The Homesteaders* or *The Cowpuncher*, that certain values and human characteristics are created or fostered by a particular physical environment.

Grant's elaborately idealistic project is to achieve social equality through communal ownership of farm land. His unorthodoxy is in itself an expression of western individualism. The "open life" of the prairie is particularly suited to such a bold project. Material considerations are spurned; the location for Grant's social experiment is determined by the magnificence of its sunsets. He conceives of himself as a king of the soil, dominating the land, which serves him in all things:

"To take a substance straight from the hand of the Creator and be the first in all the world to impose a human will upon it is surely an occasion

[8]McCourt, *Canadian West in Fiction*, p. 95.
[9]Elder, *Canadian Literature*, No. 17 (Summer 1963), 54.
[10]Stead, *Dennison Grant* (Toronto: Musson, 1920), p. 240.

for solemnity and thanksgiving. . . . Just as from the soil springs all physical life, may it not be that deep down in the soil are, some way, the roots of the spiritual? The soil feeds the city in two ways; it fills its belly with material food, and it is continually re-vitalizing its spirit with fresh streams of energy which can come only from the land. Up from the soil comes all life, all progress, all development—'' (p. 291).

Grant's enthusiasm for the fundamentals of farming is typical of Stead's fiction. Intimate contact with the soil is also contact with the spiritual basics of life. The regularity of the ploughed field suggests a land provided by God for man's nourishment. The virtues of reverence, energetic industry and progress, derived from the soil, are here sanctified. While this passage is indicative of the tone of the entire novel, such extended reflection on the divine right of the man of the soil is isolated and not developed further. In fact, Stead seems a trifle embarrassed at the passionate soliloquy and Grant is suddenly shaken from his preoccupied state by a fall from the plough.

With the fall Stead leaves metaphysical reflection to return to the romantic plot centering on the love affair of Dennison Grant and Zen Transley. As in *The Cowpuncher*, and in contrast to the earlier novels, Stead provides a more honest resolution. Grant and Zen do not suddenly overcome all difficulties to be united in eternal love. They recognize that the realities of their situation, especially of Zen's duty to her son and husband, make a continuation of their relationship impossible. This leaves Grant free to propose to his long-time secretary, the plain-looking but faithful Phyllis Bruce. Doubtless the conclusion is sentimental, but it places an emphasis on the ordinary and representative which becomes increasingly prominent in Stead's subsequent fiction.

The spiritual potential of the prairie, which Dennison Grant extols, is a central concern in Stead's next novel, *Neighbours* (1922). Set in central Saskatchewan, *Neighbours* tells of the first years of homesteading by two brother-sister teams: Jack and Jean Lane, and Frank and Marjorie Hall. The courtship and marriage of Jack and Marjorie, then of Frank and Jean are the substance of the novel's plot. Stead's use of the first-person narrator, Frank Hall, in spite of frequent inconsistencies, allows him to tell the story of homesteading with the intensity and accuracy of one actually involved in the experience. The details of selecting the quarter-section with the greatest potential, the account of working the first year's harvest as hired hands, the introduction of new settlers to the community, and the joys of a cooperative Christmas wedding feast add the dimensions of social and agricultural history to the novel, without becoming repetitious or tedious.

First-person narration does not enable Stead to present the harsh and terrifying aspect of the prairie to any extent. The dominant impression of the prairie, aside from its level immensity, is of great beauty and brilliant colours. Sunset is "a lake of saffron and champagne," with "a glory of pink and yellow and orange and crimson and burnished brass.''[11] The imagery of jewels and precious metals is ubiquitous—in the early morning dew "every blade of grass was hung with diamonds"; a snowfall is a "curtain of ivory lace"; and the land is an inexhaustible "gold mine." Truly this is a country, with its magnificence of "burnished brass," its rich luxury of diamonds," "ivory" and "gold," fit for a king. Indeed, at first sight, Frank recognizes the prairie as "a kingdom fresh from the hand of God and ready for the plow" (p. 29).

The prairie is kind not only to the cultivator of the soil, but also to the artistic spirit. Jean Lane is an artist, a woman with " 'perspective and proportion,' " who slowly educates Frank to the artist's view of the essentials of life. The prairie geography in this context has an ambiguous influence—both encouraging and discouraging the artist. " 'The deadly routine' " of a life confined to eating, working and sleeping is anathema to Jean, who finds it " 'bad enough anywhere, but on these prairies with their isolation, their immensity—unbearable.' " (p. 261). But another of Jean's observations is more typical: " 'It's too grand; it oppresses one. It's—it's all soul; no body' " (p. 93). The absence of obvious physical feature on the prairie makes it a suitable image for pure spirit, something invisible and intangible. Here Stead anticipates a metaphor which is most fully developed by W.O. Mitchell. But in not resolving, indeed scarcely considering, the impending conflict between man's will and nature's will, Stead leaves Jean's discovery of the spiritual essence of the prairie vastness seeming shallow and simplistic. Brian O'Connal's intuition of godhood in the tableau of eternally changing prairie at the end of *Who Has Seen the Wind* comes after long experience and deliberate questioning; in comparison Jean Lane's reference to the "soul" of the prairie is sentimental and self-indulgent.

Stead's handling of Frank's spiritual metamorphosis is not only incomplete, but clumsy. His supposed expanded sympathy with the things of the spirit, after the reading of a few books, is artificial. Mechanically reciting Shelley's "The Cloud" when rain threatens is apparently intended to demonstrate his new-found artistic sensibility. Instead it only serves to emphasize how inadequate and unconvincing Stead's characterization usually is.

Nevertheless, in the context of Stead's own fiction, the characterization is noticeably improved over the early novels. Although he is in too much of a hurry to recount the Ontario childhood of the Halls and the Lanes, Stead does succeed in the course of the novel in delineating the four main characters fairly well. The change in Frank's personality is actually much less abrupt than it first seems, for, as narrator, he has throughout the novel shown considerable sympathy for the aesthetic and metaphysical side of existence; the problem lies in Stead's indiscriminate shifting from Frank's point of view to omniscience. Furthermore, Stead's considerable ability for wry humour, the creation of carica-

[11]Stead, *Neighbours* (Toronto: Hodder and Stoughton, 1922), p. 31.

tures, and the evocation of accents and dialects is, with the exception of *Grain*, at its best here. The creations of Spoof, the innocent yet sensitive remittance man, and Jake, the hardened prairie hand with the heart of gold, are particularly memorable.

With Frank's dedication to a new life of expanding knowledge comes a significant definition: "Life for me was no longer a thing of the body, which is death, but a thing of the mind and spirit, which are eternal" (p. 280). Such glib philosophizing echoes Jean's description of the prairie as all soul and no body. As Jean and Frank move toward a meeting of minds, the prairie, as an image of the life of the spirit, is usually close at hand. Frank's description of the link between the spiritual and the prairie landscape is based on the figure of solitary vertical man:

> I suppose it is because of the vast sameness of the prairies themselves that we learned to turn our eyes so often to the heavens. When one's vision is hemmed about by woods and hills he is in danger of missing the greater majesty of the skies. Many a breathing spell had Buck and Bright while I turned in my plow-handles to watch the gentle drift of cloud shadows gliding over the fields, or to plunge my eyes into the blue vacuum of eternal space (p. 304).

The noble ploughman is invited by the peculiar nature of a flat landscape to turn away from earthly and material considerations in order to contemplate the ultimate majesty of the spiritual and eternal.

In spite of the superficiality and God-fearing propriety with which Stead treats this entire theme, the quest for the life of the spirit is more completely satisfied in *Neighbours* than in any of his preceding novels. On a hot summer night Jean and Frank spontaneously leave their beds, meet, and go swimming together. Jean recounts a dream which promises Frank that a beautiful maiden will arise from the sea to be taken in his arms forever. Then she disappears to arise moments later from the dark pond as the realization of that dream. The scene is extravagant, surely, and yet there is an integration here with the novel as a whole which is not found in many of Stead's works. A dreamily fantastic conclusion is at least consistent with a novel whose constant motif is the need of romance as an essential of life, especially in the midst of this vast prairie. Stead's ideal world is summarized in Jean's statement of the law by which they both must live: " 'The law of romance, which is the law of imagination, which is the law of beauty, which is the law of love, which is the law of life' " (p. 314). It is the law as well of Stead's fiction and of Stead's prairie.

The law of romance and the law of beauty just as strictly govern *The Smoking Flax* (1924). Again situated in the appropriately named Manitoba town of Plainville, *The Smoking Flax* focusses on the generation which follows the pioneers, a generation of Ford cars and agricultural prosperity. The subject matter accounts, in part, for the decreased attention to setting: the progress of the crops, the variations in the weather, and the daily details of farm life are only incidentally mentioned.

Cal Beach, a sociology graduate from an eastern university, has come to the west for his health with his adopted son, Reed, the illegitimate child of his sister. Stead, as he often does, stretches coincidence to the limit by having Cal find work on the Stake farm, to which Reed's unknown father, Jackson Stake, Jr., soon returns. The complications of plot resulting when Jackson Jr. threatens to make public that Reed is his son provide the intrigue which is consistently the weakest aspect of Stead's novels. This weakness is particularly apparent in Cal's wildly improbable plot to murder his tormentor. Strangely enough, the scene in which Jackson commits suicide beneath the wheels of a train, thus ending the threat which he poses to Cal and Reed, is successful—sensitively described and startling.

Cal Beach's aspirations echo those of most of Stead's central characters: "If he could awaken to spiritual consciousness the physical life of which the Stake farmstead was typical, and at the same time gain a livelihood for Minnie and for Reed: that, surely, would be something worthwhile."[12] In Minnie Stake, Cal finds a partner who shares with him " 'a glimpse of what it should be—of what it could be made—.' " Although the connection is not explicit, Stead's familiar benign and peaceful physical environment is clearly conducive to such naive spirituality: "Grass, green and moist, with a purple carpeting of anemones. Water shining from many tiny lakes. Coveys of white clouds, like ruffled swans, afloat in an infinite sky" (p. 7).

Cal fits the pattern of the regal farm labourer, exulting in the challenge of hard work; but when it comes to realizing their dream, as they inevitably do at the end of the novel, he and Minnie build a cottage beside a small lake, a place recommended by "its beauty, its solitude, its vast, slumbrous, brooding silence." They turn to a place which, like the gully and the pond in *Neighbours*, is both part of the prairie and yet a retreat from it—a place which reflects Stead's ambiguous feeling that the prairie is both the seat of spiritual nourishment, and, in the labour it demands, liable to frustrate the very life to which it is suited.

Cal's empathy with the natural world is further indicated by the many fables he invents in order to explain to Reed the mysteries of nature and the merits of a strict morality. The final one of these, the story of the rose and the wheat, sums up the theme of the novel, albeit in a rather mechanical manner. This fable is Cal's interpretation of Isaiah, chapter forty-two which provides the title and dominant motif of the novel: "A bruised reed shall he not break, and the smoking flax shall he not quench." Cal's recognition of the beauty of that phrase and his dedication to the life of tenderness, faith and sympathy which it provides as a model, is the central incident in the resolution of the novel. *The Smoking Flax* thus follows Stead's pattern of sentimental conclusions,

---

[12]Stead, *The Smoking Flax* (Toronto: McClelland and Stewart, 1924), p. 167.

but in this instance the sentiment does not obscure the memory of the mental anguish which has threatened the characters or of the ultimate self-denial made by Jackson Jr. The lingering impact of that episode balances the optimism in the marriage of Minnie and Reed, making the novel more serious in tone than the sentimental romance.

There is general and well-justified critical opinion that *Grain* (1926) is Stead's best novel. In this novel the elements of romantic love, elsewhere excessive or predictable, are integral to the central themes of the novel; the sensationalism, such as the near-death of Walter Peters in the threshing machine, arises naturally from the events of the novel instead of being imported from crime thrillers. Stead seems, now, to sense the inadequacy of the king of the soil image. Man in the prairie still finds himself dominating a landscape which seems conceived, despite occasional harshness, to fill his needs plenteously; but Stead recognizes that in the modern world there are attractions other than the simple enrichment that comes with tilling the soil. The hero of *Grain*, Gander Stake, finds himself pulled between the traditional love of the land and the fascinating world of machinery and technology.

Undoubtedly this tension is essential to what Stead argues is a new concept of the hero. In the opening paragraph he says:

> Perhaps the term hero, with its suggestion of high enterprise, sits inappro-priately upon the chief character of a somewhat commonplace tale; there was in Gander Stake little of that quality which is associated with the clash of righteous steel or the impact of noble purposes. Yet that he was not without heroic fibre I will not admit, and you who bear with me through these pages shall judge whether or not the word is wholly unwarranted.[13]

Historically, of course, the impulse to redefine heroism, as *Joseph Andrews* or *Tom Jones* will illustrate, is basic to the emergence of the novel as a genre. For Stead, almost two centuries later, the novel provides the same opportunity. The attempt in *Grain* to show the nobility inherent in the average man and in the commonplace event is Stead's most concerted move away from romance towards realism.

While the novel's characterization is more comprehensive, the tendency does not extend, to any degree, to the presentation of the prairie geography. The continuing dominant impression made by the landscape is one of bountiful provi-sion, most clearly indicated in *Grain* by the image of the earth-mother suckling the young prairie crops. Although Stead shows an increasing awareness of the complexities of human interaction in this novel, he tends to avoid the prairie landscape rather than alter it to conform to his theme. Gander, for example, is a solitary figure when faced with major decisions in his young life. Stead

---

[13]Stead, *Grain* (Toronto: McClelland and Stewart, 1963), p. 15.

does not attempt to link his solitude to the empty landscape as Grove or Ross would have done.

Thomas Saunders, following McCourt's lead, dwells on Gander's "inarticulate, compelling love of the land itself," finding in this aspect of his character reason to condemn the ending as contrived and "completely unconvincing."[14] The charge is quite unjustified. Much in the novel, to be sure, establishes Gander's deep love of the land: "Gander was a farmer born and bred; he had an eye for horses and a knack with machinery; the mysteries of the self-binder he had solved before he was nine, but the mysteries of the cube root he had not solved when he left school—nor since" (p. 40). Born in the prairie, Gander seems completely adapted to it:

> On afternoons when he was not needed about the farm he went skating on the lake, his thin figure a pathetic suggestion of loneliness, thinner than ever in its contrast with the great expanse of ice and the hills sprinkled white with snow and hoar frost which shouldered up from the lake to the prairies beyond. Yet Gander was not lonely; never in all his days on the farm and the prairie did Gander know the pang of loneliness. This was his native environment; he was no more lonely on these prairies than is the coyote or the badger (p. 56).

Stead uses the image of man's verticality in the prairie vastness, not to depict his exposure, but to deny it. Gander, like the native animals, is in complete harmony with the prairie. When a sudden rain comes up Gander quickly forgets the attractions of Jo Burge for the farmer's first love: "Here was rain, rain! Rain, the first love of every farmer, the bride of every dry, thirsty field, the mother of every crop that grows! Gander was a farmer. All his instincts were rooted deep in the soil" (p. 79). But the promise of rain is disappointed, leaving Gander to glare in grim defiance at the sky. Though Gander had responded exactly as a son of the soil, "he was too young to be long caught in despair over the fleeting rain; his protest had been a sort of reflex of his father, rather than a cry from his own heart" (p. 80). While the response is predictable, the impulse behind it is neither as sincere nor as total as might be expected. Gander's love of the farm and the soil in which it is rooted is secondary to his love of the machine. In similar circumstances John Harris or Dennison Grant discover much deeper, almost mystical ties to the soil.

Gander's greatest pride is his knowledge of machinery: " 'Well, I know the difference between a Deering an' a Massey Harris across a fifty-acre field' " (p. 60). Gander always operates the machinery while his father concentrates on the tasks that are done by hand. As Gander and Jo Burge watch the threshing machine rumble by at night he is touched with a strange thrill: "Although Gander was a boy not touched by the romance of books here was something

---

[14]Thomas Saunders, "Introduction," *Grain*, pp. x-xi.

that stirred him deeply—the romance of machinery, of steam, which at the pull of a lever turned loose the power of giants!'' (p. 54). The climax of Gander's romance with the machine comes with the opportunity to fire a threshing machine:

> Firing Bill Powers' straw-burner opened a new world for Gander, a world of great activity and accomplishment, in which the throbbing of the steam exhaust for a time beat down that inner throbbing which could be quietened but could not quite be killed. It was a hard life to one who weighed his work, but Gander did not count it hard because he loved his engine and delighted in its company (p. 98).

In contrast Gander's day-to-day existence is a going "on in the deepening furrow of his circle, round and round." Stead returns to the image of the furrow several times to suggest the monotonous, seemingly inescapable routine of Gander's life. It is the one aspect of the novel in which Stead seems to be altering the benign prairie to accommodate his shift in emphasis. But the image is not explicitly linked with the contours of the landscape nor does it give more than the slightest hint of the predictable and monotonous landscape as it is used, for example, in McCourt's *Home is the Stranger*. Though outwardly content to follow in the furrow his father has ploughed before him, Gander is secretly unsure that his decision is the best. Particularly, he is in a constant mental agony to justify his not enlisting to fight in the Great War. When Gander does finally make the decision to jump his furrow, to discover for himself a new definition of life, it is not surprising that the move is in a direction different from that in other Stead novels. He responds to the sense of vitality, one might even say of spirit, which he had discovered in the machine: "This—this power—this mighty thing that sprang at his touch—this was life!" (p. 101).

Gander's emergence as a hero does not come with his hunting prowess, nor with his willingness to shoulder a man's portion of the farm labour, nor even with his saving the life of Walter Peters, although all of these contribute to it. Gander's true heroism, as Stead presents it, is to be found in his gradual maturing in love and his discovery of his own individuality. It is found in Gander's reluctant rejection of his youthful infatuation for Jo Burge and his acceptance of her as a duty-bound married woman. If Gander was ever a coward, as he is the first to realize, it was not in his refusal to fight, but in his inability to communicate his love. Jerry Chansley seems to increase Gander's awareness of his inadequacies, even more than Jo had. She challenges Gander, as did Jo, to broaden his horizons. Jerry's challenge is accompanied by the prospect of the opportunity to work in the city with machines and to study at technical school. In spite of their brief contact it seems clear, considering the magnetic attraction which machinery holds for Gander, that her suggestion remains vivid in his memory. Vivid enough that when his sister Minnie tells him the story of Cal and Reed, familiar from *The Smoking Flax*, to illustrate that "sometimes it is the brave man who runs away,'' he is ready to respond. Though once unable to accept military discipline, Gander now comes to accept personal discipline by leaving his first love, his family, and farm to find a new life in the world beyond.

Saunders's objection to the ending of the novel as sentimental and inconsistent is, therefore, mistaken. It is no exaggeration to say that Gander's first love is for the machine—that its particular context is of secondary importance. When this inclination is understood, together with Gander's submerged discontent with the routine of the farm, his ultimate move to the city is quite credible. The possibility of a vital life with a spiritual dimension is found to lie in the direction of the new age of machine, rather than in a return to the land, or in a literary awakening. Yet this resolution does not involve a radical change in Stead's view of man in the prairie. Gander's prairie, that is to say Gander's world, is still an essentially harmonious one where honest industry is rewarded by spiritual and material plenty. The machine becomes an integral part of the simple rural life. The ''hard life'' of firing the threshing machine is not, in Stead's terms, a new world, but ''a world of great activity and accomplishment,'' not unlike the world of the prairie pioneer.

The reflection, in *Grain*, of the growing mechanization of prairie agriculture points to the curious irony that as man gains increasing control over his physical environment through technology, he becomes, in the pages of fiction, increasingly out of harmony with that environment. It would seem that as the machine makes the task of working the harsh land easier, the pioneer's need for the sustaining myth of an eternally beneficent land becomes less urgent. In the period covered by Stead's works the prairie writer was increasingly freed to consider more objectively man's relationship to the natural world, and, ultimately, man's own nature. The major thrust in this direction is provided by Frederick Philip Grove.

The basic geometric image in Stead's novels emphasizes the point where vertical and horizontal meet. Man is the monarch of all he surveys, rooted in the soil from which he derives both material and spiritual necessities. Prairie is primarily a metaphor for Stead's shallow conception of the spiritual in human life. The inherent ambiguity of a prairie which stimulates the life of the spirit by its magnificent vastness, yet dictates a strictly materialistic life opposed to the spirit, is implied but undeveloped. Immense flatness mirrors man's infinite opportunities, but Stead shows no sense that this was a country ''that hated a foreign and vertical thing.''[15] An awareness of this aspect of the prairie gives to Frederick Philip Grove's landscape a balance, comprehension and imaginative validity unknown to Stead.

---

[15]Stegner, *Wolf Willow*, p. 271.

III

The Implacable Prairie:
The Fiction of
Frederick Philip Grove

Nature abhors an elevation.

WALLACE STEGNER, *Wolf Willow*

While Stead's work gives proof that the Victorian age of "order in freedom; stability in progress; truth despite contradiction; hope against despair"[1] was alive well into the nineteen-twenties, Grove's fiction demonstrates the abrupt and decisive change in world view which is equally characteristic of the period between the wars. Grove, in direct contrast to Stead, emphasizes that vertical man is alien to a horizontal world. Stead's vertical figure dominating a horizontal world belongs to an era of unquestioned faith in progress; the exposure of vertical man in Grove's prairie dramatically presents the inevitability of decay. The replacement of dominant man by exposed man in this decade reminds us that chronologically prairie fiction was leading Canadian fiction as a whole into an era of a new critical, more sophisticated, more realistic novel. (Callaghan's first novel was not published until 1928.) The earnestly critical nationalism manifesting itself in the founding of the *Canadian Forum, Canadian Historical Review*, and *Dalhousie Review*, and in the first exhibitions of the Group of Seven, had its literary counterpart in the pages of Philip Grove.

Grove's protagonists have little of the king or emperor about them; they live in an implacable prairie, where "man remains distinctly an interloper."[2] Faced by a disintegration of their world picture, Grove's prairie men stand opposed to the mechanics of the universe. What was once certain becomes tentative. Man is no longer amply provided for, but must provide for himself.

Man standing upright on the prairie has no protection from the ravages of an extreme climate. While he is aware of the possible psychological extensions of this situation, Grove always gives the literal exposure of the prairie man primary consideration; man is at the mercy of natural forces. The eventual consequence of exposure, of course, is obliteration of man and man's works: "Nature abhors an elevation as much as it abhors a vacuum; a hill is no sooner elevated than the forces of erosion begin tearing it down. These prairies are quiescent, close to static; looked at for any length of time, they begin to impose their awful perfection on the observer's mind."[3] In many ways Stegner's perceptive comment describes Philip Grove's prairie. The earth itself is eternal

---

[1] W.L. Morton, "The 1920's," *The Canadians 1867-1967*, ed. J.M.S. Careless and R. Craig Brown (Toronto: Macmillan, 1967), p. 205.
[2] F.P. Grove, *Fruits of the Earth* (Toronto: McClelland and Stewart, 1965), p. 137.
[3] Stegner, *Wolf Willow*, p. 7.

while above it there is a continual state of flux, the forces of nature relentlessly returning all things to the horizontal.

In *In Search of Myself* Grove recalls the vision which defined for him the typical prairie man:

> Somewhere towards the end of my outward drive, to town, I saw a man; and what is more, he was ploughing straight over the crest of a hill to the west, coming, when I caught sight of him, towards my trail. The town which I was approaching lay on the railway, in the dry belt of the country; the general verdict was that the surrounding district was unfit for farming. The mere fact, therefore, that this man was ploughing as he came over the crest of the hill was sufficiently arresting and even startling. Besides, outlined as he was against a tilted and spoked sunset in the western sky, he looked like a giant.[4]

The abrupt vertical image obviously had great power for Grove; man in the prairie is a giant, strong and self-reliant, struggling determinedly in a barren land. But Grove saw, unlike Stead, that whatever the pioneer's measure of self-reliance and hardness, he would ultimately fail in his struggle with the land. He also recognized that the qualities which fit a man admirably to farming in this land could destroy his relationships with other men.

Elsewhere in *In Search of Myself*, the Russian steppes, as he conceived them—spare, simple, sometimes cruel, often indifferent—provided a concrete image for Grove's bleakly tragic conception of the human condition.[5] He describes the song of the Kirghiz herdsmen as a distillation of the tragic experience: "It was a vast, melancholy utterance, cadenced within a few octaves of the bass register, as if the landscape as such had assumed a voice: full of an almost inarticulate realization of man's forlorn position in the face of a hostile barrenness of nature; and yet full, also, of a stubborn, if perhaps only inchoate assertion of man's dignity below his gods" (p. 153). Grove did not again encounter such a "treeless country of an impressive and ceaseless monotony" until he came to Canada. Clearly the landscapes, if only in Grove's imagination, are the same. The staggering fact of man's presence in such a land, and the significance of constantly threatened destruction, are the inevitable concomitants of the prairie setting in his novels.

The voice of the steppes, of man forlorn, yet defiant, in the face of nature's hostility, echoes through all Grove's prairie writing. It speaks his inclination to go far beyond Stead in describing the actualities of the prairie and the realities

---

[4]F.P. Grove, *In Search of Myself* (Toronto: Macmillan, 1946), p. 259.
[5]Douglas Spettigue notes that Grove probably never visited Russia in *Frederick Philip Grove* (Toronto: Copp Clark, 1969), p. 18. On the whole question of the accuracy of Grove's autobiography see Spettigue's recent articles: "Frederick Philip Grove," *Queen's Quarterly*, LXXVIII (Winter 1971), 614-15; "The Grove Enigma Resolved," *Queen's Quarterly*, LXXIX (Spring 1972), 1-2.

of human experience. Grove represents, then, a significant advance in the attempt to embrace imaginatively and verbally the prairie world. Furthermore, a *Canadian Forum* article of 1931 indicates Grove's consciousness that the artist's efforts to know the land are necessary to a nation's knowledge of itself: "Differences in national character are most pronounced in those who are in immediate contact with the soil they sprang from; for they rest in geographic, topographic, and climatic conditions."[6]

In a later essay Grove makes his point more fully:

> What, to the members of other nations, does Canada stand for? So far, very little. Does that mean that our unrivalled sea-shores, our proud mountains, and our boundless prairies, unique on earth, have not tinged man's attitude to life and the world, or to God, whatever you care to call it? Does it mean that our broad slice of the universe as it was settled has not engendered a new human reaction to the outside world? I do not believe it.
>
> In fact, I believe that such a new reaction is to-day crying for utterance in verse and prose; for only by being uttered can it be born. Let us, then, aim at supplying a future generation with its expression.[7]

Implicit in this charge to his fellow Canadian authors is Grove's recognition that the interpretation of the physical environment in his novels has a national dimension. From the affectionate precision with which he describes his world in *Over Prairie Trails* and *The Turn of the Year*, to the harshly mysterious landscape of the Marsh novels, and the often dismal prairie in *Our Daily Bread* and *Fruits of the Earth*, the re-creation of the setting is, from his perspective, Grove's contribution to defining Canada's sense of nationality.[8]

Yet Grove is more novelist than nationalist; his first concern with the prairie setting, as even his challenge to specifically *Canadian* writers indicates, is to show its impact upon "man's attitude to life and the world." His highly developed sensitivity for place leads him to relate the attributes of his characters to the physical environment in which they exist. While human conflict—father against son, husband against wife, or even man against himself—is the focus of his

[6]Grove, "Apologia pro Vita et Opere Sua," *Canadian Forum*, XI (August 1931), 422.
[7]Grove, "A Neglected Function of a Certain Literary Association," *It Needs to Be Said* (Toronto: Macmillan, 1929), p. 20.
[8]In addition much of the unpublished fiction in the F.P. Grove Papers (University of Manitoba Library Special Collections) verifies Grove's intense interest in the prairie setting. There is, however, little that is substantially different in his use of the landscape. The settings of *Jane Atkinson*: "bare, unrelieved, rolling prairie . . . a lonely country, sparsely settled: a tragic landscape in the rising dusk" (Grove Papers, Pt. IV, No. 3, Box 16. Typescript p. 142); or of *The Poet's Dream*: "The utter barrenness of the desert-like country, . . . assumed again that cosmic air of an inhospitable landscape which was merely bridged by the road, not settled by man." (Grove Papers, Pt. III, No. 2, Box 11, Typescript p. 181), are recognizable to readers of Grove's published works. The manuscript of *The Lean Kine* is interrupted just as the land begins to show its power; except for the place names one can read *The Weatherhead Fortunes* and be quite unaware of its setting; the meticulous detective story, *Murder in the Quarry*, has little use for setting.

prairie novels, the conflict of man with his physical environment is also essential, especially as it affects human relations. In the conflict between man and land, as I have already noted, Grove sees no possibility for man's ultimate triumph. Grove's view of human experience, reinforced, if not in part stimulated, by this truth, is unremittingly tragic.

Grove defined his idea of the tragic in an essay titled "The Happy Ending":

> To have greatly tried and to have failed; to have greatly wished and to be denied; to have greatly longed for purity and to be sullied; to have greatly craved for life and to receive death: all that is the common lot of greatness upon earth. It would be misery indeed, instead of tragedy if there were not another factor in the equation. . . . The tragic quality of Moses' fate—combining the terror that crushes with Aristotle's catharsis which exalts—lies in the fact that he accepted that fate of his; that he was reconciled to it; that he rested content with having borne the banner thus far: others would carry it beyond.[9]

His conception asserts the universality of tragedy in the human experience. Both King Lear and Grove's own John Elliott are tragic figures, in spite of the fact that Elliott is much weaker, suffering a much less spectacular fate. The theme of man in conflict with the environment coexists with a sense, not unlike that found in Hardy, that man shares his tragic lot with the natural world. From this point of view man is almost an extension of the life of the soil. Grove explores the idea at some length in *In Search of Myself*:

> I believe in the unity of all life; in the unity of the urge which compels the atoms of quartz to array themselves in the form of a crystal; with the urge which holds the stars in their courses or which made me sit down to write this last will and testament of my life. . . . Only the striving after the unattainable was in any sense worth while and worthy of human endeavour. That desire, that urge was mine. That desire, that urge I saw in everything, even in the crystal or the snow-flake; and I also saw its frustration; a frustration often due to the very superabundance of the impulses making for some kind of order, exactly because there was no plan which teleologically directed that striving (p. 231).

This oneness of man and his physical environment is, then, a source of strength for Grove's heroes, as well as an anticipation of their ultimate failure.

But lest my attention to Grove's idea of tragedy mislead, I hasten to say that the critical search for the label to describe Grove's fiction is one which I wish to join only long enough to suggest his integration of character and setting. Simply, Donald Pizer's definition of naturalism is one which suits Grove's

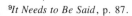
[9]*It Needs to Be Said*, p. 87.

fiction well, but not restrictively. "A naturalistic novel is... an extension of realism only in the sense that both modes often deal with the local and contemporary. The naturalist, however, discovers in this material the extraordinary and excessive in human nature." The thematic complexity of naturalism has often been disregarded. "The naturalist often describes his characters as though they are conditioned and controlled by environment, heredity, instinct, or chance. But he also suggests a compensating humanistic value in his characters or their fates which affirms the significance of the individual and of his life."[10] Man, in Grove's novels, is but one creature in the natural world, as subject as the beasts of the field to the whims of climate and topography. Yet this "controlling force" is intermingled with the "individual worth" which prompts man to defy, to endure, at moments to transcend, his physical environment.

However appropriately naturalism describes Grove's artistic aims, Grove himself rejected the term (by which he meant Zola's attempt to make the novel a scientific experiment[11]) in favour of realism. Such realism did not concern itself primarily with the documented accuracy of settings, but with that emotional and psychological accuracy which satisfies the claims of probability, and evokes the reader's response: "'There, but for the grace of God, go I.'"[12] Thus, if the achievement approaches the intention, Grove's selection of background details, and his use of setting in general, should be directed to the achievement of psychological realism.

For Grove such realism meant starting with the life of the pioneer, which he found expressed most simply, and most powerfully, his conception of the human lot. Broadly interpreted the pioneer experience is the subject of *Two Generations* and *The Master of the Mill*, of the fantasy, *Consider Her Ways*, and of the autobiographical fictions, *A Search for America*, and *In Search of Myself*. But the four novels set in Western Canada deal more particularly with the pioneer in a setting where man's struggle with the environment can be seen in starkly elemental terms. The narrator of *In Search of Myself* dedicates himself in characteristically grandiloquent terms to the task of re-creating in fiction the pioneer life:

> I, the cosmopolitan, had fitted myself to be the spokesman of a race . . . of those who, in no matter what climate, at no matter what time, feel the impulse of starting anew, from the ground up, to fashion a new world which might serve as the breeding-place of a civilization to come. These people, the pioneers, reaffirmed me in my conception of what often takes the form of a tragic experience; the age-old conflict between human desire and the stubborn resistance of nature (pp. 226-27).

[10]Donald Pizer, *Realism and Naturalism in Nineteenth-Century American Literature* (Carbondale: Southern Illinois University Press, 1966), p. 13.
[11]*It Needs to Be Said*, pp. 55-58.
[12]*Ibid.*, p. 123.

As an image for this stubborn resistance of nature, the unchanging prairie was an obvious choice. Yet Grove's prairie is not simply a world of harsh monotony, but of diversity and beauty as well.

"I love Nature more than Man," Grove states in the preface to *Over Prairie Trails* (1922). The fluidity and sincerity resulting from the congeniality of the subject matter have caused many to judge the nature sketches, particularly this volume, as Grove's best writing. In this book Grove recounts seven of some seventy-two drives made in the winter of 1917-18 between Gladstone, Manitoba, where he was teaching, and Falmouth, where his wife had a school. Two years after the drives, in the autumn of 1919, Grove drafted *Over Prairie Trails*, working, it appears, from notes he made at the time.[13]

By relating seven drives over essentially the same landscape Grove imparts an obvious unity to his work. What is remarkable about these journeys, however, is not their similarities, but their differences, the amazing variety in appearance and mood to be discovered in the same place. Grove takes what is often overlooked and, by focussing attention upon it, invests it with a new significance. His sensitivity is reminiscent of "that power," praised by William Carlos Williams, "which discovers in things those inimitable particles of dissimilarity to all other things which are the peculiar perfections of the thing in question."[14] The most passionate and lyrical passage in *Over Prairie Trails* describes the startling beauty of the hoarfrost at dawn:

> The crystals were large, formed like spearheads, flat, slablike, yet of infinite thinness and delicacy, so thin and light that, when by misadventure my whip touched the boughs, the flakes seemed to float down rather than to fall. And every one of these flat and angular slabs was fringed with hairlike needles, or with featherlike needles, and longer needles stood in between.[15]

Grove's attention to the smallest detail and nuance is evident—each minute crystal of frost is carefully, almost reverently, described. In this volume, we recognize something of Stead's constant theme in what Grove sees as "the absolute friendliness of all creation for myself" (p. 13).

Malcolm Ross's amazement at Grove's "almost incredible love for the harsh, punishing, desolate Manitoba land"[16] is shared by many readers. This love arises from two things: so intense is Grove's observation that he readily discovers the beautiful details of nature; more importantly, he respects to the point of admiration the harsh, even brutal, character of the land. Grove persuades us of the beauty in the colour and feel of the "silver grey, leathery foliage of

[13]Spettigue, *Grove*, pp. 61, 68-71.
[14]*Selected Essays of William Carlos Williams* (New York: Random House, 1966), p. 16.
[15]Grove, *Over Prairie Trails* (Toronto: McClelland and Stewart, 1957), p. 53.
[16]"Introduction," *Over Prairie Trails*, p. v.

the wolf-willow''; in the darting flight of flocks of goldfinch; or in the ''bluff of stately poplars that stood like green gold in the evening sun'' (p. 6). His descriptive appeal is mainly to the eye, though when it suits his purpose he will appeal to the sense of touch, or, as in his descriptions of birds, to the ear: the ''twittering'' goldfinch, or the tangible silence of the owl's flight.

Although no professional scientist, Grove's attempt at precision and accuracy often suggests the scientist's approach. Indeed it is one of the flaws of both volumes of sketches that the poetry often becomes lost in Grove's conscientiously scientific accounts of natural phenomena, as in the description of the origins and movements of the fog, or in the application of the terms ''exfoliation'' and ''adfoliation'' to the drifting snow and snow formations. Occasional details of this sort are acceptable, even illuminating, but they are too often amplified until the account reads more like a text book than a nature essay. This unsettling side of Grove's attention to detail is balanced by the felicitous aspect. The concentration on a small detail, for example his focussing on the pattern traced by a single snowflake, is an effective way to explain the actions of drifting snow. But, more significantly, it is an indication of the writer's reverence for nature and for life even in its smallest manifestations.

Clearly Grove's imagination is not inhibited, but stimulated, by a landscape lacking the spectacular. He himself recognizes the poetic element in his prose: ''this is only one-quarter a poem woven of impressions; the other three-quarters are reality'' (p. 41). The poetry, indeed, is stimulated by this seemingly forbidding land:

> For a moment I thought that something after all was missing here on the prairies. But then I reflected again that this silence of the grave was still more perfect, still more uncanny and ghostly, because it left the imagination entirely free, without limiting it by even as much as a sugges-tion.
>
> No wonder, I thought, that the Northerners in their land of heath and bog were the poets of elves and goblins and of the fear of ghosts (p. 33).

Grove goes on to people this foggy scene with the creatures of his own fantasy, dancing shrouds, mocking spirits and werewolves, the creatures by means of which man attempts to make comprehensible the mysteries of his existence.

Grove's delight in these creatures of the imagination contrasts with the rigid, unimaginative lives of the people of this land. Because Grove the artist, like Frost's apple-picker, is convinced that the rural life provides an almost ideal combination of work for life's essentials and stimulus to the imagination, the contrast between the potential and the actuality is often effectively poignant. The uninterrupted prairie landscape permits the survey of the land into square plots, which in turn leads to square fields, ploughed and seeded in straight rows. Grove is only one of many writers to sense that the rigid geometric pattern of agriculture becomes reflected in the predictable, monotonous patterns of the lives of prairie people. Nature abhors the straight line, as Grove asserts more than once, and man's attempt to adapt himself to the contours of the landscape is misdirected. He describes a barn on his route: "The barn was of the Agricultural-College type—it may be good, scientific, and all that, but it seems to crush everything else around out of existence; and it surely is not picturesque—unless it has wings and silos to relieve its rigid contours" (p. 9). People who farm and live according to rigid formulas are mistaken if they believe themselves to be conforming to the dictates of the landscape. Slight nuances, random wanderings and unpredictability are more characteristic of the landscape and provide the stimulus to the imagination which too often goes unfelt. This is scarcely to suggest, however, that all Grove's characters share this rigid insensitivity—indeed, most of the central characters have, or acquire, some degree of imaginative sensitivity to their environment.

I have suggested that Grove's affection for the landscape arises not only from an intelligent eye for its beauties, but also from a humble respect for its powers. Compared to Stead or W.O. Mitchell, Grove creates a predominantly harsh, or at least melancholy, prairie. Although this is least true of the two volumes of essays, the fact that it can justly be said of the total impression of even those works, only reinforces the point.

Grove, then, does not adhere to his opinion of the "absolute friendliness of all creation": he finds the winter sun "relentless," "inexorable" and "pitiless," and the landscape below reminds him of the "barren sea." The wind-blown snow seems animated and savage: "It made the impression of cruelty, and in that lay its fascination and beauty. It even reminded me of a cat slowly reaching out with armed claw for the 'innocent' bird" (p. 102). Grove finds a fascinating beauty both in the poplars at sunset, and in the power of the blizzard; but the blizzards predominate, leaving an impression at the end of the volume of man's precarious position in the face of a cruel, unyielding land. The impression is summarized in Grove's memory of the gigantic drifts: "It looked so harsh, so millenial-old, so antediluvian and pre-Adamic! I still remember with particular distinctness the slight dizziness that overcame me, the sinking feeling in my heart, the awe and the foreboding that I had challenged a force in Nature which might defy all tireless effort and the most fearless heart" (p. 72). This sense of man's vulnerability in the age-old struggle with his environment is central to all Grove's writings about the prairie.

"We merely are intruders" is the way Peter Stevens expresses the same feeling. Man as intruder is the centre of attention in *Over Prairie Trails*, for Grove is not exclusively, nor even primarily, a nature writer, even in these sketches. Arthur Phelps was to recognize the same thing in his introduction to *The Turn of the Year*.

We are almost always conscious of the observer and of the influence upon man of his physical environment. One of the most important aspects of the description of the hoarfrost is the writer's attempts to avoid disturbing the beauty with his whip. The volume is dedicated to wife and daughter, and probably its most moving feature is the devotion of this man, who defies all risk for a few brief hours with his family. Man is also present in *Over Prairie Trails* as the insensitive destroyer of the beauty of the natural environment, building drainage ditches which "lie like naked scars on Nature's body: ugly, raw, as if the bowels were torn out of a beautiful bird and left to dry and rot on its plumage" (p. 14).

In *Over Prairie Trails* man and a man's love for his family triumph over the worst that nature can muster. Yet the triumph is not achieved with certainty and exultation, but with an ever-present knowledge of the precariousness of man's status, for the slightest alterations in conditions might have spelled this man's defeat. Even in the relatively benign world depicted in these sketches, Grove recognizes man's exposure to that "force in Nature which might defy all tireless effort and the most fearless heart." The uncertainty of human existence, felt and implied here, is made explicit in *The Turn of the Year*.

In *The Turn of the Year* (1923) Grove elaborates on comments in *Over Prairie Trails* that the prairie climate is uniquely conducive to close observation:

> Nobody, I believe, who lives farther south, where winter is a mere incident, can understand how we, at these outposts, feel the summer, that short, ardent orgy of life in which only such members of the world's fauna and flora will thrive as can sum up their being in a quick, breathless growth, in a sort of revelry of germinating, blooming, fruiting. . . . We are not surfeited at any time with the sweets of the seasons: our appetites are kept sharp; and what we lack in the breadth of our nature-experience, we make up for in depth, in intensity. I doubt whether people in the south ever become quite such ardent lovers of even the most trivial things in nature as we do. Our ears, eyes, sensations are sharpened to watch for the smallest, the seemingly most insignificant things.[17]

The traditional hardy endurance of a northern prairie people is complemented, in Grove's opinion, by a delicate sensitivity. There is ample evidence of his own sensitivity to nature, particularly in the central and lengthiest of the pieces in *The Turn of the Year* which describes repeated summertime bicycle trips in the prairie and bush country near Falmouth, Manitoba. Indeed so absorbed is Grove in the miniscule details of his surroundings that he takes time to measure the shoots and leaves of a particularly fast-growing scrub oak.

The rather obvious unity of *Over Prairie Trails* is replaced here by a thematic, even a poetic, unity, which derives from Grove's relating essays on three varied aspects of life lived in the bush country on the prairie fringe. The account of his bicycling trips through the bush is supplemented by essays concentrating

[17]Grove, *The Turn of the Year* (Toronto: McClelland and Stewart, 1923), p. 24.

on the details characteristic of the transitions from one season to the next; by three vignettes tracing the stages of love between a man and a woman; and by two sketches, focussing on the solitary farmer and his intimate bond to the land. Man, his relations to, and kinship with nature, receive more attention than in *Over Prairie Trails*. The landscape takes on more definite symbolic overtones. In ''The Third Vignette: Love in Autumn'' the landscape, with its contradictory aspects of rich fullness, mellowness, impending decay and the transitoriness of life, is used primarily as a concrete image of the aging love of John and Ellen—a simple, rather ordinary device, to be sure, but in the context of prairie fiction a further recognition of the potential of local metaphor.

But for all its incidental and ennobling beauty our sense of the prairie remains, as it was in *Over Prairie Trails*, one of melancholy, of imminent tragedy. The battle metaphor is integral to Grove's account of the shifting seasons; even in accommodating himself to the natural rhythms man participates in the struggle and finds himself an intruder. The pitiless, beating summer sun, the wearying windstorm, the violence of thunderstorms and the destruction of hail emphasize the temporal nature both of man and the components of his environment.

Elemental simplicity and intimacy with the mysteries of nature and the universe give a profound religious dimension to the vocation of farming. Grove has often developed this theme, but nowhere more passionately than in this impression of an anonymous harvester:

> He became to me the man who stands squarely on the soil and who, from *his* soil—his, no matter whether he owns it or not; and likely he was no more than a hired helper on this particular farm—who from *his* soil reaches out with tentative mind, and with a great seriousness—far beyond that of a mere thinker or scientist—gropes his sure and unmistaken way into the great, primeval mysteries which are the same to-day as at the dawn of history (p. 211).

Yet this figure is not the idealized monarch of Stead's fiction. This man has the dignified aura of the powerful manual labourer, but there is little suggestion that the land will always provide generous return for his labour. Grove's account of him is juxtaposed with the story of the decay of a farming couple, the death of their son, and the triumph over all of brutal winter. While Stead saw man being served by nature, Grove recognizes that, as one small element of nature, man must accommodate himself to the cosmic rhythms; as part of these rhythms man finds his true nobility and understands, in some measure, the mysteries of his existence. ''It is from choice that we do not close ourselves in and that we do not close winter out. We want to live life as it is; we want to react to all of what exists; and we want to measure our lives by the largest unit, by the slowest and mightiest pulse which nature provides. Does not the measure, if it be such, ennoble that which is measured, even though it be human only?'' (p. 232).

For Niels Lindstedt, the central protagonist in Grove's first novel, *Settlers of the Marsh* (1925), a sense of vulnerability in the prairie landscape leads first to reckless defiance and later to a recognition of the necessity of acceptance. Niels is a pioneer, one of those whose spokesman Grove conceived himself to be, struggling to create on virgin soil a permanent and productive farm. In contrast to Abe Spalding, Niels is bound to the land not by material considerations, but by emotional, perhaps spiritual, dictates. Lars Nelson interprets the significance of the pioneer vocation to Niels:

> "I'll tell you, I like the work. I'd pay to be allowed to do it. Land I've cleared is more my own than land I've bought."
>   Niels understood. That was his own thought exactly, his own unexpressed, inexpressible thought. . . .
>   They walked on in silence, swinging along in great, vigorous strides. The last few words had filled them with the exhilaration of a confession of faith. High above, far ahead stood an ideal; towards that ideal they walked.[18]

This creed of the soil is a continuing source of strength for Niels; he "cling[s] to the landscape as something abiding, something to steady him" (p. 55). In his bleakest days Niels seems to abandon this belief, but so imbedded is it in his personality, that he can never extinguish it, and it asserts itself, almost inevitably, in the latter part of the novel.

Faith in the soil persists in face of the depressing harshness of the land. The "sheer waste of heath-like country," through which Niels and Lars are trudging as the novel opens, recalls, though it is more severe, Hardy's Egdon: "neither ghastly, hateful, nor ugly: neither commonplace, unmeaning, nor tame; but, like man, slighted and enduring; and withal singularly colossal and mysterious in its swarthy monotony."[19] Despite Pacey's sanguine observation that "nature in this book . . . yields her gifts grudgingly but none the less surely to those who seek them with sufficient determination,"[20] the prevailing sense in *Settlers of the Marsh* is of man "slighted and enduring." The reader is less conscious of the country's natural beauty than of the merciless pounding of the blizzard and the tentative nature of man's achievements in this environment. Niels, for example, escapes the ravages of drought and hail, not by determination, but by his unusual chance decision to buy hail insurance. Nature is not about to accommodate itself to man; in fact, man must adapt himself to nature. "Life had him [Niels] in its grip and played with him; the vastness of the spaces looked calmly on" (p. 34).

Opposed to this world of bland indifference is Niels's dream of a home

---

[18]Grove, *Settlers of the Marsh* (Toronto: McClelland and Stewart, 1966), p. 36.
[19]Thomas Hardy, *The Return of the Native* (London: Macmillan, 1928), p. 6.
[20]Desmond Pacey, *Frederick Philip Grove* (Toronto: Ryerson, 1945), p. 39.

and a farm where a family lives comfortably on the produce of its own soil. His dream depends on having Ellen Amundsen as the mother of his family, but that is not to be. Ellen is so sickened by the tragedy of her mother's life that she seeks to escape family responsibility rather than alter its nature. Still suffering from the shock of Ellen's rejection, Niels seeks satisfaction with the promiscuous widow, Clara Vogel, and initiates the relationship which is to end in murder and imprisonment.

Grove handles the Niels-Clara episode well. The characterization of Niels is effective and honest—it is clearly he who is responsible for the agony and failure: he insists on marriage when he wants only physical satisfaction; he is completely unable to understand the attractions of the town; he is insensitive to his wife's need for respect as a woman and companion; he cherishes a simplistic moral code which demands that crime must be mightily punished.

Inevitability, almost an air of doom, pervades the decay of Niels's marriage. The landscape is a metaphor for a world of cruel insensitivity. The scenes preceding Niels's murder of his wife are again reminiscent of Hardy's symbolic landscapes, especially of the bleakness of Flintcomb Ash. I am reminded, too, of Angel Clare's misguided morality and of his careless ignorance of Tess's needs. Specific instances of influence probably cannot be documented, but, considering Grove's expressed admiration for *Jude the Obscure* and *Tess of the D'Urbervilles*,[21] it is logical to suspect he was inspired by Hardy's example.

The sense of man's insignificance, of the inexorable facts of life on earth, dominates the scene as Niels staggers about his farm with Mrs. Dahlbeck's curse sounding in his head "like the bell of doom": "He went blindly, stumbling over roots and stumps. He was bleeding from nose and forehead. . . . He went on as an animal goes, wounded to death, seeking his lair, to hide himself. . . ." And in the same scene: "Behind him were other sloughs, swampy hollows, their soil churned up, trodden and trampled by wandering cattle into little hillocks tufted with grass, hardened by drying, with muddy holes in between where the feet of the heavy beasts had sunk deep" (pp. 182-83). The ugliness and infertility of the landscape reflect the quality of Niels's marriage, and he becomes like an animal, acting by blind natural instinct, mired, like the cattle, in an earth which proceeds by inscrutable chance.

Niels refuses to realize and accept the conditions of man's life on earth and defies them by murdering his wife. After his imprisonment he learns to accept them by renewed contact with Ellen Amundsen. The nature of his renewal is prepared for in the climactic storm scene. Grove's descriptive powers are at their peak; a sense of doom pervades: "The moment was coming. . . . It stood in front of them; and its face was not smiling; it was grimly tragical . . ." (p. 95). The turbulence of the storm externalizes the mental and emotional confusion of Niels and Ellen:

---

[21]*It Needs to Be Said*, p. 123.

> A circling festoon of loose, white, flocculent manes, seething, whirling. . . .
> Like the sea in a storm tree tops rise and fall. . . . They dance and roll,
> tumble and rear, and mutely cry out as in pain. . . . Flashes of lightning
> break on the slough like bomb-shells; rattling thunder dances and springs
> (pp. 98-99).

Grove's images emphasize the unity of the natural world: in the clouds are
the tossing manes of wild horses; like ships at the mercy of a violent sea,
the trees tremble in the wind; the death cry of a small animal is heard; and
the world resembles a battlefield. The emphasis, again, is on the capricious,
often inexplicably violent character of life in the universe. It is a character
which Ellen has seen in her father's cruel indifference to her mother, and which
she tries to escape by refusing marriage with Niels. Her eventual change of
heart is the pivotal incident in the resolution of the novel.

The resolution is not inconsistent with the novel as a whole, in spite of
the arguments of Pacey and others, for although it mitigates the tragedy, it
does not destroy the essential mood. Life, as Niels often thinks, is purposeless
and ruled by inexplicable chance. "What was life anyway? A dumb shifting
of forces. Grass grew and was trodden down; and it knew not why. He
himself—this very afternoon there had been in him the joy of grass growing,
twigs budding, blossoms opening to the air of spring. The grass had been stepped
on; the twig had been broken; the blossoms nipped by frost..." (pp. 101-2).
Niels and Ellen, close to the land as they may be, must grow into a full acceptance
of this rhythm of nature. After Clara and murder and prison, Niels realizes
the futility of defiance; Ellen, through time and the horror of Neils's experience,
recognizes the possibility of compassion and love. The grass that is trodden
down will spring up again. The fact that its existence is temporary, liable to
sudden, mysterious destruction, must be accepted, but accepted with a determination to persist, not with passivity and utter despair. Man, as animal, is part
of the natural world; yet, as Niels does, he demonstrates his humanity by a
stubborn, determined resignation which contrasts with the animal's unthinking
participation. So the final scenes, in which Niels and Ellen return to the "bower"
in the bush, are not an outburst of naïve optimism but show a determination
to accept the tragedy which is inevitable in life. Niels and Ellen find a new
relationship, which, like the white buds of the plum blossoms just bursting,
is beautiful, yet fragile. "Happiness almost ancient and a sense of infinite sorrow"
(p. 212) are mingled effectively in a resolution which summarizes the con-
tradictions lived in the novel.

Len Sterner's story, *The Yoke of Life* (1930), like that of Niels Lindstedt
involves the pursuit of a dream, but Len's dream is much grander: "One day
he was going to master all human knowledge in all its branches."[22] *The Yoke*

---

[22]Grove, *The Yoke of Life* (Toronto: Macmillan, 1930), p. 33.

of Life shares its "northern prairie" setting with *Settlers of the Marsh*, but concentrates still more on the bleakness of the setting. There are frequent waste-land images: "All about, like charred monuments burnt stumps were sticking up, bristly, from the ground" (p. 12). A devastating hailstorm, the gruesome spectacle of horses being sucked to their deaths in the mire of flooded sloughs, add to the impression of an unyielding environment. The wasteland intrudes into the most potentially pastoral scenes:

> An ineffectual morning sun glared down on the waste created by the night's blizzard. The landscape—the drifts, the bare trees, and even the sky—looked ice-cold, windswept and hostile. The absolute quiet of the atmosphere and the indifference of the sun intensified that impression, just as the song of a bird on a battlefield emphasizes its horrors (p. 26).

As the backdrop to the happenings in Mr. Crawford's school, this landscape, based on Grove's favourite battlefield image, seems incongruous. Perhaps the innocent joy of school days, like the song of the bird, only emphasizes the surrounding horror. The prairie constantly impinges, a reminder that man is an intruder doomed to a brutal struggle for existence.

The struggle of Mr. Kolm, Len's stepfather, is in its selflessness untypical of Grove's pioneers. Natural disasters force Len to abandon his schooling in order to work to ease the family debt. In accepting Len's help, ignoring his desire for education, and insisting his family accept the dictates of the land, Mr. Kolm often appears harsh; but his stature increases in the course of the novel, as we discover that the work he does on the farm is completely for the benefit of his stepsons, and that his wife is unsympathetic to the needs of both farm and farmer. In the true pioneer tradition Kolm, prompted by an instinctual bond to the land and the simplicity of the farming life, returns after one bitter failure to homestead again in the bush country.

If his ambitions are otherwise directed than those of Kolm, Len nevertheless shares the preference for the rural over the urban, and from his years spent in this forbidding country develops a deep love for nature. He too is a pioneer, instinctively preferring the wilderness world of "endeavour" to the neat farms which represent "accomplishment." But his pioneering is more likely to be metaphysical. "Whitish vapour banks of clouds enclosed the horizon, their outlines washed into the pale blue of the sky. The distance, like the future, was undefined" (p. 185). The vast spaces reflect in their unknown extent the vagaries of the future. Len's life is defined and his future dictated by his dreams, by his desires for knowledge and for Lydia, and by his yearning to see the lake, a place of beauty, fantasy and mystery where the stuff of the imagination is given concrete form.

The evolution of Len's dreams is summarized by the titles given to the sections of the novel, and by the epigraphs from *Les Fleurs du Mal*. In "Boyhood" "le monde est grand," the world's opportunities seem vast in the eyes of youth; in "Youth" the growth of knowledge leads to "amer savoir," the adolescent's bitter awareness of the real emptiness of life; "Manhood" brings with it the curse of sex, "les seins nus et pourprés"; and finally "Death," "O Mort, vieux capitaine," is greeted with enthusiasm.

Len's dream of knowledge, at first naïvely grandiose, becomes more modest as his awareness of the breadth of human knowledge grows. Len's pursuit of knowledge will involve, so Mr. Crawford philosophizes, an inevitable attempt to know himself:

> "What, in all branches of knowledge we really investigate is ourselves. Perfect knowledge would be no more than an accurate tracing out of the limitations of the human mind. You may not get all the facts. But one day, I hope, you will understand that that does not matter. A man may be learned without being fit for anything but the gathering of fact to fact unless he has the spark divine" (p. 80).

Len never achieves a very great awareness of himself, but there is something in his character of the spark divine. More the poet than the scholar, in spite of his success in high school entrance exams, Len lives for visions, which he is never able to realize nor even to articulate. His imagination turns the glimpse of a deer into a fabulous creature, embodying "the whole essence of shy, wild nature with which our northern woods surprise us" (p. 69), a representation of the beauty, the freedom and the exciting mystery which nature shows to be a possibility in life. It is a short step from this wonderful vision to the beautiful and exciting vision of a young girl. It is his obsession with the vision of an ideal love, more than the demands of the land and of economics, which finally dooms Len's dreams of great knowledge.

The reality of Lydia Housman is no more immediate to the young Len than the reality of the world of knowledge. Exulting in the "glorious sunrise" of knowledge is as immature as telling Lydia, in a particularly excruciating passage, that she is a beautiful butterfly burst from a dull, unexciting pupa. Lydia lives in Len's imagination as an ethereal goddess. While his vision of her originates at least partially in sexual yearning, Len's imaginary Lydia is absolutely pure and exclusively his. Obviously his dream does not coincide with the facts. Lydia is promiscuous in her youth, flees the district in the wake of a murder and suicide among her lovers, and eventually turns to prostitution. Only when Lydia's appearance harmonizes with his vision—she comes as ministering angel when he is near death with pneumonia—is Len able to accept her. Then, gradually, he discovers the emptiness of his vision. As they once did for the Reverend Edward Casaubon, Len's dreams of being a greatly learned man, sharing life with a chaste and beautiful woman, prove depressingly hollow.

Again the resolution of Grove's novel, for all its element of wilderness gothic, is not nearly so incongruous as it first appears. Though our acquaintance with Lydia's character is slight, her compassion for Len when he is ill is not unconvincing. She had never, except in one moment of unmeaning anger, attempted to sever her ties with him nor to abandon her memories. In the case of the more fully developed Len, the final scenes are consonant with his naïve dreams, his puritannical ideas about sex, and his fascination with the mysterious. When his hopes for love and knowledge prove bankrupt, he submits himself in a literal and lasting way to his one remaining dream. In addition, the sombre threat embodied in the landscape throughout the novel, if it does not presage the ending, at least establishes an appropriate mood for it.

Len's dream of knowledge is eclipsed by his desire for Lydia Housman, and eventually both these dreams are absorbed in his dream of the lake. In each case the dream is defeated by the bleak reality of the world as reflected in a landscape which shades from hostility to indifference. In the final section of the novel the prairie is left behind. Although the reason is not made explicit, the brutal character of the prairie undoubtedly had something to do with Len's coming to the lake, either because of the marginal existence which it provided, or simply through his desire to escape. In a sense, however, it is still the same world. Len and Lydia are exposed on a vast sea, pummelled by the relentless powers of nature. As a result, they both come to a new awareness of themselves and of the significance of their personal experience.

The final suffering of Len and Lydia, evoked in one of Grove's most memorable and exciting pieces of writing, is a metaphor for the human experience. As the sun that lights the world sinks, Len's camp fire becomes a small sun to light the world which he and Lydia share. In this "microcosm" Len and Lydia are representative of humanity at large. Lydia is aware "that this small world created by the light of the fire was surrounded by another huge world of unknown or at least unseen things. Fear drank at her heart; but fear, not of that unknown world beyond the line of light; it seemed strangely friendly as compared with that man who was working away in the shadows of the tree, preparing for the night" (p. 303). Man's world is surrounded by a vague sense of the threatening unknown, but the greatest threat is man himself and his inability to understand his fellows. This idea of the microcosm is extended to the two figures in the boat, for their voyage is an image of life as a whole; indeed the lake on which they will journey is "the sea of life." On this voyage they are threatened by external elements—their boat is almost lost in the wind—and enjoy only occasional moments of peace and rest during a trip in which they have very little personal control over their direction.

This most extended and concentrated of Grove's symbolic landscapes is rich with possibilities. The imminence of death characterizes the entire section; there is an oppressive feeling of doom, especially in the ominous chattering rocks, "which sounded like the chattering of teeth, but of teeth set in a death's head without flesh or skin" (p. 332). The geographical constriction in the lake at The Narrows marks the beginning of the "real wilderness," and reflects the gradual elimination of alternate possibilities in life as death nears. Lydia and Len have learned to face death, but their tragedy lies in their refusal to face life.

There is something finally inexplicable and irrational in Len's decision that he and Lydia must die together. But this is as it should be—the resolution of the novel derives its strange power from such inexplicability. Clearly Len desires to escape life with his conception of Lydia as an undefiled goddess intact. As an idea this is acceptable, but its evolution is not so clear. Len pleads that he has "thought and thought," but the novel provides no evidence of such careful consideration. The reader is unaware of Len's growing idea that his problem is soluble only by death.

The recognition of his status as an interloper led Niels Lindstedt to a resigned accommodation with brutal reality; Len Sterner's response admits no alternative but submission to violent death, lashed together with Lydia, in the rapids of The Narrows. After this scene of fascinating horror, Grove returns, almost by way of epilogue, to the man of the soil. Len's stepfather continues the struggle to wrest a living from the land. The birth of a son, Leonard, to Len's brother, Charlie, is a "promise" of the life which Len and Lydia had chosen to ignore in death. But it may be a reminder, as well, of the common experience which both Leonards share in a cruel and indifferent universe.

If Desmond Pacey is right, this sense of man as an intruder in an implacable universe is modified by a reading of Grove's shorter fiction.

> From the novels one tends to carry away an impression of man's puny vulnerability in the face of Nature's hostile power and Time's less spectacular but no less fatal attrition; in the stories, on the other hand, one is impressed more with the ingenuity, variety and resourcefulness of human nature, and the destructive forces of storm and decay are given less emphasis.[23]

Pacey goes on in his introduction to *Tales from the Margin* to summarize quite adequately the variety and descriptive power found in the settings of Grove's stories and makes any further catalogue of mine unnecessary. Here is further evidence of the prominence which Grove consistently gives to the prairie landscape.

One story in the collection, however, significantly advances our understanding of Grove's use of setting. The setting of "The Desert," the eastern Alberta plateau, is described in a thorough, sustained way, and deliberately explored for its symbolic richness. Alice is a disenchanted school teacher who returns to her childhood home to live the simple life in this fascinating landscape.

> All around, the horizon was even with the hill on which she stood. This bare and apparently cheerless landscape was exalted. When she stood still, she seemed to see and almost to feel how the earth was swinging

---

[23]Pacey, "Introduction," *Tales from the Margin* (Toronto: McGraw-Hill Ryerson, 1971), pp. 6-7.

eastward. The sun was suspended over the edge of the world, hanging over a bottomless abyss into which all living things had to plunge sooner or later—an unknown beyond (p. 80).

Vertical man is at once ennobled and reminded of his imminent oblivion. Deftly, almost intuitively, Grove articulates the paradox which, along with the desert metaphor, becomes increasingly familiar in the prairie fiction, for example, of Ross, Ryga and McCourt. As in *In Search of Myself* he gives the landscape its own voice: " 'Here I lie,' the landscape seemed to say, 'indifferent to the seasons. Summer or winter—to me they are both alike. They come and they go; and I remember them as though I do not distinguish between them, for there is nothing to distinguish them by. There is no past and no future; there is only a present; a present that changes and yet remains ever itself' " (p. 80).

In this indifferent world man is forced to come to terms with his own reality, his mortality, his impotence. Ultimately, however, Grove sidesteps the implications of his symbolism. Alice is subliminally aware that its very tentativeness and simplicity give life on the prairie a unique vitality. Apparently this sort of life is not sufficient; the story is crippled by a wholly sentimental conclusion, quite out of keeping with the dominantly tentative tone. (Inconsistent, disappointing endings are characteristic in *Tales from the Margin*.) Alice neither resolves the paradox of her existence, nor accepts it. Instead she can escape or ignore it when her rejected lover buys the land next to hers and prepares to share the austere life. Feeling faint, blushing from head to foot, Alice hastens to accept the best of both worlds.

Nevertheless, in "The Desert" Grove articulates with assurance what is only occasionally hinted by the writers before him. The same confident and substantial use of the landscape characterizes Grove's later novels of the west, *Our Daily Bread* (1928) and *The Fruits of the Earth* (1933). Like "The Desert" both these novels are set on the true prairie, a landscape differing in detail, but not in essentials, from the bush country of the prairie fringe. The predominantly barren landscape is in accord with the spiritual poverty of the characters and the emptiness of their human relationships.

Although pioneering is behind him when the novel opens in 1906, John Elliott in *Our Daily Bread* shares with Mr. Kolm and Niels Lindstedt the instinctual bond to the land which is the common attribute of Grove's pioneers. On the other hand Elliott's life, devoted to raising crops and a family, is more commonplace than that of Len Sterner or Niels. Summarizing the growth of the Elliott farm Grove describes "a country which was like the land of sun-set, bare, naked prairie hills, sun-baked, rain-washed, devoid of all the comforts of even slightly older civilizations, devoid at the time, even of the consolation of human neighbourhood."[24]

[24]Grove, *Our Daily Bread* (New York: Macmillan, 1928), p. 5.

Man's position in such a bare land is clear, and typical of Grove's attitude. He is exposed to sun and rain; he searches in vain for civilized comforts or even for human companionship. The crops fail in drought; the sun is either almost cruel in its strength or devoid of the light and heat which it provides as a necessity of life: "The quality of the sunlight was that of a rayless, heatless diffusion through a lens of vapour" (p. 284). The period of fecundity in John Elliott's life has passed—about him he sees his children's repeated crop failures, while Martha, his wife, who has borne him twelve children, dies from cancer of the uterus. The novel's central theme is decay—of home, of crop, of human morality and, most especially, of Elliott's cherished dream of compensating for the lack of "human neighbourhood" which he encountered as one of the first settlers in his district. The eroding, levelling prairie is at work in every phase of Elliott's existence.

Elliott envisions himself as a patriarch, as the founder of a race, however modest, which will settle about him and venerate him. Despite his large family, which is essential to its realization, Elliott's dream is doomed, not only because of its naïve idealism, but also because it fails to allow in the children the very spirit of independent self-assertion which made Elliott himself a pioneer. Grove defines the basis for Elliott's dream: "To live honourably, to till the land, and to hand on life from generation to generation: that was man's duty" (p. 189). But his conception of an honourable life comes up against the frauds of his son-in-law, Fred Sately; the ideal of tilling the land is tarnished by the crude actuality of city life and by the failures, due to laziness and greed, of those children who do take up farming; and the duty to reproduce is countered by Mary's observation to her shocked mother that birth control makes it possible to "eat your cake and have it, too."

Elliott's dream is firmly anchored in the soil. As in the prayer from which it comes, the phrase, "Our daily bread," has in Elliott's own religion both a literal and a spiritual dimension. Obviously, the land is the source of that which sustains life, and Elliott feels that man can produce almost all the necessities of life from his own land. Less obviously, though no less truly for Elliott, the task of working the land in its noble simplicity and its orientation to the essentials of life establishes contact with God. "He was proud of belonging to the hidden ground-mass of the race which carried on essential tasks, no matter under what form of government, no matter under what conditions of climate and soil: he had lived and multiplied; he had grown, created, not *acquired* his and his children's daily bread: he had served God" (p. 190).

The land itself becomes an aspect of the deity to which, in his repetition of the phrase "You can't fool the land!" Elliott attributes omniscience and superiority over man. In portraying the decay of Elliott and his dreams Grove does not question this spiritual concomitant to the life of the soil; in fact his expressed preference for farming as an occupation[25] indicates Grove probably

[25]Grove, "Democracy and Education," *University of Toronto Quarterly*, XII (July 1943), 395.

shared Elliott's inclination. Grove's view of the deity, however, is undoubtedly less sanguine than Elliott's.

The general stages in John Elliott's decay are marked by the novel's three books. Book one, focussing on Mrs. Elliott's gruesome death, and including the marriage and scattering of many of the children, shows the futility of Elliott's dream from the outset. The Elliott children are individuals who show a desire, however slight their ability to satisfy it, to establish themselves and their families independently. While the extensive filial ingratitude is often cruel, it is clear, even at this stage of the novel, that the fault is not entirely with the children. The Elliotts show a selfish inability to understand the fundamental impulse of children to move beyond parental protection and become independent. Meanwhile, the grotesquely comic scene which finds Mrs. Elliott cavorting half-mad at a community dance indicates her failure to share her husband's intimacy with the land and his love of manual labour. Viewed by Mrs. Elliott in terms of its social environment, the prairie has been barren indeed, and she asserts her pathetic defiance against the nullity of her life in this final gesture.

The title of the second book, "Chaos," indicates John Elliott's confusion as a sense of personal uselessness and the meaninglessness of his life mount up. His periodic attempts to revive his patriarchal dream, either by visiting his children or gathering them about him, prove increasingly disappointing. Faced with repeated denials of his dream, John Elliott becomes, in stages which are abrupt and unconvincing, an aged fool and miser. When Elliott seeks a family reunion at the close of this book, he is rejected in turn by each of his children.

The situation explains the title of the final book, "In Exile." This book is a montage of scenes in which Elliott encounters poverty, greed and lovelessness in each of his children's homes. In spite of the frequent changes of scene, the whole process is rather tedious for the reader. This tedium is attributable to Grove's failure to delineate the children's characters sufficiently; as a result, the entire second generation blurs into an indistinct mass. The accumulation of virtually indistinguishable secondary characters and Elliott's lack of depth make this one of Grove's weakest novels, in spite of the novel's most moving incident, the ritual pilgrimage with which Elliott, totally alienated from family and dream, concludes his life.

In the end, having lost his mental stability, Elliott revives the dream of an aristocracy established at Sedgeby and sets out to return to the family estate. He grows weaker and weaker as he draws to the end of his one-hundred mile journey, but he takes comfort in the rediscovery of the landscape which he had come to know so intimately—bare rolling hills, prickly pear cactus, and stones covered with rust-coloured lichen. Grove emphasizes the mythical nature of the return home to die with an allusion to the Ahasuerus myth and an encounter with a figure symbolic of the grim reaper. The prairie, barren, indifferent, relentless, as we saw it established in the novel's opening, is gradually reclaiming the home and farm that Elliott had established. The house is in utter disrepair, everything covered in dust and chaff; the yard is "a tangle now of sere, ripe weeds in which the shrubs lay embedded." Although man shares in the natural rhythms of the earth his brief life span makes him an intruder in a landscape which is eternal. The end of his exposure, as of the monuments he has raised, is obliteration. Elliott dies, his family, ironically, now assembled about him. Man and man's works, Grove confirms, arose from the dust and must end as dust.

As McCourt and others have shown, *Our Daily Bread* is not tragic in the classical sense, for Elliott lacks the nobility, the heart and spirit, of the true tragic hero. This seems a valid but not especially illuminating observation. That Grove conceived of the experience as tragedy, that he saw tragedy as universal, as much a part of Elliott's life as of Lear's, is surely more informative. "To have greatly wished and to be denied" is sufficient tragedy in Grove's view. "He cannot perpetuate himself or his works," Douglas Spettigue remarks in summing up Elliott's tragedy, "but he can assert their value to himself by choosing to die among them."[26] The measure of the tragedy in this novel is in the hero's persisting to the end in search of his dream, even when the dream lies buried in the prairie dust which is inevitably re-claiming him and his family home.

This image of a farm on the grand scale being inexorably reclaimed by the elements from which it arose is again central to *Fruits of the Earth*, although it is not as relentlessly exploited as in *Our Daily Bread*. In an author's note prefacing the novel Grove indicates that such an image, verified by personal observation, provided the impulse for this novel: "This farm was such as to suggest a race of giants who had founded it; but on enquiry I found that it was held by tenants who tilled a bare ten per cent of its acreage. In a barn built for half a hundred horses they kept a team of two sorry nags; and they inhabited no more than two or three rooms of the outwardly palatial house" (p. xiv). Grove's note recalls another giant man, ploughing over the crest of a hill—an image which Grove revealed was the inspiration for Abe Spalding, the hero of this novel. Together, the giant silhouette against the sun and the magnificent farm in decay embrace the two poles of the prairie experience.

The southern Manitoba setting of *Fruits of the Earth* stimulates the best descriptions Grove provides of those unique features, unrelieved flatness and rich wheat-growing soil, which are widely presumed to characterize the entire prairie. Grove's prairie, of course, is much more varied that this, yet here the landscape seems most assertive, most inevitable, for here is the reality upon which the myths about the prairie are based. The prevalent landscape is familiar: occasionally characterized by great beauty, bronzed sunlight and clear blue skies, but more often grey or dusty, conveying a sense of melancholy and occasionally becoming cruel. It is the landscape which we have seen in

[26]Spettigue, "Frederick Philip Grove in Manitoba," *Mosaic*, III (Spring 1970), 31.

variations throughout the four novels; the landscape particularly suited to the naturalistic outlook, to the conviction of the universally tragic quality of human experience.

Abe Spalding is another of Grove's representative pioneers, but he is also unique among the characters of Grove's prairie novels for, unlike John Elliott, he is shown building in stages from the virgin soil, and unlike Niels or Kolm, he attains vast material success. Later in the novel Grove delineates three more or less distinct complexes which make up Abe Spalding's consciousness: elements of his immediate surroundings, imaginatively extended both in space and time; concern about his economic situation; and his personal and family life. These aspects of consciousness define the main tensions of the novel as Abe moves from obsession with economic matters to a greater recognition of his own real needs and the demands of family responsibilities. Abe's "economic vision" dominates part one of the novel, appropriately titled "Abe Spalding." Abe conceives of the prairie in economic terms, in terms of its potential as a source of great wealth. In this light the prairie was extremely attractive and seemed, in its vastness and uninterrupted nature, to provide the opportunity Abe sought, unlimited and without major threats to its realization, "a 'clear proposition' as he had expressed it, meaning a piece of land capable of being tilled from line to line, without waste areas, without rocky stretches, without deeply-cut gullies which denied his horses a foothold. He wanted land, not landscape; all the landscape he cared for he would introduce himself" (p. 23).

This statement indicates not only Abe's lack of concern for aesthetics but also his preoccupation with the land as producer, to the exclusion of human emotions or the mysteries of man's life on earth. His neighbours, even his wife, come into Abe's consideration only to the extent that they might contribute to the realization of his dream of a baronial estate dominating the land and society round about. While asserting that the farmer lives the "freest, most independent life on earth," when he pleads: "I am not my own master" (p. 54), Abe unwittingly acknowledges the degree to which he is a prisoner of his dream.

His exclusive dedication to material success clearly marks the limitations of Abe's personality, but at the same time there is something admirable, almost heroic about him. D.H. Lawrence found this contradiction (which was noted also, for example, in Niels Linstedt) inherent in the American experience: "The spirit and the will survived: but something in the soul perished; the softness, the floweriness, the natural tenderness. How could it survive the sheer brutality of the fight with that American wilderness which is so big, vast and obdurate!"[27]

Abe's will—the will to work unceasingly, even furiously—demands, in its unflinching dedication, the reader's admiration. The prairie is a particularly appropriate place to pursue such a dream with such dedication, as Abe's concept

---

[27]Lawrence, *Selected Literary Criticism*, ed. Anthony Beal (New York: Viking Press, 1966), p. 408.

of a "clear proposition" demonstrates. The ego is particularly gratified, it seems, when success is accompanied by a startling visual equivalent. In a predominantly flat landscape man's material achievements stand out, to use Stegner's image, as "verticalit[ies]" in a "horizontal land."[28] So, following Abe's shrewd harvesting of a gigantic twelve-hundred-acre crop of wheat, his dream, and the first part of the novel, come to a climax when he can look over the miles of prairie and see on the horizon the mark he has made. "From the Somerville line he peered through the night at the pool of light on the horizon. It did not loom high but seemed rather to form a dent in the sky-line. That was the proudest moment of his life; and he raised an arm as though reaching for the stars" (p. 119).

This exhilarating success is not unqualified for, as I have implied, Abe achieves it at the expense of what Lawrence calls "natural tenderness." Abe neglects his wife Ruth's need for affection and for the relaxed moments a family should spend together. It would not be like Grove to suggest that all the responsibility for the poor relationship rests on one partner, but the key problem here is clearly the demands of Abe's extravagant dream. Abe's success is also qualified by the sense, familiar in all Grove's novels, of the potential threat to man in the landscape and climate. Ruth is disquieted by the forbidding loneliness of a barren country; Abe is always aware that his crops are threatened by drought or floods. Even at the moment of his greatest agricultural triumph Abe knows how arbitrary is his success, "how much uncertainty there is even in the most fundamental industry of man" (p. 106). In preparing to harvest his greatest crop, Abe becomes aware of the possibility of forces at work beyond man's control, of something in the universe, "whatever power had taken the place of the gods" (p. 98), that might be called fate or destiny. Perhaps this mysterious operation of fate dictates the death, at the close of part one, of Abe's favourite son, Charlie. The boy is pressed into service by his father's headlong harvest rush and dies, symbolically crushed beneath a load of the wheat with which Abe is so obsessed.

The title of part two of the novel, "The District," indicates the direction in which the novel develops—toward Abe's realization of the need for involvement, particularly involvement beyond the strictly economic sphere, in the life of his family and community. The section opens with a lengthy examination of the features of the landscape and their implications. This piece, which has many of the characteristics of his descriptive essays, Grove was able to extract and publish separately, with minor alterations.[29] That the chapter, nevertheless, is carefully integrated in the novel and, indeed, sums up the novel's major themes, demonstrates the major development which Grove represents in the progress of prairie fiction to a mature, artistically sophisticated use of the natural setting.

[28]*Wolf Willow*, p. 10.
[29]"The Flat Prairie," *Dalhousie Review*, XI (July 1931), 213-16.

The key development in the novel, as I have indicated, is Abe's growing awareness of the restrictive nature of the economic vision which has dominated his thinking. This awareness derives, to some extent at least, from the experience of literature. Abe had begun to read and his reading revealed hitherto undetected spiritual constants, "that background of life which no so-called progress can change" (p. 132). His growing sense of the futility of material success also derives—and the two are interrelated—from a new awareness of landscape, an awareness, to use Grove's own distinction, of "landscape" rather than "land." By his use of landscape Grove is able to amplify the three major aspects of Abe's growing consciousness.

Gradually Abe comes to recognize the necessity for greater involvement in the affairs of family and community. The social imperatives are reinforced by the visual characteristics of the prairie; the frequent mirages seem to magnify distant objects and bring them close to hand. "A town or a group of farmsteads, ordinarily hidden behind the intervening shoulder of the world, stood up clearly against the whitish sky which only overhead shaded off into a pale blue" (p. 135). Similarly, the unrelieved horizon causes the smallest object to be visible at great distance and, significantly, permits Abe to watch the course of the automobile in which his daughter is seduced and later to note the mysterious arrival of Frances to confess her pregnancy to her mother. Thus Abe becomes involved in his family's affairs almost in spite of himself. The image of Abe as marsh-hawk has the same implications: "His mind seemed to hover over the landscape as in flight." The hawk's low, soaring flight takes in great sweeps of the landscape in detail, suggesting Abe's intimate acquaintance with an entire community and his inescapable duty to participate in its direction.

The second aspect of Abe's awakening consciousness is summed up in the phrase: "Man remains distinctly an interloper." Although the comment is specifically prompted by the threat of floods, the entire context establishes the link between the vertical interloper and the horizontal world: "The moment a work of man was finished, nature set to work to take it down again." As Abe looks closely at his mansion, he sees with shock that it is already becoming weathered, that even the bricks are turning to dust. Stegner's contemplation of the prairie forces him to conclude that "nature abhors an elevation" Abe, long before, had sensed the same truth: "And so with everything, with his machines, his fields, his pool; they were all on the way of being levelled to the soil again" (p. 134).

Abe becomes aware of the temporary nature of human achievement, of the mutability of all things, both natural and human. The spatial vastness of the landscape becomes also a vastness of time in which man is still less significant, his life span telescoped into perspective against the stream of time: "It is a landscape in which, to him who surrenders himself, the sense of one's life as a whole seems always present, birth and death being mere scansions in the flow of a somewhat debilitated stream of vitality" (p. 137). Exposed on the prairie, Stegner observes, "you become acutely aware of yourself." Something of this awareness of self is now Abe Spalding's. He begins to see and assess the significance of one human life, his own, in relation to other men and to all eternity.

Finally, there is something in Abe's encounter with his landscape—far more sombre, more cerebral than anything found in Stead—to stimulate a recognition of the spiritual aspect of existence. Grove finds on the prairie "a distinct local character and mentality" arising, perhaps, from some "predilection for this peculiar, melancholy landscape, bred into the blood by some atavism of sentimental tendency" (p. 137). "The characteristic impression of the landscape," an observation which could apply not only to this, but to each of the novels discussed,

> is neither noon nor midnight but the first grey dawn of day, especially a dull day; or the first dim dusk of night, that dusk in which horizons become blurred and the height of human buildings seems diminished. And similarly the time of year most in harmony with the scene is neither summer nor winter; but rather the first few days of spring while the snow still lies in dirty patches and, from the heights in the west, the floods send down their first invading trickles which follow the imperceptible hollows of the ground; or the first drear approach of November days, with indurating winds and desolate flurries of snow in the air (p. 138).

The predominant landscape, then, is one of transition, one where the sense of struggle so typical in Grove is immediate. It is a landscape more bleak than beautiful that leaves one more melancholy than exhilarated. The prevailing "silence, like the flat landscape itself, has something haunted about it, something almost furtive. . . ." Such furtive, haunted silence is, I think, the silence of the eternal, the representation of a power and a truth beyond human knowing. Beneath the changes of season and climate the flat landscape is unchanged, a reminder that change itself is eternal. In this massive serenity lies the landscape's "awful perfection"[30] which Abe now seems ready to accept.

In the course of the novel, as his farm and family disintegrates, Abe grows to recognize the incalculable, the mysteriously spiritual, in the landscape and in his life. He comes to see the windbreak surrounding the farm as a "rampart which, without knowing it, he had erected to keep out a hostile world." Now he knows that the windbreak, too, will eventually be destroyed. If the hostile world cannot be kept out, then he must confront it and attempt to comprehend it.

For Abe this means stoic acceptance of life's disappointments, social involvement, and renewed concern for others. Knowledge of the ultimate passing of

---

[30]Stegner, *Wolf Willow*, p. 7.

things human, and consciousness of some mysterious indeterminate power beyond human control enable Abe to recover from political disgrace and family scandal. At the end of the novel Abe quietly accepts his duty to wife and children and determines to lead the community once more with a new dedication to service. The novel ends with Abe's gesture of new responsibility which represents neither a total change in character nor a plunge into sentimentalism (at least if we ignore the awkwardly intrusive final sentence), but clearly marks his abandonment of exclusive preoccupation with material ends and social stature.

Grove disagrees that starkness in fiction is necessarily ugly: "Ideas of beauty change according to the capacity of finding it."[31] The beauty of the prairie so obvious in the essays is often difficult to perceive in the novels. Or, better, beauty is to be found not as prettiness, but in the stark flatness and noble simplicity of the landscape and in the purity of the elemental forces manifested in the prairie storms. The landscape's beauty inheres in an absoluteness such as Grove expresses in the final pages of *Fruits of the Earth*: "Man passes, they say; his work remains. Does it? It seemed vain in the face of the composure of this prairie" (p. 262).

The inevitable conflict of the elemental forces in man with the elemental forces of the prairie environment is a central theme of these novels. The struggle to win a living from the soil is universal and for all time. That man, from Niels Lindstedt to Abe Spalding, is doomed to failure in that struggle is Grove's vision of the human tragedy. The prairie, level from prehistoric times and forcing everything to conform to its horizontal norm, is a setting especially suited to this view. Man exposed on the prairie is often a magnificent figure, yet, ultimately, he can not resist the forces battering him. Man's struggle with the natural environment is only one of the many conflicts that take place in the wider world of nature. Thus, while there is dignity and nobility in man's persistent struggle with his environment, the struggle, Grove repeatedly insists, is one which must take place with knowledge and acceptance of the mutability of man and man's achievements. In acquiring this knowledge Niels and Abe come to know the harsh, vast and primitive prairie world in a way which eludes Len Sterner and John Elliott.

These men, particularly Elliott and Spalding, bowed before the relentlessly levelling prairie, prefigure all later developments of the image of vertical man in a horizontal world, from Ross's Philip Bentley to Robert Kroetsch's *Studhorse Man*. Beginning with Martha Ostenso's *Wild Geese*, published the same year as *Our Daily Bread*, the focus begins to shift from man's literal relation to the landscape as tiller of the soil, to his metaphysical and psychological relationship to the landscape as twentieth-century man. To be sure, Stead's concept of the prairie, as the next chapter will illustrate, endures almost unchanged in much of the minor fiction. But in most mature fictions the prairie as a

---

[31]Grove, *Canadian Forum*, XI (August 1931), 421.

symbol of spiritual essence, becomes, especially as the dust bowl of the thirties makes its massive impact on fiction, the symbol of a debilitating spiritual emptiness. Both these new emphases depend, of course, on the continuing primacy of Grove's figure of the interloper in an implacable prairie. Confronting "mile after mile of stupefying space,"[32] and recognizing that "with a single twitch, the prairie could snuff us out,"[33] proves essential to whatever measure of understanding his successors achieve.

[32] John Peter, *Take Hands at Winter* (Garden City: Doubleday, 1967), p. 54.
[33] Robert Hunter, *Erebus* (Toronto: McClelland and Stewart, 1968), p. 121.

IV

The Invisible Prairie:
Representative Minor Fiction

out of sight of land

FREDERICK NIVEN, *The Flying Years*

Canadian prairie fiction in the period spanning the two world wars was dominated first by Robert Stead and then by Frederick Philip Grove; their works sum up the principal shift in the artist's perception of the landscape and of man in that landscape. Behind these representative writers, however, stand surprisingly large numbers of less significant novelists and romancers.[1] So legion were these that by 1954 the editor of *Maclean's*, considering the 125 novels submitted for the Maclean's Award Novel, apparently discarded automatically those about the prairie: "The most popular subject has dealt with children growing up on the Canadian prairies. Unfortunately this subject has been dealt with pretty often before."[2] But ignoring his questionable critical principles, one can find some sympathy with the editor's feeling; most of the novels which he vaguely recalls are slight, lacking in seriousness, often insipid. Remarkably, genres popular in Canadian literature in the late nineteenth century survive almost unchanged. Similarly, the typical fictional treatments of the relationship between mind and prairie landscape remain virtually unaltered. Most of the writers incline to romances (or very romantic novels) or to historical romances; their approach to setting resembles Stead's—man is a king in an idyllic setting suited to his edification and material provision. Some of the best known of these writers, such as Nellie McClung and Arthur Stringer, who began to publish in the first decade of the century, have been discussed in chapter I. So persistent are their attitudes that they merit further attention, if only to provide one measure for the achievement of later writers.

The relationship between man and his physical environment is almost invariably poorly presented in the romance. A contradiction seems inevitable between an author's recognition or instinct that the land is essential to his characterization and the tendency of romantic fiction to the extravagant and remote in incident and setting. In a genre particularly vulnerable to writing to formula, the result is often neglect of a local and recognizable setting for a plot mingling crime, mystery, and passionate love affairs. Although the writers under study invariably take some account of landscape, their recurrent settings, wholly idealized and described inadequately with romantic cliché, leave the actual prairie quite invisible. Since melodrama, the literary form devoted to the production of strong emotional response, was essential to most of these fictions, the usual "function

---

[1]See *Literary History of Canada*, pp. 296-99, 660, 663-68.
[2]"In the Editors' Confidence," *Maclean's Magazine*, LXVII (January 15, 1954).

of setting," as Gordon Roper notes, was "to reinforce the emotional effect of the action."[3] With this aim uppermost the romancer presented the reader with an extravagantly coloured and exaggeratedly productive prairie.

This approach to setting is typified by the first view of the prairie in Harold Bindloss's *Ranching for Sylvia* (1912):

> The prairie ran back to the horizon, brightly green, until its strong coloring gave place in the distance to soft neutral tones. It was blotched with crimson flowers; in the marshy spots there were streaks of purple; broad squares of darker wheat checkered the sweep of grass, and dwarf woods straggled across it in broken lines. In one place was the gleam of a little lake. Over it all there hung a sky of dazzling blue, across which great rounded cloud-masses rolled.[4]

The bright colours, abundant flowers, ordered fields, small lake, and peaceful sky combine to present a scene of pastoral contentment. When the more brutal prairie of drought and hail storm obtrudes, it is more as a test of man's moral fibre than as a threat to his prosperity. The driving blizzard through which George Lansing struggles to get the mail from England illustrates the use of setting to reinforce emotional effect. The cruelty of Sylvia's letter rejecting George's planned visit to England is not only in harmony with the cruelty of the storm but is accentuated by our awareness that George is willing to risk death in his devotion to her. But with upper lips stiffened George, and fellow Englishman, Edgar West, soon discover a fondness for the prairie. The hard work which it demands becomes a pleasure and a source of nobility. Both men are attracted by the conventional freedom of vast spaces, clear air, and bright sunshine. Simultaneously, George finds the chaste severity of Flora Grant, a true "daughter of the stern, snow-scourged North," preferable in a prospective wife to the more obvious charms of a devious English socialite.

Slightly superior is Francis Beynon's *Aleta Day* (1919), a love story which, in spite of its obvious melodrama, avoids such a pat resolution of the conflict of character and idea. Virtue is not rewarded, at least not with the traditional happiness and fortune, nor is villainy punished. The main theme is Aleta Day's fear of her parents, of God, of social conventions, and her eventual triumph over that fear. The contradictory pressures in Aleta's personality are expressed by the prairie setting: "There was nothing but a few shacks between me and the far away edge of the world. I felt very tiny under that immense black dome, and I was glad even of the barbed wire fence which shut me in from those immeasurable distances."[5]

Alone on the prairie she feels insignificant and fearful of the vast world

---

[3]Gordon Roper, "New Forces: New Fiction, 1880-1920," *Literary History of Canada*, p. 274.
[4]Harold Bindloss, *Ranching for Sylvia* (New York: A.L. Burt, 1913), p. 48.
[5]Francis Beynon, *Aleta Day* (London: C.W. Daniel, 1919), pp. 29-30.

outside herself. At the same time, however, the "far horizons" of Aleta's "prairie birth-place" urge her to assert her own personality, to escape the relentless pressure of social conformity and ethical compromise. But in the novel as a whole the prairie is not an organic element. More often, when the winter storm blows while Aleta's brother is dying, or when raw spring winds accompany the news of her lover's war wounds, the setting has the predictable limited function of increasing the agony. Yet, despite their minor importance in the novel, the descriptions reveal an eye for evocative detail; the wind, for example, "would go wailing off around the corner, only to come tearing back between two high buildings with a handful of grit to throw in one's teeth." The hint of sensitivity to the distinctive qualities of things and people in these few passages from *Aleta Day* is characteristic of the entire novel, particularly of the concluding account of Aleta's courageous sacrifice for her beliefs.

Even Beynon's slight verbal facility seems rare enough. Sixteen years after *Ranching for Sylvia*, Ethel Kirk Grayson's *Willow Smoke* (1928) is the same indigestible dish. Set in a small Saskatchewan town, it is the story of a young woman's lost love and her discovery of happiness with a new admirer. A gap yawns between the author's sense of the importance of the land and the distinctly false and affected tone of her description, as inadequate a reflection of the physical environment as Parker's *Pierre and His People* provided in the late nineteenth century. If one could lean over far enough to justify Miriam's description of the creek: "'like a smoke and purple shot silk ribbon,'"[6] as a reflection of her own personality, he would still topple at the author's description: "Peach and daffodil dappled a tender sky; low gray hills, like cautious vestals, dipped gently to a sedgy water-splash in a long coulee." Romantic description, just as realistic description, derives authenticity from being rooted in the environment described. Except for reference to the coulee, this combination of pastels, tenderness and mythological figures is better suited to an eighteenth-century English garden than to the broad prairie. Grayson shows an occasional awareness of the complex influences of this landscape: the ambiguity inherent in vastness ("A towering immensity of space had become a prison") makes man "morbidly self-reproachful." But such allusions are isolated and without thematic development in the novel. While the structural or symbolic use of landscape is certainly not essential to fiction, the reader looks for Grayson, having implied the landscape's importance, to treat it with some originality and insight.

Wilfrid Eggleston's novel *The High Plains* (1938) manifests a more assured grasp of the landscape and its effect on man. Its familiar theme is the growth of a young boy to manhood; the setting is the arid district of southern Saskatchewan and Alberta known as Palliser's Triangle. Eric Barnes, like Gander Stake, is more fascinated by machinery than by soil. Yet Eric, and the entire Barnes family, find the forbidding country both cruel and seductive: "It was

[6]Ethel Kirk Grayson, *Willow Smoke* (New York: Harold Vinal, 1928), p. 174.

the edge of the desert, and it had some of the desert's ineluctable charm."[7] Eggleston describes the prairie and man's place in it in terms closer to Grove's than to romantic formula: "He [Eric] went out and looked over the grand sweep of country—the range of hills, the distant canyon of Milk River, the cerulean sky. For once they left him cold. He saw only the encroachment of sagebrush and cactus, the unendurable bareness of the landscape, the penury of the land. Life was incredibly harsh and cruel, and he could see no promise of alleviation" (pp. 237-38).

While there is nothing brilliant about his accounts, Eggleston avoids, except for the adjective "cerulean," the shallow pretentiousness of Grayson's descriptions. Typically, "the first settlers' shacks were sparsely dotted here and there, lost in the infinity of earth and sky." This acute sense of man's insignificance, and the unremitting labour and frequent despair which are part of farming in this region, mingled with the melodramatic suspense of a murder mystery, are the main elements of Eggleston's novel. It is indicative of the tone of the novel that while the mystery is solved by young Eric, the struggle with the land does not end, as might be expected, with either the death, or the stoic endurance of the principals. Hope and confirmation of man's ultimate ability to triumph over nature characterize the ultimate removal of the Barnes family to the almost Edenic irrigated region near Lethbridge.

Once the grossest excesses of a Bindloss or a Grayson are left behind, this pattern, already noted in Stead and in Grove's "The Desert," becomes quite usual. The realistic account of the rigours of prairie agriculture is again betrayed by a sentimental conclusion in Nell Parsons's *The Curlew Cried* (1947). A fortnight after landing from Liverpool, Victoria Sewell is married to the stranger Lane Jarvis and transplanted to his farm on the southern Saskatchewan prairie. As Parsons repeatedly notes, "Lane and the land were strangely alike. Big, virile, ruthless. The land had a purpose to which all must conform, the inexorable spread and growth of life. Lane had a purpose too—to force the land to yield to *him*."[8] Lane, like the prairie, is remote, expressionless, and even his voice has the rasp of dry grass. In the light of this identification Tory's adaptation to her new environment, the movement from scepticism that there could be beauty in "illimitable space and almost total emptiness" to conviction that "she belonged to it completely," also marks the growth of love between herself and Lane. To the basic love story are added Melsie's shooting of her cruel husband, and the nagging mystery of Lane's past, but such melodramatic elements are underplayed. The description, though occasionally extravagant, is, in its simplicity and awareness of psychological implications, far removed from that of earlier romances:

Tory loved to watch the wind spread chords of light and sound and scuttling

[7]Wilfrid Eggleston, *The High Plains* (Toronto: Macmillan, 1938), p. 258.
[8]Nell W. Parsons, *The Curlew Cried* (Seattle: Frank McCaffrey, 1947), p. 85.

shadow down the silver-green, grassy slope. Rippling grass had the beauty of a fluted melody, with now and then a faint cessation of the theme, into which the trill of a lark, or the shrill whistle of a gopher, fell, as if the universe had paused just for that. There was an urgent power in the wind and the land (p. 58).

The sight of silver-green slopes, and the sound of flutes and trilling larks do not quite obscure Parsons's reaching for the distinctiveness of this landscape: its unspectacular yet very real beauty, its urgent power, and the sudden intrusion of sound into silence, which seems an assertion of presence like the abruptness of vertical man in the horizontal world. "The descriptions of the Canadian prairie," writes the author in her Foreword, "are true to the land I knew as a child." When she approaches such fidelity to details, particularly to express a dispiriting loneliness, one senses that Grove's fiction, *Wild Geese*, and the more recent *As For Me and My House* have established a tradition which is being felt, if only vaguely, by even the minor writers of the region.

The resolution of the novel, the culmination of a hard-won love for Tory and Lane, comes about only with the almost total levelling of the Jarvis farm and ambitions by prairie fire. The land, which had demanded so much that it made meaningful human relation impossible, ironically becomes less powerful when it does its very worst. The unrelieved optimism of this resolution is a flaw in a novel which often deals effectively with the complex interplay of man and land, and with the struggle, sorrow, and hope in human experience.

Laura Goodman Salverson is distinguished from these other writers only because she treats a quite different theme. Being of Icelandic descent, Salverson's special interest is the peculiar problems of Icelandic and Scandinavian immigrants in the prairie provinces. Her fiction, then, straddles the boundary between the romantic novel and the historical romance. Unfortunately, the rich possibilities of her subject are usually left unexplored, while the characters and melodramatic incidents proliferate endlessly. For example, in *The Viking Heart* (1923), the first four years of the Icelanders' experience in Manitoba, the first four years of Borga and Bjorn Lindal's marriage, are dismissed in a paragraph.[9] Such hasty treatment of the years when the community is struggling to establish foundations in a new land suggests the sense of incompleteness and lack of authenticity which characterize the novel.

Since the Icelanders are fishermen rather than farmers, the land is of less importance to them and less emphasized in Salverson's fiction. Salverson repeats the standard descriptions of the invigorating influence of the clean northern air. The immigrants' first predictable view of their new country is of a sunset "bathing the river in a crimson and amber glory, casting a ghostly glimmer over the ragged autumn woods on either side." The glories of this paradisiacal

---

[9]Laura Goodman Salverson, *The Viking Heart* (Toronto: McClelland and Stewart, 1923), pp. 50-51.

scene augur well for the immigrants, but the entire picture, especially the mysterious glow over the woods, could as well be Europe as Manitoba. The abrupt experience of an old civilization in a new land is, Salverson's novels would suggest, quite significant. But the Icelandic community as she presents it has little interaction with other groups, and the descriptions of the land have little in them to suggest that this country seemed different to the immigrant. Salverson's prairie, or more correctly the scrub forest on the prairie fringe, is like that discovered by the child of nature, Balder Fjalsted, all "thrush and singing river." Her references to the desolation of the prairie, or to the "wild freedom" of the "untrammelled prairie," are occasional and of little significance. A continuing theme of the discovery of nationhood through a growing love of the land can be found, culminating in Borga's "sudden passion for this wide, quiet land." But this motif, like the novel's conclusion in which the land's potential is a comforting promise to those mourning the death of the young Thor, seems a mechanical afterthought, rather than something which rises with inevitability from the complexities of the novel.

Salverson's remarks in the foreword to *The Dark Weaver* (1937) indicate her chief concern is with intellectual and cultural history. Part of this foreword is worth quoting because it says a great deal about her use of landscape and the flaws of the novel:

> To those who cannot know how the great plains unfolded to the settler like some Arabian Night's tale full of dark mystery, yet of an infinite variety of alluring charm, inestimable resources and, over all, a brooding hint of destruction to the fearful heart and unprogressive spirit, this tale may seem full of anachronisms. Its crude beginnings will, quite conceivably, appear unreal, its tragedies melodramatic, its joys artificial, and the underlying unity of creative purposes be entirely lost.[10]

Certainly Salverson seems to have been her own best critic. Again the landscape does not seem essential to the story; the reader does not have a strong sense of its distinctive features or influences. Setting creates emotive atmosphere — the vastness of the plains, the darkness of the forests, are brooding, mysterious, even terrifying, like the inscrutable "Dark Weaver" weaving the destiny of human lives. To Salverson the prairie is a "quiet, spacious land, designed and destined for wide, heroic gestures."

The location of the new Scandinavian settlement is described in terms which emphasize the picturesque and charming: "Like an oblong tapestry when viewed from an elevation, whose variegated greens are interlaced with the dull silver of the little stream and the mottled brown of slow-drying marshes" (p. 7). There is little in the delicacy of tapestry and lace, the generalities of "variegated

---

[10]Salverson, *The Dark Weaver* (Toronto: Ryerson, 1937), p. 5.

greens" or in the cliché of silver streams to suggest the immigrant's encounter with a unique land. Against this backdrop are played out the vicissitudes of the love of the cavalier, yet endlessly noble Manfred for the pure, long-suffering Greta. While the novel ends with the death of these two figures in the welter of the First World War, it does not avoid sentimentalism. Greta's sacrifice, Manfred's shooting down of his best friend, and finally Manfred's flying off to his end in the sun's eternal flame provide a spectacle of unrestrained emotional indulgence which seems to have little connection to the struggle to form a new Scandinavian community within Canada, or to the clash of ideas which Salverson sees that process representing.

The historical aspect of Salverson's fiction suggests the continued hardiness of the historical romance, as of the romance itself, on the Canadian prairie well into the 1940s. In the face of urbanization and technological progress, the appeal of remote adventure was to some extent replaced by nostalgia for a simpler, more vital life. Such nostalgia seems to account for the endless succession of popular histories and memoirs recounting pioneering days on the prairie. Whatever the reason for its endurance, however, the historical romances, particularly those of Frederick Niven, merit some mention in the spectrum of literary interpretations of man in the prairie landscape.

Although the historical romance places a high premium on action, the fictions to be discussed here do not neglect setting entirely. Setting is only invisible in the sense that, like background music, it is designed to be unobtrusive and pervasive. Certainly there are few attempts to delineate or describe in detail specific aspects of the prairie. This lack of attention to man's interaction with landscape is symptomatic of the writer's attention to romance rather than history.[11] Jane Rolyat's *The Lily of Fort Garry* (1930) is a case in point. The heroine, Margaret Moore, asserts her independence by marrying a half-breed voyageur who embodies the heroic nobility of a life close to nature. Clearly the myth of the north, the excitement and toughness associated with water, pine trees, rocks, and snow, is of central importance. Margaret, and her creator, seem quite unaware of the prairie around, of the flatness, the wind, or the shifting light; it is the magic of a far-off world which appeals so intensely to Margaret.

Among historical novelists of the prairie, Frederick Niven is distinctive. There is something of a prose epic about his attempt to recount the settling of the Canadian West in three volumes. The first of these, *The Flying Years* (1935), is also the best. It is the story of the growth and adventures of Angus Munro in the west during the second half of the nineteenth century. The novel is filled with incident, adventure, and movement from one place to another. Not surprisingly, then, it lacks unity and focus, though Angus is a more dominant

---

[11]W.L. Morton's *Manitoba* (Toronto: University of Toronto Press, 1967), which puts considerable emphasis not only upon the economic importance of the land, but also upon its psychological importance, provides an effective contrast in this respect.

and interesting figure than the heroes of the later novels. Occasionally Niven expresses the immensity of the prairie effectively, most notably when he speaks of being "out of sight of land"[12] in describing the experience of travelling for days over the level sea of grass. So flat, so uninterrupted does the land become that it seems to disappear altogether, leaving man utterly alone. Such felicitous expression identifies another invisible prairie, one which holds an increasing fascination for later writers; here, unfortunately, it is isolated and no attempt is made to make the landscape integral to characterization.

Niven's most exuberant description is saved for the Rockies, both here and in the last novel of the trilogy. It is indicative of the quality of Niven's account of the Canadian West that the best portion of *The Flying Years* is the Dickensian sense of detail and atmosphere in the account of Angus's brief career in an Edinburgh book store. He seems incapable of such a sure literary touch in a Canadian setting. McCourt's summary of this limitation is excellent:

> When Niven writes of his native land he writes of something that is a part of himself, and his scenes are sketched with the assurance that comes of knowing by instinct what is important. But when he writes of the Canadian scene that assurance vanishes; he relies on knowledge rather than feeling; and because he is not sure of what is important tends to crowd his canvas with unnecessary and distracting detail.[13]

The second novel of the trilogy, *Mine Inheritance* (1940), is the journalist David Baxter's account of the beginning of settlement in the west at Red River. Again the book is crowded with historical detail based on Niven's considerable research, and again it suffers from prolixity and a disjointed rhythm. The prairie's influence is only vaguely felt. For Niven apparently the vastness of the land is appropriate to a story in which he sees so many heroic deeds, stirring adventures, and epic undertakings. The immensity of the country defies expression:

> "My dear Alec!" exclaimed the Governor. "Think of the extent of the land, the vastness of the land."
> I pulled myself together and had no difficulty in thinking of the vastness of the land. I was filled with a sense of its vastness, aware of expansive Rupert's land round me.[14]

This crazy repetitiveness deserves enshrining as one of the classic passages of prairie writing. In its ridiculous way it illustrates not only Niven's limited use of landscape, but also the massive task which all writers faced in articulating their sense of this world; yet, at the same time, it looks forward, like Henday's

---

[12]Frederick Niven, *The Flying Years* (London: Collins, 1935), p. 59.
[13]McCourt, *Canadian West in Fiction*, p. 54.
[14]Niven, *Mine Inheritance* (London: Collins, 1940), p. 34.

despairing: "We are still in the Muscuty Plains," to the bewildering prairie of recent fiction.

The third novel of the trilogy, *The Transplanted* (1944), deals with the coming of industry and technology to the west in the twentieth century. There are many references to the characters' deep love for the land, but since the novel is set entirely in the British Columbia interior it has little importance for this study. The novel is also the weakest of the three, largely neglecting the wealth of historical detail which gave some interest to the earlier volumes.

The fiction discussed in this chapter verifies the almost inevitable insistence on the significance of the land in works set on the Canadian prairie in a still largely rural society. But, when compared to the more realistic and psychologically complex fiction of Grove, of Ross, or of many recent writers, these works seem to ignore setting for love stories and spellbinding action. In fiction where the plot must be neatly resolved with ample reward provided for the virtuous, the prairie will necessarily contribute, as it did in Stead, to man's ultimate spiritual and material enrichment. If man is exposed on this prairie, the exposure must enhance his stature. The prairie will add to his self-confidence and he will be, like Bindloss's George Lansing, a figure larger than life. The landscape in which he moves will be idealized, just as the life he leads will be presented, not as it is, but as the author wishes it could be. Actual details of land and climate are neglected or shown to be temporary obstacles on the path to man's ultimate happiness.

V   The Obsessive Prairie: Martha Ostenso's *Wild Geese*

we ran west

wanting
a place of absolute
unformed beginning
. . . .
but the inner lakes reminded
us too much of ancient oceans
first flood: blood–
enemy and substance

MARGARET ATWOOD "Migration: CPR"

In stark contrast to the attitudes of such writers as Bindloss, Parsons, or Salverson is the serious and comprehensive vision of man on the prairie in Martha Ostenso's *Wild Geese* (1925). This first, and usually considered the best, of Ostenso's many novels draws most explicitly on her experience of the Manitoba prairie, where she lived from 1921 to 1925. Unlike the fiction discussed in chapter IV, Ostenso's presentation of man's overwhelming loneliness in a barren, empty land has a continuing freshness of imaginative insight. Except for Grove's novels, with which it shares many attitudes, *Wild Geese* is the most important Canadian prairie novel to be published between the wars. Like Grove, Ostenso is conscious of the inherent cruelty of the prairie and of the great emptiness which encircles man in this landscape. In the haunting "level monotony"[1] of Ostenso's prairie, one feels *Wild Geese* making its contribution to the gradually intensifying impression, if one reads more or less chronologically through prairie fiction, of total nothingness, of vacancy, of a completely exhausted world. Ostenso is aware of the loneliness that comes to man in this landscape, but her central concern is with the loneliness of the human heart, even among men in close physical contact with their fellows. Through the story of a proud man and his rebellious daughter, she looks at the very core of the "unmeasurable Alone surrounding each soul" and tries to comprehend the "nameless and undreamed . . . forms that drift within that region" (p. 57).

Ostenso makes a conscious effort to create in Caleb Gare a human equivalent of the prairie landscape: "Caleb, who could not be characterized in the terms of human virtue or human vice—a spiritual counterpart of the land, as harsh, as demanding, as tyrannical as the very soil from which he drew his existence" (pp. 35-36). The force which had attracted men to the west, the desire of each

---

[1]Martha Ostenso, *Wild Geese* (New York: Grosset and Dunlap, 1925), p. 147.

individual to become self-supporting on land he owns himself, runs wild in Caleb. His obsession is to possess not only more land and more of the land's products but also the hearts, minds, and bodies of his wife, his children, and even the community's school teacher.

Between the land and Caleb, the land's counterpart, as between like magnetic poles, there is a fundamental antagonism. "The impulse that bound him to the land" is neither so innocent, nor so enriching as that cherished by Stead. Caleb wishes to dominate the land and to extract from it the greatest possible amount of produce. Ostenso reinforces this inclination by repeated tableaux of the gigantic figure as vertical intrusion in the level land. Caleb, the giant solitary figure, stands at twilight on a small rise and looks out over his domain:

> Caleb felt a glow of satisfaction as he stood there on the ridge peering out over his land until the last light had gone. He could hold all this, and more—add to it year after year—add to his herd of pure bred Holsteins and his drove of horses—raise more sheep—experiment with turkey and goose for the winter markets in the south—all this as long as he held the whip-hand over Amelia (pp. 14-15).

This obsession with expansion is most obvious in the attention Caleb devotes to his crop of flax: "There was a transcendent power in this blue field of flax that lifted a man above the petty artifices of birth, life, and death. It was more exacting, even, than an invisible God. It demanded not only the good in him, but the evil, and the indifference" (p. 171). Ostenso is adding another dimension to the theme that the demands of the land jeopardize the intimacy of human relations. In its seductiveness, the land has become a substitute for Caleb's wife; in its transcendence, the land has become a substitute for God.

Caleb's maniacal need to dominate extends to everyone he knows, but it falls most heavily on his wife, Amelia. Caleb relies for his power upon knowledge of the relatively minor moral lapses of his fellows: Thorvald Thorvaldson's stealing fish, Bjorn Aronson's financial indiscretion, Judith's moment of wild temper, and especially Amelia's bearing of an illegitimate child, Mark Jordan. Caleb makes an elaborate, ego-gratifying game of keeping Amelia subservient and accommodating of his every whim. The most despicable of many instances is his action upon learning that Anton Klovacz has just visited at the Gare farm. Travelling by a circuitous route, Caleb arrives back at the farm and plays on Amelia's reluctance to tell him of this slight break in her daily routine. He draws her further and further into her lie until he springs upon her in a fury designed to convince her of her unworthiness: "'So—you'd lie, too, eh? What else have you done, tell me that, can you?'" (p. 233).

By virtue of the control he exercises over Amelia, Caleb controls the entire family. His threat to reveal Mark Jordan's parentage causes Amelia to become an unwilling ally in discouraging rebellion among the children: "Amelia had determined to isolate herself wholly from Caleb's children, so that she might not weaken in her resolve. She would be as hard with them as he had been, lest they dare break for freedom and so bring ruin on Mark Jordan'' (p. 195). This tendency to withdraw, forced upon the entire Gare family, creates the overwhelming sense of loneliness in the novel. It is essential to Caleb's approach to the farm to discourage any love within the family or without. In this effort he almost succeeds. Martin, the elder son, dreams of a new, more comfortable house as a monument to his creative hard work, but his father's intolerance of "frivolity" forces him into pitiable resignation. Caleb's daughter, Ellen, is the nearest that Caleb comes to successfully creating someone in his own image. Ellen, a frustrated artist, momentarily considers going off with the half-breed, Malcolm, but Caleb's grip on her is too strong. She withdraws into self-righteous imitation of her father and comments austerely on the conduct of her brothers and sisters. Even Caleb's favourite, Charlie, is but a pawn in the game, to be pampered as an illustration to the others of their inferior status. Isolated individually, these people are also isolated collectively, having never been beyond a radius of ten miles from home, nor even allowed, excepting Martin, to attend church.

Among the Gare children only one, Judith, having grown up with more of her mother than her father in her, constantly fights Caleb's tyranny. If Ostenso characterizes Caleb quite explicitly in terms of the land upon which he lives, so, more obscurely, and hence, to my mind, more interestingly, does she portray Judith. In spite of his devotion to his crops, Caleb is fundamentally opposed to the land. Judith, who longs for an escape from the farm, has established a deep and meaningful connection with the land and its rhythms. In direct opposition to Caleb's oppressions and the hypocritical strictures of society is this magnificent rebel, a young woman "vivid and terrible, who seemed the embryonic ecstasy of all life." Undoubtedly Ostenso was influenced considerably by D. H. Lawrence in her characterization of Judith.[2] Looking at *Women in Love* (though parallels could be found in most of Lawrence's writing), I find a similar admiration for the "powerful sweet fire" at the core of life, a similar desire for the "'freedom *together*'" which is true love, and a similar disgust with the acquisitive society, the world of "'sordid and foul mechanicalness.'"[3]

Judith, searchingly, tentatively at first, and then finally more positively, breaks out of her version of the immeasurable solitude which surrounds each of the Gares by establishing mental, emotional, and physical ties with Sven Sandbo. One of the early scenes in which Judith and Sven are together reveals the two lovers in a strange, strongly Lawrencean ritual struggle, dominated by naked animal passion, but ending in a deep, conciliatory kiss. The significance of the struggle is seen from Sven's point of view: "Then something leaped

---

[2]The same suggestion is made by Linda Jane Rogers, *Environment and the Quest Motif in Selected Works of Canadian Prairie Fiction* (Unpublished M.A. Thesis, University of British Columbia, 1970), p. 109.

[3]Lawrence, *Women in Love* (New York: Viking Press, 1960), pp. 122, 143, 347.

in Sven. They were no longer unevenly matched, different in sex. They were two stark elements, striving for mastery over each other" (p. 117). Slowly Judith realizes the necessity of asserting her selfhood which Sven intuits here. She recognizes "in herself an alien spirit, a violent being of dark impulses, in no way related to the life about her. She was alternately seized with an agony of pity for Amelia, whose reticence she could not fathom, and futile rage at Ellen and Martin for their endurance. And beneath it all her passion for Sven pressed through her being like an undercurrent of fire" (p. 124).

Judith's vital spirit is reflected in her private relation with nature, her desire to identify with the uninhibited freedom, and true passion of the natural world. Thus Judith stretches out nude, pressing against the warm earth of the ravine:

> Oh, how knowing the bare earth was, as if it might have a heart and a mind hidden here in the woods. The fields that Caleb had tilled had no tenderness, she knew. But here was something forbiddenly beautiful, secret as one's own body. And there was something beyond this. She could feel it in the freeness of the air, in the depth of the earth. Under her body there were, she had been taught, eight thousand miles of earth. On the other side, what? Above her body there were leagues and leagues of air, leading like wings—to what? The marvelous confusion and complexity of all the world had singled her out from the rest of the Gares (p. 67).

The tentativeness of Judith's understanding emphasizes the mystery at the heart of Judith's quest; yet it is by identification with this very mystery that Judith finds her strength. Hers is a world in which "every living thing caressed, or was caressed" (p. 235). Her father's limitation is his closing his eyes to this fascinating mystery. Judith's intimacy with nature includes the animal world—an intimacy developed in scenes which are again reminiscent of Lawrence, especially of his use of the horse to symbolize vitality. Lind Archer looks on with quiet admiration as Jude struggles stubbornly to break a young colt, "slender and glossy as black satin, with a fine blazing eye," to the saddle. Just as Lou Witt thrills at the "dark, invisible fire"[4] of life in St. Mawr, so Judith sympathizes with the defiant, animal passion of the untamed colt.

The "unmeasurable Alone surrounding each soul" is intensified, the novelist suggests, by an empty and demanding land. Amelia thinks to herself that "the precious flame [of affection] had been sucked into the very earth upon which and by which they lived" (p. 24). Amelia's attitude is wholly understandable, considering her extremity, but not necessarily anything more than one character's momentary view. When similar sentiments are put into the mouths of Lind Archer and Mark Jordan, characters who serve an essentially choric function in the tragedy, they have implications for the novel as a whole:

[4]Lawrence, *St. Mawr*, in *The Short Novels* (London: Heinemann, 1956), II, 11.

They talked of the strange unity between the nature of man and earth here in the north, and of the spareness of both physical and spiritual life.

"There's no waste—that's it," Mark observed, "either in human relationships or in plant growth. There's no incontinency anywhere. . . . Think of the difference there would be in the outward characters of these people if the land didn't sap up all their passion and sentiment" (pp. 104-5).

Though Lind agrees with Mark about external appearances, she realizes that human passions are not absent, but confined:

"We are, after all, only the mirror of our environment. Life here at Oeland, even, may seem a negation but it's only a reflection from so few exterior natural objects that it has the semblance of negation. These people are thrown inward upon themselves, their passions stored up, they are intensified figures of life with no outward expression—no releasing gesture" (pp. 105-6).

To this theory of characterization in which man is made the mirror of his environment can be opposed the equally valid theory that the environment is a product of the mind, that the metaphor can be reversed so that the landscape mirrors the individual. Judith, one suspects, is more likely to fit the latter theory, for she is able to sense, albeit inexactly, a delicacy and mysterious rhythm in the natural world which so often seems to be her enemy. This fundamental sympathy with a world in which both love and brutal passion are stripped of masks causes Judith to make the move which will define her individuality. Ostenso describes her decision, again in typically Lawrencean idiom:

She had wanted none of them to know [of her pregnancy]. They were not fine enough to know. They would denounce her for the thing she regarded with pride. She belonged to another, clear, brave world of true instincts, she told herself. They were muddled, confused souls, not daring to live honestly. Living only for the earth, and the product of the soil, they were meager and warped (p. 332).

This last phrase does not, I think, negate the previous argument, but rather points to the failing of Caleb, to his obsession with what the earth can provide, to his living *for* the earth, unlike Judith who lives *as* the earth. In love Judith has discovered a new, self-fulfilling freedom from responsibility and the dictates of social conscience; she will obey the primal forces in her being, the "brave world of true instincts."

In spite of Amelia's subdued acceptance of life under a tyrant, Judith is very much her mother's daughter; mother and daughter have a mutually strengthening influence on one another. The instincts which Amelia has stifled are manifest in Judith's self-assertion. Like Judith, Amelia empathizes with the rhythms of nature, but the family situation severely inhibits her: "Always before, the sight of growth had somewhat thrilled her, had struck a vital, creative chord within her that was otherwise left unsounded in his barren life. Now her mind was dulled by the sight of it. Growth—with death in its wake" (p. 121). Amelia's apparent willingness to sacrifice the Gare children to protect her illegitimate son is her rebellion against Caleb and the debilitating life he represents. Through the bleakness of the novel's resolution shines the hope of Amelia's final defiance of Caleb, a more temperate form of the self-assertion that Judith makes. With the discovery of Judith's pregnancy Amelia recognizes her own youth in her daughter. She decides that Caleb must not be allowed to ruin his daughter's life as he has ruined her own. To Judith she gives her tacit assent for flight with Sven, despite her conviction that Mark would now come to know his parentage. Strengthened by her resolution to see her daughter free, Amelia now triumphs over Caleb by passive defiance in the face of his brutal whipping: "His face was twisted with disbelief. He could not bring himself to admit that she had beaten him—beaten him in the very crisis of her life" (p. 345).

Caleb meets a cruel death in a fire which destroys the flax to which he had given his most tender devotion. He dies symbolically trapped in the very land which he had tried to master; in the grip, as Ostenso describes it, of an "insidious force in the earth [which] drew him in deeper" (p. 351). As Mark Jordan observes, there is an obvious justice in such an end: "'The only thing he really cared for claimed him in the end'" (p. 355). Nevertheless, the resolution is too hurried and too mechanical. The suddenness with which the fire follows Amelia's critical defiance and Caleb's moment of "shame and self-loathing" is inconsistent with the subtle development of the novel to this point. The interplay of characters and the complexity of response to Caleb, which ranges from disgust and rage to pity for the weakness and loneliness of a jealous ego-maniac, seem undercut.

But so perceptive is the novel that it would be a distortion to end on a negative note. Inherent in the symbolic motif established by Ostenso's title is an evocativeness and complexity which is worth particular attention. The wild geese relate directly to the central themes of loneliness and freedom. Like the loon and the wind elsewhere in the novel, the call of the geese is a lonely sound, a "trumpet-call" which causes Mark to comment: "'They sound as if they know something about it—something about being alone'" (p. 61). Mingled with the loneliness, however, is a stirring, yet ambiguous, freedom: "Their cry smote upon the heart like the loneliness of the universe . . . a magnificent seeking through solitude—an endless quest" (p. 57). In their flight "to a region beyond human warmth . . . beyond even human isolation" (p. 34), these wild geese come to represent both the mystery, the great imponderable at the heart of human existence, and the human impulse to seek an understanding of this mystery.

The distribution of references to the geese in the novel, the great concentration of them near the beginning and end, reinforces the simple identification of the migratory birds with the cycle and pulse of nature, with the "beginning and the end of the period of growth." Clearly Caleb was unaware of the beautiful mysteries of life; to him life was clear-cut: "'Every man for himself, that's what I say. Nothing matters to me but myself'" (p. 283). The measure of the strength of Amelia and Judith, of Mark Jordan and Lind Archer, is their ability to touch the mystery, to accept the mingling of joy and sorrow, of life and death, as nature's order; to come to the tentative recognition that Lind Archer achieves:

> Lind felt humble as she heard the wild geese go over. There was an infinite cold passion in their flight, like the passion of the universe, a proud mystery never to be solved. She knew in her heart that Mark Jordan was like them—that he stood inevitably alone. But because of the human need in him, he had come to her. It warmed her to dwell on the thought (p. 355).

Ultimately, then, the "unmeasurable Alone surrounding each soul" is not debilitating, but nourishing. It is the source of each man's personality and individuality. Man is beset by a landscape of utter "negation"; he is an insignificant intruder: "Here was the prairie, spare as an empty platter—no there was the solitary figure of a man upon it, like a meager offering of earth to heaven" (p. 161). In the absence of external reassurance he must search the depths of his own being. Attempts such as Caleb's to dominate the world outside himself, either the land or other men, are doomed. The real negation lies in the denial of one's own essential nature. Escape from human loneliness, from the isolation of individual from individual lies in the natural wellsprings of love; the vital love which drives Judith to meet and flee with Sven in the face of social strictures; the love which is felt in the irrepressible changes in the mood of the earth. Concerning the relation of man to man Ostenso is renewing the urging found in one of her own poems:

> Draw near to me, lest we be two,
> I, alone, and alone, you.[5]

---

[5]Ostenso, "First Snow," *In a Far Land* (New York: Seltzer, 1924), p. 52.

VI The Prairie Internalized: The Fiction of Sinclair Ross

> The sun's clear-edged heat
> parches minds to dry bone
> but we grope for firmness;
> we see brush holding on
> huddled in blurred clusters.
>
> PETER STEVENS, "Prairie: Time and Place"

"Level monotony" and "negation" are the aspects of the setting in *Wild Geese* which dominate the mood of Sinclair Ross's prairie. Ross's prairie is the Saskatchewan of the Depression years when the bleakness of the landscape was accentuated by drought and dust. Unlike Caleb Gare, or Grove's pioneering men of the soil, the central characters in Ross's novels are a small-town minister and his wife, a young criminal fleeing from Montreal, and a young musician fleeing from Saskatchewan. They still may "feel exposed,"[1] but they are exposed as much to community prejudice and feelings of personal inadequacy as to the extremes of summer heat and winter blizzard. Ross's typical man on the prairie is much more conscious of the implications of the emptiness around him than of the forces of nature pounding against him. In the face of an indifferent and meaningless universe he "'can't bear to admit his insignificance.'"

The taut and poignant *As For Me and My House* (1941) is Ross's best expression of this sense of futility. Only in several bleakly memorable short stories has he approached the accomplishment of his first novel. As Claude Bissell observes, *The Well* (1958) is "a superior novel," but without "sufficient intensity and power to weld together theme and action."[2] Ross continues his exploration of man's feeling of insignificance in *A Whir of Gold* (1970), a novel with little subtlety of characterization and an almost inconsequential action. Throughout this apparently declining achievement Ross has always shown interest in the relation of his characters to the Saskatchewan landscape; *As For Me and My House* and his short stories particularly mark an important new direction in the literary use of the prairie.

In Ross's fiction the prairie is first significantly internalized. "The inner and outer worlds of the Bentleys," Roy Daniells remarks, "correspond perfectly."[3] In his creation of character, Ross incorporates features and descriptive terms which apply equally to the prairie landscape. Mrs. Bentley's landscape is completely subjective. It is integral to her way of thinking and

---

[1]Sinclair Ross, *As For Me and My House* (Toronto: McClelland and Stewart, 1957), p. 13.
[2]Bissell, "Letters in Canada: 1958," *University of Toronto Quarterly*, XXVIII (July 1959), 370.
[3]Daniells, "Introduction," *As For Me and My House*, p. vi.

expression, so that not only major themes, like the yearning for assurance of one's "existence and reality," but minor details, like Philip's tone of speech, are expressed in terms which involve the surrounding prairie. In other words, Ross is the first writer in Canada to show a profound awareness of the metaphorical possibilities of the prairie landscape. More particularly, and hence the term "internalization" is appropriate, Ross introduces the landscape as a metaphor for man's mind, his emotions, his soul perhaps, in a more thorough and subtle way than any previous writer.

As For Me and My House is the study of the life and thoughts of two people during one Depression year in a small prairie town. In choosing to tell the story in diary format from the point of view of Mrs. Bentley, Ross achieves both unity and fascinating psychological complexity. He delicately exploits the tension between Mrs. Bentley's point of view and the reader's perspective. Our understanding of Philip's character must be coloured by an awareness that this small-town minister, who is almost completely dominated by his wife, might have an outlook on things quite different from that which his wife detects. Similarly, Mrs. Bentley presents herself in a light that Daniells, for example, calling her "pure gold and wholly credible," accepts unquestioningly. But Mrs. Bentley's point of view need not necessarily be identical to the author's and, indeed, it is the effective counterpoint of her opinions and the objective judgment the reader is encouraged to make which enhances the sense of psychological complexity.

The prairie setting is indispensable to Ross's psychological portrait. Horizon itself, representative small town as it most assuredly is, takes its name from a dominant feature of the prairie landscape. It is, as Daniells comments, a place "at once nowhere and everywhere," with the elusive, beckoning quality of a dream, but it is also where sky and land inevitably meet, where, it seems, the dream must confront the inalterable reality. The people of Horizon, as Mrs. Bentley describes them, mirror the physical environment's dry and featureless visage, and yet they are not at home in it. The bewilderment of being vertical and exposed is an essential factor in the characterization of Mrs. Bentley and Philip. The geometric figure is inevitably implicit in the attempt to discover self.

Early in the novel Mrs. Bentley describes the precariousness of the town and herself:

> It's an immense night out there, wheeling and windy. The lights on the street and in the houses are helpless against the black wetness, little unilluminating glints that might be painted on it. The town seems huddled together, cowering on a high, tiny perch, afraid to move lest it topple into the wind. Close to the parsonage is the church, black even against the darkness, towering ominously up through the night and merging with it. There's a soft steady swish of rain on the roof, and a gurgle of eave troughs running over. Above, in the high cold night, the wind goes swinging

past, indifferent, liplessly mournful. It frightens me, makes me feel lost,
dropped on this little perch of town and abandoned (p. 5).

The surrounding immensity is almost overwhelming. The sense of being upright
and exposed, like the church's tower and the town "on a high, tiny perch,"
is strong throughout her description. It is as if the blackness of night is oblivion,
with man placed uneasily at its edge, insignificant and waiting to be reclaimed.
He is unable to illuminate the darkness; he cannot make a lasting mark in
it; he cannot see into the future; he is not even aware of himself. The wind,
which blows ceaselessly through this novel, is the agent of oblivion, constantly
threatening to topple man and his achievements indifferently into the void.
The fear of the void, the sense of being lost, describes the essential experience
of Philip and Mrs. Bentley. *As For Me and My House* is the record of their
search for courage and comfort.

Vulnerability in the landscape, and in the universe, is an experience Philip
shares with the farmers assembled on Sunday morning in the Partridge Hill
schoolhouse. Mrs. Bentley feels that their vigorous singing of the orthodox
hymns is somehow a response "to the grim futility of their own lives." For
"five years in succession now," she reflects, "they've been blown out, dried
out, hailed out; and it was as if in the face of so blind and uncaring a universe
they were trying to assert themselves, to insist upon their own meaning and
importance" (p. 19). Here is the recurrent prairie theme, man's desire to assert
his presence. These men are insisting on their "right to be in sight on the
prairie."[4] For Gander Stake, who feels quite at home on the prairie, the insistence
is slight; but for Abe Spalding it means raising a house and barn majestic
in their proportions. For the Bentleys the assertion becomes a more intellectual
and imaginative one, in which the escape from their sense of insignificance
involves principally religion and art.

The false-front mode of architecture has repeatedly served the prairie writer
as a symbol of man's obsession with asserting himself, with raising a significant
equivalent to his own abrupt but awesome position in an almost limitless landscape. In Ross's novel the false-fronted stores dominate the architecture of
the prairie town, becoming a memorable symbol of man's facile self-deception.
Each character erects his own false front. The minor characters have theirs,
be it the scholarly veneer of Paul's glib comments on etymology, or the assumed
superiority of Mrs. Bird, the doctor's wife. But those which Mrs. Bentley and
Philip erect are of much greater interest.

Philip's false front is, of course, his religion, his entire vocation. In the
face of each town's expectation that their minister be strongly fundamentalist,
Philip lacks the courage to voice his more contemporary views. "The Word
of God as revealed in Holy Writ—Christ crucified—salvation through His

[4]Stegner, *Wolf Willow*, p. 271.

Grace—those are the things that Philip stands for'' (p. 4). These are the things, that is, which the public Philip stands for; the private Philip cannot accept the rigidly literal interpretation of scripture. When Steve, the Bentley's adopted son, puts grave doubts into a friend's mind ''as to the likelihood of a Noah's Ark capable of the cargo credited to it by scripture'' (p. 111), Mrs. Bentley has to assure the community that modern theology is something which Philip may discuss, but to which he does not adhere. Philip himself is torn, Mrs. Bentley observes, between deceiving Steve, and revealing himself to Steve as a hypocrite.

Clearly, Philip's false front is not so much an assertion, or gesture of defiance, as a mask, as something like his study door behind which he can retreat. Like Abe Spalding's wind-break, Philip's religion is a ''rampart . . . erected to keep out a hostile world.''[5] The religious vocation, which in Horizon, especially, demands not only doctrinal adherence but piety and propriety in every phase of one's public and private life, is for Philip a simple matter of economic expediency. He pretends to be what he can never be, for the sake of a meagre existence, and yet he is heartsick with awareness of the futility of his pretense. When he paints the false-fronted stores Mrs. Bentley assumes his own identification with them: ''False fronts ought to be laughed at, never understood or pitied. They're such outlandish things, the front of a store built up to look like a second story. They ought always to be seen that way, pretentious, ridiculous, never as Philip sees them, stricken with a look of self-awareness and futility'' (p. 4).

The ease with which Mrs. Bentley makes such absolute judgments about her husband's shortcomings conceals her arrogance. The implication here that Mrs. Bentley is always able to laugh at the false fronts is denied by her later actions. Her own deceptions, to be sure, are more defiant than those of Philip. Her hypocrisy, unlike Philip's, is deliberate, insolently regarded as essential to survival in this social environment:

> I resigned myself to sanctimony years ago. Today I was only putting our false front up again, enlarged this time for three.
> Philip, Steve and I. It's such a trim, efficient little sign; it's such a tough, deep-rooted tangle that it hides.
> They spy and carp and preen themselves, but none of them knows. They can only read our shingle, all its letters freshened up this afternoon, *As For Me and My House*—*The House of Bentley*—*We Will Serve the Lord* (p. 61).

She is delighted, almost proud, to be called on again and again to outwit the congregation and keep the mask of piety intact. But behind the mask is

[5]Grove, *Fruits of the Earth*, p. 138.

a scarcely acknowledged "tangle" of personal and family problems. She comes to sense in herself the very contradiction she describes in Philip: their deception is both utterly futile and grimly inevitable. Particularly when she has to maintain a false front of disinterested solicitude for the welfare of Philip's child and for Judith, its mother, she is as plagued by doubt, guilt and lack of resolve, as she insists Philip is.

The complexity of Ross's characterization can be sensed here. It is legitimate to speculate as to the veracity of Mrs. Bentley's view of her husband's character.[6] How much of the responsibility for their situation is truly his? Perhaps, had Mrs. Bentley not been so ready to usurp Philip's role and so quick to cultivate the absurdly pious image to which they were to conform, they might have escaped the deadening cycle of Horizons long ago. Philip's allowing himself to be so dominated in itself suggests a weakness, but at the same time one senses the inadequacy of Mrs. Bentley's conclusions. Philip may have a reserve of resolute determination, hinted in his relations with Steve and Judith, which is obscured by the quickness with which Mrs. Bentley presumes to make his decisions.

False fronts are, by nature, precarious. The prairie, as Grove had earlier recognized, exerts a relentless pressure to return all things to the horizontal. The unending wind which fills the novel threatens to sweep away everything, and leave the false fronts collapsed: "Mile after mile the wind poured by, and we were immersed and lost in it. I sat breathing from my throat, my muscles tense. To relax, I felt, would be to let the walls around me crumple in" (p. 38). Beyond the effective detail and evocation of Ross's descriptions of the wind lie a variety of symbolic implications. In the preceding passage the wind represents the meaningless turmoil of existence. The wind, as in Anne Marriott's poem, is the enemy and Mrs. Bentley prefers to "be out in the wind and fighting it." The wind carries the totality of possibilities which life offers, possibilities which cannot be grasped or merely pass unnoticed: "I've felt that way so many times in a wind, that it's rushing past me, away from me, that it's leaving me lost and isolated. . . . I think how the winds and tides of life have left me just the same, poured over me, round me, swept north, south, then back again" (pp. 159-60).

Essentially, then, wind in this novel symbolizes the passage of time. Seated in Philip's library, listening to the rattling windowpanes, Paul and Mrs. Bentley think "of wind and men, and the mystery of passage." The three things are appropriately linked; the wind is the symbol of the agent of passage, and man and his pretensions are carried in and out of this life as inevitably as the prairie wind carries things before it. The wind, as the metaphor of the town's perch made evident, threatens to topple man and his achievements into the void. Caught themselves in the winds of time, winds which destroy their delusions

[6]W.H. New discusses the ambiguities inherent in Mrs. Bentley's diary in "Sinclair Ross's Ambivalent World," *Canadian Literature*, No. 40 (Spring 1969), 26-32.

and leave them in confusion, the Bentleys must face this threat of extinction. Their attempt, primarily metaphysical, to deal with feelings of purposelessness and fear, necessitates, on Ross's part, a more thorough and symbolic use of prairie landscape than anything previously attempted.

Landscape and climate become an integral part of *As For Me and My House* in a way which is new to the prairie novel. The wind is more than a device descriptive of the rigours of Depression agriculture; it is more, even, than a convenient symbol. It is so pervasive in the novel that it seems essential to Ross's, or, more correctly, to Mrs. Bentley's mode of thinking. The impact of the wind, in fact of the environment in general, is primarily psychological; as Peter Stevens expresses it: "The sun's clear-edged heat/parches minds to dry bone."[7] Similarly, the horizon, which has been an influential, if distant, feature of the prairie landscape, becomes the name of a community and, in turn, the shorthand for a corporate mentality, ironically narrow-minded and selfish. The horizon is no longer distant and beckoning man, as in Stead, to the "adventure of life untrammeled by traditions,"[8] but near at hand, closing the people in and smothering them.

The manner in which other features of the physical environment permeate the novel is summarized by W.H. New:

> The overall impression left by the book is certainly one of aridity: of dust and heat, the Depression on the prairies and the drought which went with it. And accompanying the unproductivity of the land is the dryness of the people: Mrs. Bentley, who cannot bear a child; Philip, who does not believe in his church and cannot comfort the people; the people themselves, who in Mrs. Bentley's eyes cannot appreciate anything or anyone beyond their own restricted world.[9]

In a physical sense, of course, the wind and dust are everywhere.

> It's been nearly dark today with dust. Everything's gritty, making you shiver and setting your teeth on edge. There's a crunch on the floor like sugar when you walk. We keep the doors and windows closed, and still it works in everywhere. I lay down for a little while after supper, and I could feel it even on the pillow. The air is so dry and choking with it that every few minutes a kind of panic seizes you, and you have an impulse to thresh out against it with your hands (p. 62).

But as the latter part of this passage indicates the dust represents suffocation in all respects, particularly emotional and intellectual suffocation.

[7]Stevens, "Prairie: Time and Place," *Nothing But Spoons* (Montreal: Delta Canada, 1969).
[8]Stead, *The Cowpuncher*, p. 198.
[9]New, *Canadian Literature*, No. 40 (Spring 1969), 28.

The landscape and climate become internalized. They are part of Ross's imagination, part of the community he portrays, part, especially, of his characters. The comparisons between man and his environment are no longer mechanical, restricted to facile similes. Man and environment are totally integrated so that adjectives chosen to describe the natural environment could as well apply to character, and vice-versa. Light, both indoors and out, is "colorless and glum"; Mrs. Bentley's furniture is "dull and ugly," the walls of her home "dingy"; the town is "barren"; and the people of Horizon "become worn so bare and colorless." Such a technique is finely ironic, for the characters of the novel are influenced by the environment, and yet they themselves contribute to its oppressiveness. The irony is especially evident, since the entire novel is told from her point of view, in Mrs. Bentley's description of Philip. Philip's eyes are "dry" or "flat," with a "half-frightened stillness"; his voice is also "dry" or "neat and brittle"; and both his words and hers seem "stilted, lifeless," like their life together.

This internalization of the landscape is subtle, yet remarkably effective. As winds and sun and dust, both external and internal, persist, the feeling of suffocation mounts. Mrs. Bentley comes increasingly to feel there is no escape. Finding her garden "bare, inert, impaled by the rays of sun and left to die," she identifies with it. Walking through the town she feels "an alien in its blistered lifelessness" (p. 90). In the depth of despair she is no more able to survive in her family and social environment than the plants in the drought: "I haven't roots of my own any more. I'm a fungus or parasite whose life depends on his. He throws me off and I dry and wither. My pride's gone" (p. 151).

The oppressive atmosphere in *As For Me and My House* is emphasized by Ross's insistence on the repetitive cycle of the lives of his characters. Though the novel describes only the one year which the Bentleys spend in Horizon, the reader is as uncomfortably aware as Mrs. Bentley that this town is a duplicate of the ones before and the ones to come. Horizon's Main Street is not unlike that of Gopher Prairie, Minnesota. "Gopher Prairie was merely an enlargement of all the hamlets which they had been passing.... The huddled low wooden houses broke the plains scarcely more than would a hazel thicket. The fields swept up to it, past it. It was unprotected and unprotecting; there was no dignity in it nor any hope of greatness."[10] Likewise, the inhabitants of Gopher Prairie: "The people—they'd be as drab as their houses, as flat as their fields." Isolated, exposed, and ugly, the prairie town, whether viewed by Ross or Sinclair Lewis, offers the same monotonous succession of people living the drab life that their physical environment dictates.

Consistent with the patterns of the novel, Philip, himself from a small town and the bastard son of a student preacher, in turn, as preacher in the town of Horizon, fathers an illegitimate child. That he tries to remake his adopted

[10]Sinclair Lewis, *Main Street* (New York: Grosset and Dunlap, 1920), pp. 26-27.

son, Steve, in his own image extends the predictability in time beyond the pages of the novel, creating the expectation that the tedium will continue in future generations. The overpowering monotony of the novel remains, however, a problem for the characters and does not become, as Daniells suggests, boring in itself. Mrs. Bentley despairs of "the next town—the next and the next," concluding that "there doesn't seem much meaning to our going on" (p. 103).

It is appropriate that a novel which devotes so much attention to life's meaninglessness should have an aspiring artist as a central character. Philip's paintings and pencil sketches are his attempt to interpret his experience on the prairie. His art involves, although in a different medium, the same internalization, the same attempt to suggest human psychology through the subtle use of landscape features, that is so much a part of Ross's technique. Philip's painting of a schoolhouse is not simply a photographic representation, but a powerful, if not totally successful, expression of man's lonely defiance in a "distorted, barren" world.

Discovery of one's own significance involves, in Philip's opinion, religion and art:

> "Religion and art . . . are almost the same thing anyway. Just different ways of taking a man out of himself, bringing him to the emotional pitch that we call ecstasy or rapture. They're both a rejection of the material, common-sense world for one that's illusory, yet somehow more important. Now it's always when a man turns away from this common-sense world around him that he begins to create, when he looks into a void, and has to give it life and form" (p. 112).

Though, for the Bentleys, neither religion nor art is particularly satisfying, Philip's recognition that one has to face the void and attempt to comprehend it through imaginative creation is of fundamental importance to the resolution of the novel. Furthermore, Philip's acknowledgement points to a principle which has motivated most artists dealing with the prairie vastness.

It is through Philip's drawings, perhaps more so than in her own writing, that Mrs. Bentley is able to articulate her sense of the community and their own position in it. She is able to see the false fronts, for example, as "they stare at each other across the street as into mirrors of themselves, absorbed in their own reflections" (p. 69). Is it through a change in Philip or in herself that Mrs. Bentley comes less and less to challenge the tone and composition of Philip's paintings and more and more to accept the truth of his insights? The drawing of the white country schoolhouse seems especially expressive because, in its vertical isolation, standing up "lonely and defiant on a landscape like a desert," it is so typical of the prairie artist's vision. This is, thinks Mrs. Bentley, an important representation of "faith, ideals, reason—all the things that really are humanity—like Paul you feel them there, their stand against the implacable blunderings of Nature" (p. 80). There is no real escape from the void, rather discovery that the void is not to be escaped, only to be feared less and known more. Man on the edge of the void is like the farmhouse in one of Philip's paintings: "erect, small, isolated." He is both vulnerable in his insignificance, and yet resigned in his endurance.

Something of the possibility and the nature of escape from Horizon is suggested by Mrs. Bentley's many walks up the railway track to the open prairie, with its ravine and small creek. From this vantage point Mrs. Bentley is able to gain a perspective on the town and on herself. She senses that her world is not always "bitter" and "implacable" but occasionally somehow "curious and wondering," creating "a lost, elemental feeling, as if I were the first of my kind ever to venture there" (p. 148). When the experience of isolation also involves the thrill of pioneering, the break from the oppressive pattern becomes easier.

As For Me and My House, as W.H. New notes, derives much of its effectiveness as a novel from its ambiguous resolution. The novel is not open-ended, but it carefully avoids a pat or sentimental solution to the dilemma which it so powerfully presents. The penultimate diary entry confirms what Mrs. Bentley had realized, but which neither she nor Philip had been fully able to accept. That the wind indeed is master is affirmed physically by a steady April gale at the conclusion of which "most of the false fronts were blown down." In a fit of rage Mrs. Bentley confronts Philip with his responsibility for Judith's child. Rather than putting further strain on their relationship, this confrontation serves to relieve tensions. The elimination of the false fronts which both have tried to maintain with regard to this child allows the possibility of an improved marriage on a more honest basis. Similarly, the false front of piety, the necessary concomitant of the ministerial vocation, is discarded with the decision to move to the city and open a bookstore. The collapse of this false front is symbolized when Philip unhesitatingly smokes the new pipe which his wife has given him. The Bentleys become less hypocritical, more self-reliant, and more honest with themselves as the novel proceeds. This development is neither abrupt, nor absolute; it is gradual, relative, even slight, but it is undoubtedly there.

The loss of Steve forces Philip to the realization that " 'you're a fool not to be just as casual with life as life is with you. Take things as they come—get what you can out of them. Don't want or care too much for anything' " (p. 119). This cynical voice of despair is not representative of the end of the novel, but it does anticipate a significant discovery for the Bentleys. Pummelled as they are by the winds of time, their attitude must be not constant regret of the past and despair of the future but a resolution to "take things as they come," to live in the present. The feeling of being on the edge of the void, empty landscape and empty future, is not erased, but simply made less important by an increasing acceptance of their position. Mingled with the acceptance of their smallness and isolation is a determination to stand erect and persist despite their vulnerability.

Such a determination originates neither totally in religion, nor in art, but in the impulse which Philip finds basic to both. Philip and Mrs. Bentley rediscover that it is not art so much as aspiration which is truly genuine in life. Their discovery is not the panacea for all ills; in fact the aspiration is much less modest at the novel's conclusion than the dreams Mrs. Bentley builds of marriage to a great artist and operation of a thriving business. But the aspiration embodied in their determination to forget the past, to raise the young Philip, and to initiate a new career, tempered, as it is, by the memory of twelve years of monotonous frustration, is the indication of a new direction in their lives. The quality of the aspiration of the moment, rather than the quantity of realization in the future, is the apparent key to contentment.

In one sense the reader is not so aware of place in *As For Me and My House* as he is in earlier prairie novels. Ross avoids the pockets of landscape description which bring the reader up abruptly with an awareness of locale which may have faded from consciousness. The reader of *As For Me and My House* is both less aware of the prairie and, because it is a continuing experience, more conscious of it. Locale permeates the fabric of the novel as it is internalized, and thus Ross represents both an escape from self-conscious local colour and a much more profound, if unconscious, feeling for place. The same cannot be said of Ross's second novel, *The Well* (1958), and for this reason, among others, it is a much less successful work.

The Well echoes familiarly with key elements from *As For Me and My House*: Larson's longing for a son, the mystique of the railroad, the domineering wife, and Chris's fascination with horses. But without the cohesive factors of the earlier novel, they are only mechanical reworkings of themes that once proved successful. The loss of impact attributable to the change from first to third person is most noticeable. Ross sacrifices the unifying vision, the irony, and the complexity he had achieved in his first novel. The change to less ordinary subject matter leads him into the sensationalism of melodrama, and the attempted exploration of the criminal psyche degenerates into the pallidness of a conventional thriller.

The prairie in *The Well* is noticeably less severe than it is in *As For Me and My House*. The crops are plentiful; drought and dust are scarcely mentioned. Ross does use the basic image of man in the prairie in a similar way, but he pays much less attention to it. Donald Stephens described the effect of the first novel: "There is a feeling approaching claustrophobia, yet the vastness soars over the people."[11] Ross introduces a similar ambiguity in *The Well* with less success. Accustomed to the enclosed feeling of city streets, Chris feels lost in the "stark, sky-and-earth immensity." His exposure in the landscape mirrors a social and emotional exposure:

It was his first contact with the open country; the bare expanse spread

---

[11]Donald Stephens, "Wind, Sun and Dust," *Canadian Literature*, No. 23 (Winter 1965), 19.

out before him now seemed gaping, mutilated, as if a giant shovel had sheared away something essential, like features from a face. He would never fit in, never survive. The feeling of exposure and inadequacy was so strong that it cost him an effort not to retreat to the truck and slam the door.[12]

Coexisting with the feeling of exposure is Chris's sense of being trapped, not only in his "close, cupboard-like room," but also in the oppressive, almost palpable, sunlight or darkness. Like this faceless landscape Chris, travelling under an alias, is without an identity.

With the passage of time Chris becomes less frightened that his crime will be discovered and begins to feel more at home on the prairie. But he continues to be terrified by "the wet black void that lay beyond." The limitless prairie night represents the unknown fate facing Chris, aware he is a criminal, uncertain if he is a murderer. The confrontation with the stark realities of birth, life, and death in this environment and his consequent growing concern for the horses and then for his fellow men enable him eventually to face the forbidding void. Confronted with Sylvia's challenge to escape his past and gain wealth and sexual favours with a gun, he rejects her, and with her, his former way of doing things. Ross summarizes Chris's decision with a return to the metaphor from the environment:

Ever since it happened he had let his mind look only to the escape side of his future. The other side, for the simple reason that he had refused to look at it—the side of arrest, trial, conviction—had taken on the terrors of the unthinkable and unknown. It had filled half his sky, had piled up behind him like a thunder cloud. But now he turned and met it squarely (p. 253).

Considered in the light of Ross's fusion of men and environment in Horizon, Chris's meeting of the thunder cloud, his leap into the void, seems easy and mechanical. Such a pat resolution, with the promise of eventual material wealth and Elsie's simple love, is, from the creator of the haunting ambiguity of *As For Me and My House*, most unsatisfying.

A Whir of Gold (1970), Ross's most recent novel, reverses the situation in *The Well*, placing a Saskatchewan boy in the heart of Montreal and tempting him with a life of crime. The shift in setting does not mean that Ross has entirely forgotten the prairie. Sonny (or Saskatchewan, as the narrator sometimes refers to himself) carries rawness and a sense of alienation with him from his native environment: "I'm from the farm and a prairie Main Street where people are exposed, comparatively simple. Easily taken in; not fit to judge."[13] His

---

[12]Ross, *The Well* (Toronto: Macmillan, 1958), p. 13.
[13]Ross, *A Whir of Gold* (Toronto: McClelland and Stewart, 1970), p. 120.

dream, to make a name as a clarinetist in Montreal nightclubs, is linked with the flicker, "flashing like a whir of gold" in the prairie morning. But as the flicker captured loses its magic, so, at the core of the dream, Sonny finds pain and disillusionment. The novel ends with only the emptiness of dreams. That Ross should continue to use such symbols is interesting evidence of the great power which the prairie environment holds over the writer. But beyond that the novel is unremarkable—the characters are slight, their motivations unconvincing, and the action uninteresting.

Unlike *The Well* and *A Whir of Gold*, many of Ross's short stories show the artistry demonstrated in *As For Me and My House*. Almost all of these stories make use, to a greater or lesser extent, of the prairie setting. The farmer, directly involved in trying to grow crops on the harsh prairie, is, with his wife, a central figure. In spite of this more literal relation of character to landscape, Ross continues to internalize the prairie, to make the prairie an essential factor in his characters' psychology. The most noticeable recurring theme is one central to so many prairie novels from Stringer's trilogy to Ryga's *Ballad of a Stone-picker*. The demands of the prairie are so overwhelming that the farmer is almost inevitably forced to disregard human affairs. The isolated vertical figure, once lonely because he was without companionship, now, with companions, finds himself unable to make the vital human connections. The land, Margaret Laurence writes, is the "chief protagonist,"[14] and the struggle of man with land results in isolated, lonely men and women. The neglect of human intercourse is a result not of conscious neglect, nor of boredom, but seemingly of gradual necessity; it is in the truth of this facet of human affairs that the power of Ross's stories lies.

"The Lamp at Noon" is a representative story, telling of a prairie farm family in the bleakest days of the Dust Bowl. The characters are shown as they attempt to accommodate themselves to the unrelenting wind and dust. Paul's reaction to the dust is not despair but continually reinforced determination.

> Dust and drought, earth that betrayed alike his labour and his faith, to him the struggle had given sternness, and impassive courage. Beneath the whip of sand his youth had been effaced. Youth, zest, exuberance—there remained only a harsh and clenched virility that yet became him, that seemed at the cost of more engaging qualities to be fulfillment of his inmost and essential nature.[15]

The wind is cruel and destructive, but it makes a worthy antagonist against which Paul can measure his manhood. So unyielding is the wind and drought that in order to maintain his faith in the land and his faith in his own ability

---

[14]Margaret Laurence, "Introduction," *The Lamp at Noon and Other Stories* (Toronto: McClelland and Stewart, 1968), p. 7.
[15]Ross, *The Lamp at Noon*, p. 15.

to restore the land to productivity Paul must match sternness with sternness. He cannot tolerate a show of his wife's weakness and to attempt to comfort her would be in effect an admission that the land was stronger.

Ross makes a vivid contrast between the responses of Paul and Ellen to this "dust-mad wilderness." To Ellen, Ross observes, "the same debts and poverty had brought a plaintive indignation, a nervous dread of what was still to come. The eyes were hollowed, the lips pinched dry and colourless. It was the face of a woman that had aged without maturing, that had loved the little vanities of life, and lost them wistfully" (p. 15). Paul's stoic endurance and determination that things would get better is balanced by Ellen's fear that things might get worse. The landscape, its dryness and lack of colour, is internalized, man and land becoming indistinguishable parts of a bleak world. The prairie emptiness can be seen in Ellen's eyes, the reflection of a life devoid of affection and promise. Ellen, like the wheat, has aged without maturing.

Paul finds a sympathy for his wife's "lonely terror" when he recognizes that his dream of better times is not shared. The howling of the wind seems suddenly to represent Ellen's cry of lonely outrage. Ironically, when he is finally stripped bare of faith and manhood by the same wind that has stripped his fields to naked desert, Paul finds his wife has already fled. Caged in the small house and stifled by dust and loneliness, Ellen flees in the wind to the ultimate and cruelest suffocation. Smothered by dust and his mother's frantic efforts to protect him from the elements Ellen's infant son dies in her arms. The poignancy of this resolution is accented especially by the understated way in which Ross presents Ellen's deranged inability to realize what has happened. This is one of Ross's most relentless visions of the consequences of human solitude. The brutal prairie erodes all human sensitivity and sympathy, leaving man exhausted and beaten.

Drought, dust, and wind are the centre of man's attention in "The Lamp at Noon." In "Not by Rain Alone" the focal event is the violent force of an early blizzard; in "A Field of Wheat" the impact of the less relentlessly inevitable, but still more devastating, hail storm is examined. Though the list of stories in which Ross explores facets of the prairie experience could be greatly extended, a comment on his best-known story will better serve to summarize his theme and technique.

In "The Painted Door" the prairie setting is again crucial, used not merely to evoke an atmosphere, but to establish dimensions of character and human experience. "The outer situation," Margaret Laurence comments, "always mirrors the inner. The emptiness of the landscape, the bleakness of the land, reflect the inability of these people to touch another with assurance and gentleness" (p. 11).

Mirroring one environment with another is, of course, precisely the technique of internalization which was discussed in *As For Me and My House*. In "The Painted Door" the "long white miles of prairie landscape seemed a region alien to life," a region alien to the meaningful emotional and intellectual life which human beings can share. Man's feeble vertical intrusions into this world serve to accentuate each individual's utter solitude. "Even the distant farmsteads she could see served only to intensify a sense of isolation. Scattered across the face of so vast and bleak a wilderness it was difficult to conceive them as a testimony of human hardihood and endurance. Rather they seemed futile, lost, to cower before the implacability of snow-swept earth and clear pale sun-chilled sky" (p. 100).

The frozen silence of the prairie winter and the frozen silence that exists between John and his wife, Ann, are one. Again the harsh physical environment seems responsible, for the unending work it demands becomes a religion, and leisure, frivolity, basic human contact become sins. The abrupt conclusion, like that of "The Lamp at Noon," is starkly memorable. The effect lies not in the magnitude of Ann's guilt; her brief affair with Steven does seem a forgiveable assertion of her womanhood. But the discovery of John frozen to death, white paint smeared on his hand, confirms that he has justified Ann's faith in his return despite all odds. It is a dramatic visual image of the cowering loneliness and uncertainty of man's existence. For John, it is now clear, had not lost his feeling for his wife, indeed it may have become stronger than ever, and the agony lies in the recognition that two people so deeply in love were so tragically unable to communicate that love.

The intense feeling of emptiness that is caused by man's inability to communicate, or by his fear of communicating, is characteristic of the fiction of Sinclair Ross. Suggestions of the psychological impact of the prairie in Grove become integral to Ross's technique. The prairie is both externally real and absorbed as part of the mentality of the characters. An empty, unproductive, and oppressive existence in an empty, unproductive and oppressive landscape makes an intense fictional impact. The discovery of meaning in this existence, particularly in *As For Me and My House*, makes Sinclair Ross one of Canada's best novelists. Novelists who follow Ross have his internalization of this awesome landscape as background. Christine van der Mark, George Ryga and Robert Kroetsch, discussed in chapter VIII, see the same dry, flat prairie from new perspectives, creating fresh significances. In the work of W.O. Mitchell a rather different prairie becomes both question and answer in the adolescent's diligent probing of the ultimate meaning of existence.

VII   The Eternal Prairie:
The Fiction of W.O. Mitchell

Eternity is a peneplain.

WALLACE STEGNER, *Wolf Willow*

In Ostenso's *Wild Geese* Mark Jordan finds that a world of " 'so few exterior natural objects' " throws people " 'inward upon themselves.' " In *As For Me and My House* Philip and Mrs. Bentley consider their own significance from a precarious perch at the edge of emptiness. Man on the prairie, or so the fiction suggests, is inclined to intense introspection. Ironically, the theme is closely linked to the familiar sense of emancipation in a boundless landscape. As usual, Wallace Stegner provides a perceptive description of the paradox:

> You become acutely aware of yourself. The world is very large, the sky even larger, and you are very small. But also the world is flat, empty, nearly abstract, and in its flatness you are a challenging upright thing, as sudden as an exclamation mark, as enigmatic as a question mark.
>
> It is a country to breed mystical people, egocentric people, perhaps poetic people.[1]

The focus of W.O. Mitchell's fiction is on man as question mark. His pages are filled with mystics, egoists and poets; his best characters, indeed, combine something of the qualities of all three. For Mitchell upright man in the prairie flatness is essentially a thinker. He is forced by the contours of his environment to ponder his own meaning in the universe. Yet his questioning is not exclusively inner-directed. Knowing oneself involves knowing one's world.

The great distance to the horizon, characteristic of the relatively flat prairie landscape, suggests the even greater distances of infinity. With the low prairie horizon there is an unusual amount of sky visible, which, in its vastness and seeming depth, reinforces the idea of endlessness. Like Frank Hall in Stead's *Neighbours*, watching "the gentle drift of cloud shadows gliding over the fields" or plunging his "eyes into the blue vacuum of eternal space,"[2] most characters in prairie fiction are drawn almost automatically to the horizon and the sky. So man on the prairie looks not only inward, but also to the surrounding vastness. His visual focus on sky and horizon is a metaphor for man's emotional and intellectual focus on the nature of the infinite, upon that which is normally beyond human comprehension. In Mitchell's fiction, then, man the intruder is completely unconcerned with his physical exposure, and given increasingly

---

[1]Stegner, *Wolf Willow*, p. 8.
[2]Stead, *Neighbours*, p. 304.

to meditation and reflection—a shift particularly obvious, because it is so sustained, in Mitchell's first novel, *Who Has Seen the Wind* (1947).

The childhood growth of Brian O'Connal is the centre of attention in this novel. Being very much a creature of the prairie, Brian's character and development are repeatedly linked to his physical environment. At the outset Mitchell insists on the importance of landscape: "Here was the least common denominator of nature, the skeleton requirements simply, of land and sky—Saskatchewan prairie."[3] The parallel is clear: a simple, elemental landscape stimulates, or at least harmonizes with, consideration of simple, elemental questions. Apparently Grove sensed the same thing when he explains his choice of a prairie home by the desire "to *flatten* out my views. I wanted the simpler, the more elemental things, things cosmic in their associations, nearer to the beginning or end of creation."[4] Paul Shepard's description of the desert expresses the notion evocatively:

> This [the desert] is the saturation of solitude, the ultimate draft of emptiness, needing courage and sanity to face. It brings introversion, contemplation, hallucination. Space and time and silence are metaphors of the eternal and infinite. To the desert go prophets and hermits; through deserts go pilgrims and exiles. Here the leaders of the great religions have sought the therapeutic and spiritual values of retreat, not to escape but to find reality.[5]

In this sort of landscape there are no diversions, no irrelevancies to distract one from the consideration of ultimate reality. For me the prophets, hermits, pilgrims and exiles in *Who Has Seen the Wind* are analogous to the inhabitants of Shepard's desert; Mitchell's brief preface makes the theme unmistakeable:

> I have tried to present sympathetically the struggle of a boy to understand what still defeats mature and learned men—the ultimate meaning of the cycle of life. To him are revealed in moments of fleeting vision the realities of birth, hunger, satiety, eternity, death. They are moments when an inquiring heart seeks finality, and the chain of darkness is broken.

Various adults in the community try to articulate their own versions of this struggle. For instance Milt Palmer, harnessmaker and amateur philosopher, has his own primitive conception of these realities: " 'What's real. I'll tell you—the beginnin'—that's gittin' born, the end—that's gittin' dead.... Both of them is real—good an' real' " (p. 162). Palmer speaks with conviction. Brian's speculations are less arbitrary, even less articulate, yet ultimately more profound.

---

[3] W.O. Mitchell, *Who Has Seen the Wind* (Toronto: Macmillan, 1947), p. 3.
[4] Grove, *Over Prairie Trails*, p. 51. My italics.
[5] Paul Shepard, *Man in the Landscape* (New York: Alfred A. Knopf, 1967), p. 44.

Mr. Hislop, "herder of God's Presbyterian sheep," is another of the novel's searchers after reality. His meditations on Berkeley (a philosopher discussed later by Digby and Milt Palmer) suggest the direction of Brian's mental probing: "Self and not-self; what was the relationship? He had separated himself from the phenomena of his experience. He could say to himself, 'I see the yard—John Hislop sees the yard and the lawn mower.' But—who was John Hislop? What was 'seeing'? Was the chipped greenness of the mower a quality inherent in the mower, or was it only . . .'' (p. 26). He is trying to understand both the self, that is the way he responds to people and things, and the not-self, the true nature of God. These two, of course, are not mutually exclusive. The search for a satisfactory God involves an understanding both of the external world and of the self.

We can only fully understand Brian's development if we realize that the answers to his questions are ultimately less important than his knowing what questions to ask. "It wouldn't be so bad, Brian thought, if a person knew, or even knew what it was he wanted to know" (p. 198). The consideration of fundamental questions in itself necessitates maturity and experience. Brian must learn what questions, asked in what form, are primary and essential, and which are irrelevant or inconsequential.

Repeatedly, as Mitchell presents them, the primary questions are posed by the prairie; the essential discoveries are almost always linked to the prairie. The link between boy and landscape is most obviously made, as the title suggests, by the omnipresent prairie wind. Brian is probing, sometimes consciously, often intuitively, the nature of human existence, and the "why" of birth and death; at the same time he is trying to understand more fully the nature of God. While these two quests cannot be simply distinguished, they can, for convenience's sake, be discussed separately. In each case Brian's inquiry is closely associated with the wind.

In a landscape without shelter the wind is peculiarly immediate and persistent—readily associated, as in *As For Me and My House*, with temporality and the mysteries of the cycle of life. The conscienceless "prairie wind . . . lift[s] over the edge of the prairie world to sing mortality to every living thing" (p. 31). Representing time, the wind itself is timeless and thus an apt symbol for God. Mitchell makes it explicit in his preface that he is drawing on a long-established symbol: "Many interpreters of the Bible believe the wind to be symbolic of Godhood." Brian's search for God is invariably accompanied by the wind's presence. Mitchell's epigraph, from the Christina Rossetti song, makes clear the appropriateness of the association.

> Who has seen the wind?
> Neither you nor I:
> But when the trees bow down their heads,
> The wind is passing by.

The wind, like God, is invisible and ubiquitous, intangible yet strongly felt. Brian can see neither the wind nor God, yet the power of each is everywhere manifest, most particularly in the small, delicate details of nature, such as the rustling of the tree's leaves.

Brian's early efforts to discover God's true nature are firmly rooted in his day-to-day experiences. God becomes a very human figure: "When God ate His porridge He had a dish as big as the prairie. He had to squirt milk onto it from a long hose; if it was hot He turned a cooling wind on it" (p. 21). Brian grasps at, but cannot possess, the notion of transcendence. For him God is only another man, albeit a giant. Typically God's size is expressed in terms of the immediate geography, his actions closely associated with the prairie wind. The four-year-old's comprehension of God is indicated by Brian's drawings: "He made a yellow God, yellow for the round part, and green legs, and purple eyes, and red arms, and that was God. He made another God and another and another until there were Gods all over the paper. He added arms and more arms, legs and more legs; those were spider Gods, of course" (p. 32). He senses God is superhuman, almost a monster, yet he does not hesitate to try to render God in visual terms. The figures crowding on the page suggest a power that is not restricted to one place at one time. This strange-looking God also derives from Brian's religious upbringing. Calling on the vindictive Old Testament God nurtured by strict Presbyterianism, he anticipates, almost with glee, the Deity's impending discipline of his grandmother.

Notwithstanding God's sitting down to his morning porridge, Brian's instincts about God are not entirely misdirected. Just as one can detect the wind in the bowing of the trees' heads, so can God be discovered in the details of the natural world. Mr. Hislop points Brian in this direction early in the novel, in reply to the boy's query about what God concerns himself with: "'Flowers —birds—people—things. He makes meadow larks sing. If an ant climbs a grass-blade—a—a grasshopper spits tobacco juice—that's God.'" (p. 23). Brian has already sensed God's tender view for himself. At the end of chapter one, after his first contact with the Young Ben, Brian fixes his eyes on the sky and muses. It is a moment for discovery of the beauty and congeniality of the prairie:

> After the boy's [the Young Ben's] figure had become just a speck in the distance, Brian looked up into the sky, now filled with a soft expanse of cloud, the higher edges luminous and startling against the blue. It stretched to the prairie's rim. As he stared, the gray underside carded out, and through the cloud's softness was revealed a blue well shot with sunlight. Almost as soon as it had cleared, a whisking of cloud stole over it.
>
> For one moment no wind stirred. A butterfly went pelting past. God, Brian decided, must like the boy's prairie (p. 12).

Although Brian himself may not realize it, this experience is very much a revelation of God. The flash of sunlight, the palpable stillness, the glimpse of a butterfly, such are the fleeting moments, as Brian becomes increasingly aware, when man makes contact with his God.

This instant when the wind is stilled is significant. It is one of the properties of the wind which make it so effective as a symbol of God that it is capable of such variation, from hushed calm to violent fury. When Brian knocks at the church door, innocently hoping to meet God person to person, the wind rustles his hair. The stilled wind or the breeze's caress suggests a benign God, but more often in the early part of the novel Brian finds a threatening God: "The wind cried long at the eave troughing outside, then was suddenly sibilant again at the screen. It was a frightening and lonely sound, fading into nothingness" (p. 20). Here are the themes of fear, loneliness and proximity of the meaningless void which are so familiar in prairie fiction. When Brian is caught lying at school, the vengeful Presbyterian God becomes even more imminent:

> He felt a gathering Presence in his room as the wind lifted high, and higher still, keening and keening again, to die away and be born once more while the sad hum of the weather stripping lingered on in the silence. Fearful—avenging—was the gathering wrath about to strike down Brian Sean MacMurray O'Connal, the terror-stricken Brian O'Connal, who had lied about his hands (pp. 94-95).

The terrifying God is very real, but he is not the only God; Brian's search is for a God that offers relief from fear, companionship in his loneliness, and meaning in the midst of nothingness.

Brian will not find God nor meaning, of course, merely by listening to the wind keening in his ears. He has to experience those elemental realities which Mitchell stresses in his prefatory note. In order to accommodate this theme *Who Has Seen the Wind* is divided into four parts, each separated by two years. The novel opens in 1929 when Brian is four years of age; in part two he is six and starting school; in the latter sections he is eight and, finally, eleven. During these years Brian experiences the ever shifting daily and seasonal cycles, the hope of spring, the dry hot summer, the fulfillment of harvest and the exhilarating cold of winter. He marks the growth and death of plants and, more importantly, he is touched by the ecstasy of birth and the vacancy of death. As he lives through this superbly varied cycle Brian grows in the awareness of the possibilities and limitations of his own life.

When Brian sees new lives being created he is naturally led to ponder the origin of things. Questions to his father about the origin of the baby pigeons are easily satisfied, but his questions four years later about the birth of young rabbits become much more probing. Thus at the age of eight Brian seems able to understand the mechanics of conception in mammals. His father's explanations, however, leave him only briefly satisfied and his grandmother must point out the problem: "'What ye tell is the how—all right. The why—that's another thing. That's for the Lord'" (p. 170). The basic truth of this observation remains with Brian. The rebirth of prairie in spring comes closer in explaining the "why": "Here and there meadow larks were suddenly upon straw stacks, telephone wires, fence posts, their song clear with ineffable exuberance that startled and deepened the prairie silence—each quick and impudent climax of notes leaving behind it a vaster, emptier prairie world" (p. 103).

The "why" is somehow embodied by the principle operative in the prairie spring. The principle is a burst of exuberant vitality, essentially inexpressible, which is more hint than answer, emphasizing the vast unknown which impinges on man and defines his existence. So, when confronted by the question of the Parsons' many children, Brian does not turn to the scientific explanation but affirms simply: "'God sends them'" (p. 204). His quiet conviction marks not a return to the literal God of the earlier part of the novel but the growing discovery of an abstract, ineffable, but no less real, power in the universe.

Brian's experiences of birth are balanced by contacts with death. His baby pigeon dies and is buried, according to Brian's wishes, on the open prairie. The killing of the gopher by the Young Ben is more complicated in its impact. Art's swinging the gopher to break its tail off brings Brian abruptly face to face with the heart of darkness. Suddenly he is made aware of man's spontaneous, inexplicable cruelty. After the Young Ben reacts to such cruelty by thrashing Art, Brian finds a new sympathy with him. When Brian re-encounters the rotting gopher carcass, his sorrow is not so much for death in itself, but, like Ralph in *The Lord of the Flies*, he mourns "for the end of innocence, and the darkness of man's heart."[6] Mingled with this sorrow is a new exultation that comes from his complete assurance in "the justness, the rightness, the completeness of what the Young Ben had done." But neither the death of the pigeon nor of the gopher touches Brian as personally as the death of his dog Jappy. Whereas he sensed the propriety of returning the pigeon to the prairie dust, Brian feels only loss and disbelief as he buries Jappy. There is no quiet thrill "of completion and of culmination." In a sense part of Brian's own personality has been eliminated, and in its absence is only "an emptiness that wasn't to be believed."

Each death in Brian's experience leaves him more aware of the inevitability of death. The emotional indulgence associated with the pigeon's death is replaced by a stoic acceptance. Maturity comes not so much from understanding death as from realizing its essentiality in the scheme of things. Knowledge of death may bring sadness but not despair. For Brian the realization that death is part of the human experience, part of the how and why of living, makes him more complete. The sadness he feels at his father's death is accompanied by his inability to cry: "'I can't Fat. I tried it but I can't. It's just like—nothing

---

[6]William Golding, *Lord of the Flies* (Harmondsworth: Penguin, 1960), p. 192.

was any different'" (p. 241). He returns to the prairie, as he had after each death: "He walked on with the tall prairie grass hissing against his legs, out into the prairie's stillness and loneliness that seemed to flow around him, to meet itself behind him, ringing him and separating him from the town" (p. 245).

Stillness and loneliness are what Brian now feels when he responds to death—there is a very meaningful empathy with his landscape. As the sole human figure on this spread of level land, Brian is absorbed in thought, acutely aware of his own apartness, his individuality and his humanity. This awareness of his own humanity is, in such circumstances, the unconscious acknowledgement of his own mortality. The prairie stillness is indicative both of the peace which comes with acceptance and the ultimate silence which confronts those who speculate on life's basics. His loneliness is first for the loss of his father, but it also marks an awareness that the individual is dependent only upon himself for the discovery of purpose and meaning.

W.H. New describes Brian's growth as the gradual abandoning of reliance on sense perception as he becomes "increasingly aware of conceptual and emotional abstractions which sensory perception cannot explain."[7] While New's description of Brian's development has a good deal of validity, it still seems true that whatever insight there is into "the ultimate meaning of the cycle of life" (and Mitchell has stated: "I didn't have an answer. It was just a question."[8]) originates in sensory perception of natural phenomena. A sense impression implies a concomitant emotional response. In Brian's case particularly, emotional and even intellectual response is so closely bound up with his sense impressions that it is misleading to suggest that sense perception is not essential to his approach. Mitchell's basically romantic outlook is that meaning is somehow to be detected in the prairie itself. Like Wordsworth he is not content simply with a carefully realized sense of place, but must look *through* the place to find its "spirit." Whatever measure of abstract knowledge Brian derives from this spirit, however, is almost wholly intuitive and clearly grounded in sense impressions.

As I have noted, the prairie is often seen as being in special accord with the contemplative temperament. From the moment early in the novel when the four-year-old boy first finds himself alone in the prairie, until the novel's lyrical conclusion, Brian repeatedly speculates at greatest length and with most result when he is alone on the vast prairie. It is not merely that the prairie is a suitable backdrop, but that in itself it is the object of the speculation. Prairie is both the question and the answer.

The significance of the prairie in Brian's development is reinforced by

[7]New, "A Feeling of Completion: Aspects of W.O. Mitchell," *Canadian Literature*, No. 17 (Summer 1963), 25.
[8]Patricia Barclay, "Regionalism and the Writer: A Talk with W.O. Mitchell," *Canadian Literature*, No. 14 (Autumn 1962), 55.

Mitchell's introduction of two characters who are virtual embodiments of the prairie ambiance. When Brian first encounters the Young Ben, he feels intuitively this connection between boy and land: "'This is your prairie,' Brian said" (p. 12). His first words to the Young Ben are more a recognition than a query. The Young Ben's inscrutability, like that of the prairie, is accentuated by his silence. He is invariably alone, yet not necessarily lonely, and he spurns society not by deliberate rebellion, but by utter indifference. The prairie, landscape least interrupted by visual or geographic restrictions, is in perfect accord with the Young Ben's longing for freedom. Brian repeatedly marvels that the Young Ben "'doesn't live in a house,'" empathizing with this free spirit wandering happily and at random over the prairie. In the absence of spoken communication, the bond which is forged and strengthened between the two boys is instinctive, prompted by Brian's sympathy for the Young Ben's freedom and confirmed by the Young Ben's natural and uncomplicated reverence for life and justice. This reverence is manifested particularly in the Young Ben's silent support when Brian is unjustly disciplined in school, and in his punishing Art for cruelty to the gopher. The combination of these characteristics: reticence, solitude, exemption from restrictions, and love of life in all its forms links the Young Ben to the simple, primary elements of his familiar landscape. In addition the Young Ben shows a maturity far beyond his years. As his father delights to relate: "'Thuh goddam kid was borned growed-up'" (p. 85). This violation of the dictates of time suggests the timeless in the Young Ben's nature. Like the prairie he has something eternal about him. In the conduct of his life and in his responses to life's vagaries the Young Ben illustrates something of the essentials, which, like the skeletal nature of his environment, are to be distinguished from the unnecessary adornments. In other words, the Young Ben's life is a plea for a simplicity which is neither idle nor shallow, but profound.

Saint Sammy, like the Young Ben, is an embodiment of the spirit of the prairie. He is similarly solitary, spurning a society which seems to give inevitable rise to immorality and materialism. His devotion to his Clydes and his awareness of the insects and plants of the prairie are not unlike the Young Ben's great respect for the life impulse. However, unlike the Young Ben, Sammy is never at a loss for words but always ready to rant and prophesy in ringing tones. Successive years of crop failure in this demanding environment had apparently driven Sammy Belterlaben mad. He had become a hermit, living in a piano box on Magnus Petersen's pasture with his Holstein and his Clydes. He lives with only his animals, his "tin box with its broken glass and pebbles and twigs and empty matchboxes and labels," and especially his God, for company.

Sammy is a fervent mystic, in frequent direct communication with God. The prairie is a very real extension of God's kingdom on earth—the location of the garden of Eden, as we learn from Sammy's version of Genesis:

"An' He got to thinkin', there ain't nobody fer to till this here soil, to one-way her, to drill her, ner to stook the crops, an' pitch the bundles, an' thrash her, when she's ripe fer thrashin', so He took Him some topsoil—made her into the shape of a man—breathed down into the nose with the breatha life.

"That was Adam. He was a man.

"He set him down ontuh a section to the east in the districka Eden—good land—lotsa water" (p. 197).

For Sammy man's noblest vocation—indeed the reason for man's creation—is farming the prairie. Brian's later dedication to the career of "dirt doctor" adds validity to Sammy's eccentric view. God himself speaks to Saint Sammy in the idiom of the prairie farmer: " 'Sammy, Sammy, ontuh your fifty-bushel crop have I sent hailstones the sizea baseballs. The year before did I send the cutworm which creepeth an' before that the rust which rusteth' " (p. 264). The effect of this prairie version of the creation and the Creator is to humanize God, not so much by making him a man, as by making him more accessible to humans. Saint Sammy's God, removed from the traditional conception of the established church, becomes more immediate without losing his fascinating inscrutability. Brian is impressed, despite his knowledge that Sammy is strange, if not completely mad. To the account of creation Brian responds with rapt attention. He feels somehow that he is closer to knowledge, but he resists: "A thing couldn't come closer through a crazy man gone crazy from the prairie." Yet if insight is not possible he is certainly inspired by Saint Sammy with a new, more fervent aspiration: "And yet for breathless moments he had been alive as he had never been before, passionate for the thing that slipped through the grasp of his understanding and eluded him. If only he could throw his cap over it; if it were something that a person could trap" (p. 199). Enthusiasm, faith, simplicity, love of the fundamentals of life and landscape—these are the characteristics of Sammy's weird existence which, in their variations, become important to the maturing Brian.

Since, as W.H. New observes, the Young Ben and Saint Sammy are at one with the prairie, it is impossible, when considering Brian's growth, to distinguish rigorously between the formative influence of his companions and the direct influence of the physical environment. That Sammy and the Young Ben seem to have all their needs satisfied by the prairie undoubtedly confirms Brian's instinct that nature, especially on the prairie, is a key to his search for meaning. Attention to minute detail usually suggests great reverence for nature. Brian's fascinated study of the raindrops is an example:

They lay limpid, cradled in the curve of the leaves, each with a dark lip of shadow under its curving side and a star's cold light in its pure heart. As he bent more closely over one, he saw the veins of the leaf magnified under the perfect crystal curve of the drop. The barest breath of wind stirred at his face, and its caress was part of the strange enchantment too.

Within him something was opening, releasing shyly as the petals of a flower open, with such gradualness that he was hardly aware of it. But it was happening: an alchemy imperceptible as the morning wind, a growing elation of such fleeting delicacy and poignancy that he dared not turn his mind to it for fear that he might spoil it (p. 107).

This phenomenon brings Brian closer to true holiness than anything he can find in church. Both magnifying the vessels of life blood and reflecting the universe round about, the raindrop is a perfect microcosm of the natural world. But Brian is reluctant to examine the experience intellectually, and when he yearns for a return of this elation, his passion is less for knowledge than simply for emotion. Wordsworth's comment in "Tintern Abbey" on the limitations of adolescence illuminates Brian's response; looking back on the emotional indulgences of his youth the poet remembers himself as

> more like a man
> Flying from something that he dreads than one
> Who sought the things he loved. For nature then
> . . . .
> To me was all in all.

When emotion is recollected in tranquillity, however, youthful raptures are replaced by quiet speculation. Whereas Brian had at first avoided diluting the pure emotion with thought, he now begins to consider the origin of his feeling, the complexity of which is suggested by oxymoron: "He was suddenly sad, his throat aching, his heart filled with unbearably sweet and maddening melancholy" (p. 175). The origin of the feeling is closely associated with the pure life impulse as found, for example, in the bee's industry at the heart of the Canterbury bell. Brian is sure that babies are sent by God; his desolation when Art ridicules this notion demonstrates how closely his feeling of fulfillment is connected to questions of origins and faith in his own God. The extent to which Brian's notion of God has matured is best indicated by his attempt to understand the discussion of Berkeley between Milt Palmer and Digby. Digby answers Palmer's puzzlement over " 'who "me" is' " with Berkeley's assertion that man is an idea of God. Brian's willing struggle to understand this concept at age eleven marks the degree to which he has moved intellectually beyond the porridge-eating God of the early part of the novel.

The questioning itself, then, is more important than the answer. Brian himself must sense the necessity of questioning—he certainly seems less frustrated at the novel's conclusion, even while thinking that "some day . . . when he was older than he was now, he would know; he would find out completely and for good." Coexisting with his recognition that "it was awful to be human" is Brian's depth of feeling for the unique beauty of the individual human life. Gazing over the "platter-flat" prairie he discovers the singularity of vertical man: "He looked up at rime-white wires, following them from pole to pole to the prairie's rim. From each person stretched back a long line—hundreds and hundreds of years—each person stuck up" (pp. 298-99).

The summation of the novel, with Brian caught up in the rhythms of the prairie, indicates less despair at the inscrutability of things, a greater readiness simply to accept inscrutability. Such answer as might be lies simply in something permanent. It is transience which is mystifying, and permanence is reassuring for its own sake. The prairie provides this reassuring permanence:

> People were forever born; people forever died, and never were again. Fathers died and sons were born; the prairie was forever, with its wind whispering through the long, dead grasses, through the long and endless silence. Winter came and spring and fall, then summer and winter again; the sun rose and set again, and everything that was once—was again—forever and forever. But for man, the prairie whispered— never—never (p. 247).

Here is the message of the wind, itself ever moving yet unchanging. The land is permanent, changing in feature, yet in essentials unaltered. Change is like the land because it is permanent and predictable. Just as death is permanent, so is renewal and rebirth. The exquisite sensitivity of the novel's conclusion repeats this idea less directly.

The prairie eternity is evoked by the shift to present tense narration on the novel's last page: "The day grays, its light withdrawing from the winter sky till just the prairie's edge is luminous" (p. 300). The sudden use of the present tense telescopes the changes so that all seem to be happening simultaneously at the moment of reading. Changes are seen in ever-widening spheres—from variations in wind speed and nuances of light, to the diurnal cycle, the seasonal, the annual, and beyond to the cycle of passing ages:

> Light then dark, then light again. Day then night, then day again. A meadow lark sings and it is spring. And summer comes.
>
> A year is done.
>
> Another comes and it is done.

Death, marked by the "gravestones," the eternity of the prairie's "endless silence," and the promise of new growth in the rich soil are part of the same scene, each an essential of the experience of life. From "the skeleton requirements simply, of land and sky" the novel has moved to another unpeopled landscape. Yet in the prairie of the final scene there is a sense, unknown at the novel's opening, that this is the boy's landscape and that it has somehow brought him understanding. The tenantless prairie has drawn man outside himself to the wider world and the eternity in which man's life occupies such a brief span. Ironically the energetic life of an ant goes on in the hollow eyesocket of a dog's skeleton. Where there is death and emptiness, there too is new life. Finally Brian feels again the wind. Being silent and invisible yet always palpably there, it is a token both of continuing mystery and of reassurance. The whirlwind of time is sweeping all before it and yet is leaving the essentials unchanged: "The wind turns in silent frenzy upon itself, whirling into a smoking funnel, breathing up topsoil and tumbleweed skeletons to carry them on its spinning way over the prairie, out and out to the far line of the sky."

The eternal prairie is less central, but still significant, in Mitchell's second novel, *The Kite* (1962). Like the Young Ben and Saint Sammy, Daddy Sherry is an embodiment of the prairies. A man one hundred and eleven years old is an appropriate personification of the eternal landscape. The symbolic kite of the novel's title is an extension of vertical man in the horizontal prairie. In its ever-upward yearning, its thriving on the wind, and its defiance of the prairie's horizontal pressures the kite is suggestive of man's desire to assert himself in the strongest possible way.

The novel, like *Who Has Seen the Wind*, is concerned with primary realities. Again a young boy, Keith Maclean, probes the meaning of human existence: " 'Why does stuff have to die?' "[9] But in this novel his query is shared by an adult, the thirty-nine-year-old journalist, David Lang, who has come to Shelby, Alberta, to write a story about Daddy Sherry. What knowledge these two gain comes from contact with Daddy, who is thus, despite Mitchell's problems with the novel's focus, the central figure in the novel.

Daddy has "dandelion-down hair," moods that shift like the prairie shadows when " 'the clouds slip over the sun,' " and a nostalgic passion for the " 'bonny perfume' " of wolf willow. Although he is not farming, his life is governed closely by the cycle of the seasons, as Mr. Spicer, the barber, explains: " 'Wintertime he holes up at home—hibernates like a grizzly. But as soon as the sky is blue and the run-off starts—down town every Saturday morning. Law nature' " (p. 25). Such descriptions and characteristics, like his love for Paradise Valley and his refusal to let it be ravaged by technological progress, reinforce the identification of Daddy Sherry with landscape and the natural world.

Even at one hundred and eleven Daddy is filled with an unquenchable enthusiasm for life, which no doubt accounts in part for his having reached such an age. When David remarks on the stillness of the prairie, Daddy is quick to contradict him: " 'Nope. Prairies an' foothills is never still. . . . Always a meadah lark—gophers squeakin' . . .' " (p. 194). This sensitivity to the vibrant sounds of vitality on the prairie indicates where Daddy Sherry's sympathies lie. The doctor observes that he thrives on excitement and Reverend Finlay confirms that " 'the life force sparkles . . . through him' " (p. 80). Helen Maclean describes Daddy Sherry's vitality as being dependent on surprise and unpre-

---

[9]Mitchell, *The Kite* (Toronto: Macmillan, 1962), p. 142.

dictability: "'Daddy comes to everything as though it were fresh and new
—like a poet'" (p. 136). Each of these explanations senses a pure life
force incarnate in Daddy which can be likened to the meadow lark's enthusiastic
assertion of his presence in the midst of silence. This characteristic vitality
is confirmed by David's realization that Daddy Sherry was no historian. This
man was living history, unconcerned with the recall of stale facts. His history
was most bound up with the sense impressions of the land:

> He knew now that he had expected more than he should have from the
> old man, who had been too immersed in living to build historical
> significance out of his days. And when he went over his notes, he realized
> that he had a wealth of sensuous detail; rough as they were, the prairie
> perfumed them; the foothills sun had warmed them; ever so faintly one
> could catch the gay and martial impudence of fife and drum; this was
> the sort of material to stain his narrative with immediacy (p. 124).

Daddy has his own formula for longevity: "'Jist keep outa drafts—keep
reg'lar—lots buttermilk,' Daddy said. 'Don't give a whoop—be a dangerous
acerobat—sail over the tops the circus crowds. Don't give a damn whether
she rains or thaws or freezes—whether you live or die'" (p. 191). He is quite
indifferent to clock time and lives for the excitement inherent in each passing
moment. This refusal to be bullied by time is most obvious in his smashing
the grandfather clock which is presented to him as a birthday gift. Here is
the essence of immortality—the involvement in the excitement and life which
is part of each moment, the refusal to give over life to a preparation for death.
Unlike *Who Has Seen the Wind*, where the answer to the mystery of mortality
could only be vaguely felt or intuited, *The Kite*, or at least Daddy's observations,
serves to make mortality less of a mystery. Death, Daddy comments, is natural,
universal, and needs no practice to be accomplished successfully. Acceptance
of these truths enhances the quality of life, and makes the living of life fully,
in all its variations, more essential and meaningful.

When Helen and David grope after the significance of Daddy Sherry's life
and character they turn again to the prairie as a possible explanation:

> "It must be a lot easier to get along with grass and earth and sky than
> with other men. You know where you stand with them," said David,
> "most of the time."
> "Not exactly a Sunday School picnic," she said. "But there were the
> dependable rhythms of the seasons—the lunar cycle—planting and harvest.
> Earth and leaf and grass and water and sky—what sort of imprint do
> they leave on a man?" (p. 199).

Natural time, as manifested in the rhythms of the prairie, is more congenial
to Daddy than clock time. He lives in a non-human time which is eternal.

Death, like harvest, is a fruition, accepted in the full knowledge that it will be followed by new growth. There are no abrupt beginnings and endings here, but a gradual shifting in which the decline to death contains the seeds of new growth. Rigid timetables are extraneous and best rejected.

The novel's ideas about mortality are summed up in the symbol of the kite which frames the work. Daddy receives the kite, his birthday gift from Keith, with great delight. Mitchell himself explained the symbolism involved: "The idea of a kite, a lively thing held by a thin thread of life, is comparable to man and his mortality, and the novel is a study in mortality, and awareness of the shortness of man's days upon the earth."[10] Consequently the wind, as in Mitchell's first novel, is an important factor. Early in the novel the sky, "celestial neighbourhood too rare and lonely, proper province only for the eagle and the hawk," is associated with the "emptiness" of the prairie. The kite tumbling in the sky is like man in the empty world. Man is buffeted by the winds of time, yet it is on those same winds that he is borne, "yearning ever upwards." David receives the simple message of Daddy Sherry's life: "He had lived always with the awareness of his own mortality" (p. 209).

Such awareness does not imply a steady consciousness of death, nor a race with it, but an acceptance of mortality as a natural part of the condition of life. "It was for such a short time that the string was held by anyone. For most of his hundred and eleven years Daddy had known that, and knowing it, with his own mortality for a touchstone, he had refused to settle for less. Quite simple after all. Time and death and Daddy Sherry insisted: never settle for anything less" (p. 210). So Daddy explored what facets of life he could, yearning after more life, not in fear of death, but in order to make of his life all he could, to live it with zest simply because it was there to live. He does not merely hang on in fear or despair but like the exuberant meadow lark, asserting his presence in the prairie silence, he greets life and lives it for the joy of living.

The same exuberant presence is found in *Jake and the Kid*, a collection of stories both less profound and more consistently humorous than Mitchell's novels. Again Mitchell relies for his effect upon skillful re-creation of the adolescent point of view, but, in contrast to the novels, he uses the Kid as first person narrator. This absence of the balancing objectivity of third-person narration accounts for the stories' less serious tone.

The descriptions are affectionate and impressionistic, based on naïve sensation and intuitive perception; the prairie in winter is "all lard-white . . . stretching wide to where the sky started, soft grey the way it is in winter. You could hardly tell where the prairie quit: I never heard her so still—clean, cold, still."[11] The Kid's account of Mac's coulee is impressive in its selection of significant detail:

[10]Barclay, *Canadian Literature*, No. 14, 55.
[11]Mitchell, *Jake and the Kid* (Toronto: Macmillan, 1961), p. 33. Most of the stories originally appeared in *Maclean's Magazine*, 1942-1955.

Still, still as water, with the sun coming kind of streaky through the wolf willow along her edges—what you might call stiff sunlight the way she's full of dust dancing all along her. And when you lie on your belly at the bottom of Mac's coulee, you're in a world; she's your own world and there's nobody else's there, and you can do what you want with her. You can look close at the heads on the wild oats all real feathery; you can look at the crocuses and they're purple, not out-and-out purple, but not blue either. If you look real close they got real, small hairs like on a person's face close to a mirror (p. 65).

Like Keith or Brian, the Kid, alone in the vast world, is engrossed, lost in thought about the significance of it all. Furthermore, the prairie provides ready metaphor for other descriptions: "He [the horse, Fever] ran like the wind over the edge of the prairie coming to tell everybody they can't live forever—slick as the wind through a field of wheat, slicker than peeled saskatoons" (p. 142). Such passages indicate the immediacy of the prairie in the young boy's experience. The importance of landscape is not made so explicit as it is in the novels, but the obvious affection for it has the same roots. "Prairie," expressed baldly without modifying article, is not only a specific landscape in a particular area but an enveloping ethos, a spirit as well as a geographical fact. The inarticulate attempts to express the feeling of the prairie through sky and earth, the smell of wolf willow, the throat of a tiger lily, run throughout these stories. The feeling has something to do with simple natural beauty, with the basics of life embodied in the prairie rhythms and with the sense of man's insignificance and responsibility in the midst of vastness. "'You do a lot of wonderin' on prairie,'" says Jake (p. 26).

Man's search for the meaning of his existence, occasionally despairing, often whimsical, always important, is central in Mitchell's imagination.[12] The nature of this search, largely inarticulate, assisted by nature rather than by books, and concentrating on only the most elemental aspects of life, makes the prairie an appropriate setting. Indeed, the relation between mind and landscape may seem to the novelist's imagination even closer than this. Perhaps the starkly elemental make-up of prairie landscape: "earth, sky, water, fire/in the sky

---

[12]If a short excerpt is reliable, then Mitchell's next novel will be as alert to the impact and fictional possibilities of the prairie as anything he has written, perhaps moving towards the frightening, disorienting prairie of the sort examined in chapter VIII.

When his [Carlyle's] drawing was finished it was shocking; his eye travelled straight and unerring down the great harp of prairie telephone wires strung along tiny glass nipples of insulators on the cross bars, down the barbed wire fence lines on the other side of the highway. And as the posts and poles marched to the horizon, they shrank and crowded up to each other, closer and closer together till they all were finally sucked down into the vanishing point.

W.O. Mitchell, "Old Kacky and the Vanishing Point," *Canadian Forum,* LI (October 1971), 26.

at night, that's all,"[13] not only conforms to the spirit of man's questioning, but causes the questions to be asked. In Mitchell's fiction the prairie's influence seems that strong. Mitchell's prairie is both question and answer. It is the eternal prairie described in John Newlove's poem, "East From the Mountains."

On a single wind, followed
by lonely silence, the snow
goes by. Outside
everything is gone; the white
sheer land answers no questions
but only exists.[14]

---

[13]George Bowering, "the plain," *Rocky Mountain Foot* (Toronto: McClelland and Stewart, 1968), p. 34.

[14]John Newlove, "East From the Mountains," *Moving in Alone* (Toronto: Contact Press, 1965), p. 50.

VIII   The Bewildering Prairie: Recent Fiction

> Je ne concevais pas, entre moi et ce rappel de l'énigme
> entière, ni collines, ni accident, passager contre lequel eût pu
> buter mon regard.
>
> GABRIELLE ROY, *La Route d'Altamont*

The right verbalization of the prairie experience—simple yet emotionally resonant, at once unique and characteristic—is most often found in Stegner's *Wolf
Willow*. Stegner's childhood memory of repairing the family Model T on the flats
of southern Saskatchewan is typical, and suggestive enough to summarize the
attitude to the prairie in Canadian fiction of the last twenty years:

> We sat baldly on the plain, something the earth refused to swallow, right in
> the middle of everything and with the prairie as empty as nightmare clear to
> the crawl and shimmer where hot earth met hot sky. I saw the sun flash off
> brass, heliograph winking off a message into space, calling attention to us,
> saying "Look, look!"
>   Because that was the essential feeling I had about that country—the sense
> of being foreign and noticeable, of sticking out.[1]

Man on the prairie, as Stegner observes elsewhere in *Wolf Willow*, is an intrusion
"as abrupt as the elevators that leap out of the plain to announce every little
hamlet." He may feel "foreign," cowering before the forces of a threatening
environment, or "noticeable," clearly dominating a vast landscape. In any case he
will almost certainly wish to meet the challenge of this land, to say "Look, look!"
in whatever way he can, by raising a crop or a monument, by interpreting his
experience in paint or in words.

Reading through prairie fiction since Ross and Mitchell reveals no diminishing
in the imperative of setting. The prairie continues to issue its challenge, and the
comtemporary novelist responds with an enthusiastic exploration of its metaphorical possibilities. Perhaps surprisingly, in an era when technology increasingly
tends to insulate man from his physical environment, the function of prairie
landscape is almost as great in the urban novel as in the rural.

In the rural novel realistic representation of setting is completely dominant.
Melodrama, sentimentalism and improbability can still be found in character and
plot, but now against a backdrop which is often detailed in its reference to local

---

[1]Stegner, *Wolf Willow*, p. 269.

vegetation and contour, and which emphasizes, often to the exclusion of reference to the prairie's beauty, the harshness of the land. This predominant bleakness is due, in great part, to the memory of the Depression. Economic conditions, compounded on the prairies by drought, made a profound impact (as political events in themselves show) on the people of the Canadian West. To understand the horror of those years, it seems that the prairie psyche had to re-create and relive that period in art. We have already seen that Ross and Mitchell focus on the prairie of the Depression years. The writers who follow them depict a still bleaker, still more frightening landscape. The setting of recent prairie novels is usually a variation, to return to Stegner's phrasing, of "prairie as empty as nightmare." Confronted with the enormity of emptiness, the introspective thinker of Mitchell's novels becomes the tortured neurotic. The mental and emotional sterility which Ross depicts becomes still more acute in the pages of George Ryga, Patricia Blondal or Robert Hunter.

In both rural and urban fiction the prevalent landscape is empty and nightmarish, peopled by bewildered, frightened men. Recent fiction radically interprets the vertical-horizontal image. Man finds himself "sticking out." In its stark simplicity—solitary vertical man against the uninterrupted, empty horizontal—this image is an ideal expression of the situation of existential man. Edward McCourt initiates this fundamental interpretation of the image by a tentative exploration of the prairie as metaphor for the meaningless, an idea which is, of course, implicit in many earlier works. The tendency toward the existential prairie is evident in the evocation of the wasteland in the work of Christine van der Mark, Blondal and Ryga.

The idyllic prairie of Gilbert Parker's romances has not, however, entirely lost its hold. As recently as 1962, in W.A.S. Tegart's *In the Face of the Winds*, the author asserts that "the immensity of distances, the clear snappy air, the wide open freedom, and that indefinable mysticism that murmurs through the ever-moving prairie grass, is far more intoxicating than any other type of terrain can claim."[2] Just as enthusiastic is the description of the countryside, "a haze of shimmering air, an enamelling of wild-flowers,"[3] in Vera Lysenko's novels. In *Yellow Boots*, and particularly in *Westerly Wild*, the "impression of suffused gold"[4] made by the prairie landscape harmonizes with the glib, excessive emotions which are Lysenko's staple in fiction. But happily such crudely exaggerated depiction of landscape, once the exclusive note in prairie fiction, is now a distinctly minor key. More typical is the prairie setting of McCourt's novels. Certainly, considering the references to climate and contour in *The Canadian West in Fiction*, his emphasis on physical setting is not surprising.

Music at the Close (1947) recounts the education and maturing of Niel Fraser in the period between the world wars. The prairie where Niel grows up has

[2]W.A.S Tegart, *In the Face of the Winds* (Saskatoon: Modern Press, 1962), p. 84.
[3]Vera Lysenko, *Yellow Boots* (Toronto: Ryerson, 1954), p. 28.
[4]Lysenko, *Westerly Wild* (Toronto: Ryerson, 1956), p. 108.

much of the wasteland about it: "shallow stagnant sloughs... covered with a thick green scum," oppressive heat, dust in "fine grey particles that stung the skin," and a general monotony.[5] A "bleak, treeless" cemetery, Niel later decides, harmonizes well with the landscape. This environment is not likely to be conducive to the fulfillment of Niel's dreams of being a great novelist and poet married to a dark, remotely beautiful woman. His artistic dream is dashed by a vicious, but apparently perceptive, English professor. His dream of marriage is doomed when his ideal of womanhood, Moira Glenn, marries Gil Reardon. When he later marries the widowed Moira, his dream cannot accommodate the prosaic elements of day-to-day wedded life.

The prairie's fascination for Niel is the essentially negative fascination "of an harmonious combination of elements undiminished by detail, awe-inspiring in its colossal monotony." He appreciates the beauty of the bond to the land which shaped his Uncle Matt's life: "It was no small thing to be on intimate terms with the earth itself, no ignoble life that was dedicated, however blindly, to the nourishing of life" (p. 132). Yet Niel himself seems incapable of being on such "intimate terms with the earth." Greed and drought combine to defeat his own grandiose agricultural schemes. In the landscape Niel is the vertical intrusion: "There were no other sounds to destroy the illusion that he was a solitary human being in the midst of a vast plain" (p. 165). This illusion may have its attractions but it leaves Niel unaffected. The landscape, its emptiness and his utter aloneness in it, is, of course, symbolic of Niel's life: "Life so far had been a series of seemingly unrelated episodes and nothing more." The "dreary fields" and "unchanging landscape" aptly reflect his bewilderment at a life devoid of meaning and pattern. Only in his death on a Second World War battlefield does Niel find meaning. The sacrifice for freedom, however slight his contribution may be, ennobles him. McCourt develops the ambiguity, mingling peace and music with absolute silence and darkness; for, ironically, Niel finds meaning and a dream fulfilled in the ultimate meaninglessness of war.

McCourt is utilizing a dimension of the prairie metaphor which is first elaborated by Sinclair Ross. The prairie effectively suggests man's quandary in a totally meaningless universe. McCourt's theme in *Home is the Stranger* (1950), the familiar account of the immigrant's accommodation to a new environment, dictates an emphasis on the prairie as battlefield, a return, that is, to an earlier image of the prairie particularly obvious in Grove's works.

In a silent, lonely world devoid of living things, Norah Armstrong becomes " 'increasingly filled with the terror of infinite space.' "[6] She tries to escape the terror by withdrawing into the limited circle of home and family. But domestic bliss is illusory. Because of the conditions of prairie agriculture, the farmers' "essential selves tended to disappear behind an elaborate defence mechanism

[5]McCourt, *Music at the Close* (Toronto: McClelland and Stewart, 1966), pp. 15-16.
[6]McCourt, *Home is the Stranger* (Toronto: Macmillan, 1950), p. 51.

created to meet a sustained crisis.'' With Jim having to devote so much of himself to the struggle with the land, Norah finds herself as lonely within her home and family as she is in the immense landscape. Her eventual reaction to this condition, recalling Ann's response in Ross's ''The Painted Door,'' is a fleeting but intense moment of passion with her neighbour, Brian Malory. Brian serves as a ready vehicle for Norah's rebellion against the monotonous round of life on the prairie, yet, predictably, her illicit attachment has no lasting significance.

The death from pneumonia of her son Phillip reinforces Norah's opinion of the harsh prairie: ''The earth was cruel, the earth was hungry. The earth had claimed him'' (p. 248). When she turns the blame on herself and attempts suicide the land is again evoked as a destructive force: ''She had been defeated by the forces which defeat nearly all men, forces inherent in the earth itself, and which had nothing to do with good or evil as manifested in the petty actions of mankind.'' If some ''malignant power'' was particularly nurtured in this severe climate and empty landscape it was also, as McCourt makes clear here, a universal force affecting human destiny.

But McCourt has not entirely forgotten the prairie's dreary monotony:

> Within the range of vision of an observer standing in the centre of the great circle of plain, the congregation of life intensified at a dozen points, each point marked by the upthrust from the plain of from two to six or more tall bleak towers standing red-walled and black-roofed in a precise row like the guardsmen of some historic busbied regiment on parade. Within the shadow of each row of elevators lay a village, and the villagers, like the elevators, were distinguished only in their conformity to a rigidly conceived design: a single street, at right angles to the highway, false fronts rising on either side; ... Into each village roads led from four points of the compass, roads that ran long miles as straight as the surveyor's chain could make them, thick pencilled lines across the surface of the plain dividing it with geometric precision into two-mile squares (pp. 17-18).

McCourt starts with the usual image of man in the landscape, a solitary figure upright in a vast, flat land. The configuration of the landscape, and by extension the conduct of everyday life, is inescapably patterned. There is order here, but it seems to have no point. Pattern without variation is as meaningless as chaos. These surroundings are, as Norah comments despairingly, so '' 'obvious.' '' An essential of life—imagination, mystery—is missing. There are no little people, no leprechauns, here, because such creatures of the imagination only have reality if one can also conceive a place for them to hide. Similarly, perhaps, the prairie seems almost a godless place, looking ''like a region from which the hand of God had been withdrawn before the act of creation was complete; the foundation was there, but nothing lifted above its flat uniformity except a few bleak ridges'' (p. 32).

This potential meaninglessness, impinging on Norah's consciousness, aggravates her despair before the cruel prairie. When Jim makes the decision to move to the west coast, however, Norah must reject his suggestion. Because she loved Jim, who "loved the vast grey sweep of prairie better than anywhere else on earth," she knows she must stay. She recognizes the necessity of coming to terms with the earth, here, in this forbidding land. So she resigns herself to a life amidst the cruelty, the monotony, and the powerful inhuman forces which are part of life as they are of the earth.

Again in *Walk Through the Valley* (1958) McCourt concentrates on the brutal prairie, though it is not as integral to the novel as the setting of *Home is the Stranger*. McCourt is diverted into the paths of juvenile melodrama dealing with whisky running in the early 1920s. Criminal melodrama and serious themes prove immiscible with the result that neither is successfully realized.

The prairie is dry, bleak, dusty and repeatedly described as "desert." With Michael's father dead at the end of the novel, the young boy's mood harmonizes with the surrounding plains: "The landscape below was desolate, dead. Green down the long slopes where the pines grew heavy and tall; but beyond, as far as the eye could see, only the drab grey fields, no alleviating touch of colour anywhere, running at last to merge with a drab grey sky at the very limit of human sight."[7] Earth and sky join in a universe of dull monotony, markedly contrasting with the nobility, mystery and vitality of the hills and the great lone stag which symbolizes their spirit. Michael's ultimate attitude to life is defined by these polarities. Like Norah Armstrong, he would face the fear, death, and evil that was "part of the fabric of life itself," but with defiance, with a reverence for the wild pride and freedom which was the spirit of the magnificent stag.

Of McCourt's novels *Music at the Close* most clearly points the way to the oppressive nothingness imaged by the prairie in his urban novels. The agony of living in the dreary, desert-like prairie of *Home is the Stranger* and *Walk Though the Valley* is still more acute in other recent novels. In *Honey in the Rock* (1966), for instance, Christine van der Mark uses an unusual metaphor to describe the prairie setting, a metaphor anticipated in the opening chapter of her first novel, *In Due Season* (1947). For Lina Ashley and her family the gaunt, scarred prairie is a world to be escaped as they pursue the dream of rain and rich pasture in the northern bush. In the later novel the dust-bowl prairie in 1936 is overwhelmingly bleak, a "desolate land, brown, dried out, hailed, soil-drifted."[8] For the community of German immigrants, transposing the story of Moses striking the rock to their own experience, that prairie is the rock. And they have faith that, in the words of the evangelical hymn, there is "Honey in the Rock." The metaphor is starkly effective. It goes farther even than the comparison of the prairie with desert to emphasize the barren,

---

[7]McCourt, *Walk Through the Valley* (Toronto: McClelland and Stewart, 1958), pp. 216-17.
[8]Christine van der Mark, *Honey in the Rock* (Toronto: McClelland and Stewart, 1966), p. 22.

utterly unproductive aspect of the prairie in periods of prolonged drought. Stripped by wind or battered by sleet the prairie is as unyielding as solid rock. Only toward the end of the novel, stimulated by spring rains unknown for many years past, is there "honey" in the landscape: "The buffalo beans. Blue vetch. Sweet clover. And new green wheat. A three-day rain had soaked the land, and there was great hope for the crop after its second seeding" (p. 219). But there had always been "honey" in the lives of the people. Even when their existence is the rockiest, they show humility, tenderness, determination, friendliness and faith. To Dan Root, the school teacher from whose point of view the story is largely told, the "rock" has come to have great appeal: "Those rough hills... That vast rim of prairie and sky... it gets you..." (p. 221).

Like Dan Root, Rudy Wiebe, a still more religious novelist than van der Mark, is moved by the "vast rim of prairie and sky":

> The grass crunched dry as crumbs and in every direction the earth so flat another two steps would place me at the horizon, looking into the abyss of the universe. There is too much here, the line of sky and grass rolls in upon you and silences you thin, too impossibly thin to remain in any part recognizably yourself.[9]

But Wiebe's reflection on life on the land might mislead about the place of the prairie landscape in his novels; none of the three novels could accurately be called a prairie novel. In *Peace Shall Destroy Many* (1962) the intensely Mennonite community is isolated in the northern bush nourished by a rich soil and feeling the prairie, if at all, as the hint of distant possibilities from which it is hemmed off. *First and Vital Candle* (1966) is a novel of northern Ontario; the brief opening section set in Winnipeg depicts a distinctive city, but not one, as described later in this chapter, particularly conscious of the surrounding landscape. *The Blue Mountains of China* (1970) has a global setting, but the prairie feeling of insignificance before the universe is more prominent here than in either of the earlier novels. In the novel's final bitterly lyrical passage Jakob Friesen, representative of the eternally homeless Mennonite, wanders the prairie as it merges mentally with west and north, a vague symbol of both peace and the elusive spirit which governs man's life.

Similarly bleak yet strangely comforting is the prairie of *The Stone Angel, A Jest of God* and *A Bird in the House*, fictions which derive much of their inspiration from Margaret Laurence's youth in Neepawa, Manitoba. *The Stone Angel* is the story of a ninety-year-old woman who is nearing death in a west coast city. Hagar Shipley, having been born, brought up, and married in Manawaka, still has strong memories of this fictional town in which all Margaret Laurence's prairie fiction is set. Manawaka is in many ways an untypical prairie

[9]Rudy Wiebe, "Passage by Land," *The Narrative Voice*, ed. John Metcalf (Toronto: McGraw-Hill Ryerson, 1972), pp. 258-59.

town. It is obviously on the edge of the prairie, as Neepawa is, where the land is often rolling and the trees are more plentiful. The Manawaka countryside in early fall, with its "oak leaves mottled with brown, the maple leaves dappled green and that queerly translucent yellow, the leaves of berry bushes colored cochineal, and goldenrod dusty with pollen shining like coinage,"[10] clearly has a gentler atmosphere than Ross's Horizon or even Stead's Plainville. Yet the theme which Mrs. Laurence detected in Sinclair Ross's short stories, "the inability of these people to touch another with assurance and gentleness," by epitomizing the narrow puritanism of Manawaka, fits her own fiction exactly.

Laurence's work suggests that this puritanism can, in some way, be traced to the influence of the prairie landscape. It is the sort of landscape which discourages romance and imagination, as Hagar makes clear in telling of her father's having left the Highlands:

> How bitterly I regretted that he'd left and had sired us here, the bald-headed prairie stretching out west of us with nothing to speak of except couchgrass or clans of chittering gophers or the gray-green poplar bluffs, and the town where no more than half a dozen decent brick houses stood, the rest being shacks and shanties, shaky frame and tarpaper, short-lived in the sweltering summers and the winters that froze the wells and the blood (p. 15).

The prairie, particularly in the Depression years, reflects this restricted society: "Rippled dust lay across the fields. The square frame houses squatted exposed, drabber than before, and some of the windows were boarded over like bandaged eyes. Barbed wire fences had tippled flimsily and not been set to rights. The Russian thistle flourished, emblem of want, and farmers cut it and fed it to their lean cattle" (p. 168).

The parallels, while not explicit, are obvious. The people, like their homes, are exposed, drab, blind to new ideas and possibilities. There is an overriding sense of decay and of want about this world. And in it Hagar, agonizingly and inexorably nearing the end of her life, is like the pieces of rusty machinery, an "aged body gradually expiring from exposure, ribs turned to the sun." She is both of the narrow-minded, puritan Manawaka and a rebel against all it represents. The awkward moment when Hagar lies undiscovered in the same room where her son John makes love to Arlene sums up this paradox. Hagar fumes at the shameless immorality of her children while she thrills that "such a spate of unapologetic life should flourish in this mean and crabbed world."

Having always wanted "simply to rejoice," trying desperately in her last moments "to recall something truly free" that she has done, Hagar so often manifests that "spate of unapologetic life" for which she feels such admiration.

---

[10]Laurence, *The Stone Angel* (Toronto: McClelland and Stewart, 1968), p. 122.

"Unchangeable, unregenerate" Hagar Shipley shows the same defiant vitality, the same eternal quality as those "wild and gaudy flowers" that cling to life against the worst that man and prairie can do.

In Laurence's prairie fictions landscape is most pronounced in *The Stone Angel*, but it has a palpable significance in all three. Mrs. Laurence herself acknowledges the influence of place in her fiction:

> When one thinks of the influence of a place on one's writing, two aspects come to mind. First, the physical presence of the place itself—its geography, its appearance. Second, the people. For me, the second aspect of environment is the most important, although in everything I have written which is set in Canada, whether or not it is actually set in Manitoba, somewhere some of my memories of the physical appearance of the prairies come in. I had, as a child and as an adolescent, ambiguous feelings about the prairies, and I still have them, although they no longer bother me. I wanted then to get out of the small town and go far away, and yet I felt the protectiveness of that atmosphere, too. I felt the loneliness and the isolation of the land itself, and yet I always considered southern Manitoba to be very beautiful, and I still do. I doubt if I will ever live there again, but those poplar bluffs and the blackness of that soil and the way in which the sky is open from one side of the horizon to the other—these are things I carry inside my skull for as long as I live, with the vividness of recall that only our first home can really have for us.[11]

Loneliness, isolation, beauty, the rich promise of the soil, the openness of a vast sky: these are the responses to the prairie which Margaret Laurence makes and which, in some often subtle way, affect her fiction.

In *A Jest of God*, Rachel Cameron, spinster school teacher in her early thirties, yearns for freedom from Manawaka and yearns to make meaningful, fulfilling contact with another person. A brief summer of passion with Nick Kazlik followed by the agonizing fear of an unwanted pregnancy scarcely satisfy this yearning. But perhaps these events will make fulfillment possible in the future. Rachel's fear of "one of those yellowing summers, with no rain, and the green seeping away from the grass and leaves,"[12] suggests that dryness and dust are not only physical but descriptive of the small town's social atmosphere. An atmosphere of death pervades the novel, a point which Paul Newman's film version, *Rachel, Rachel*, made with monotonous persistence. The incessant wind and dust are definitely in sympathy with this atmosphere, which extends even to Rachel's love-making with Nick, in a place he unfeelingly describes as being "'private as the grave.'" For Rachel to escape this atmosphere, the feeling

---

[11]Laurence, "Sources," *Mosaic,* III (Spring 1970), 82.
[12]Laurence, *A Jest of God* (Toronto: McClelland and Stewart, 1966), p. 60.

of being boxed in, is to become, "'More outspoken. More able to speak out. More allowed to—both by your family and yourself.'" She reaches out to touch her "clamped, rigid" mother, realizing that, with her sympathy and help being called upon, "I am the mother now." Suicide and death are rejected; God's inexplicable jests are accepted; and Rachel gives herself to the spirit of the prairie wind: "The wind will bear me, and I will drift and settle, and drift and settle. Anything may happen, where I'm going" (p. 201).

In summing up the importance of the physical environment in these two novels, McCourt concludes that Hagar Shipley's "fierce independence, her resourcefulness, her love of the wide earth and empty sky are obvious manifestations of a distinctive and unsophisticated environmental influence." In *A Jest of God*, on the other hand, McCourt notes that "the struggle of man against his physical environment is no longer of much significance."[13] These observations are correct, as far as they go, but they do neglect to mention that in some understated way, which Mrs. Laurence herself admits she does not completely understand, the prairie landscape has shaped the themes of loneliness, the desire for freedom, and the agonizing lack of human contact. The Vanessa MacLeod stories, collected under the title *A Bird in the House*, illustrate this influence of landscape more directly.

These short stories are closer to autobiography than anything else Margaret Laurence has written. While the stories are told by Vanessa, they are dominated by the memorable and often richly humorous portrait of Gandfather Connor. In young Vanessa's opinion if Grandfather Connor is a representative prairie pioneer she has little use for pioneers: "To me there was nothing at all remarkable in the fact that he had come out west by a sternwheeler and had walked the hundred-odd miles from Winnipeg to Manawaka. Unfortunately he had not met with any slit-eyed and treacherous Indians or any mad trappers, but only with ordinary farmers who had given him work shoeing their horses, for he was a blacksmith."[14]

One of the themes of this volume, which reads as much like a novel as a series of short stories, is Vanessa's establishment of contact with the adult world, her gradual acquisition of a respect for the pioneering spirit of her Grandfather. Through the writing of *The Stone Angel* and, presumably, of these stories Margaret Laurence came to realize "just how mixed were my own feelings towards that whole generation of pioneers—how difficult they were to live with, how authoritarian, how unbending, how afraid to show love, many of them, and how willing to show anger. And yet—they had inhabited a wilderness and made it fruitful. They were, in the end, great survivors, and for that I love and value them."[15] Hers is a realization, simply, of the tremendous odds that faced the pioneer, encountering an often cruel prairie climate, and a depress-

[13]McCourt, *Canadian West in Fiction*, p. 115.
[14]Laurence, *A Bird in the House* (Toronto: McClelland and Stewart, 1970), pp. 9-10.
[15]*Mosaic*, III (Spring 1970), 82.

ing landscape. It is a realization paralleled in Vanessa's later respect for Grandfather Connor's "energy that was partly physical and partly sheer determination" and her admiration for his handsome face with its "eyes a chilled blue like snow-shadows." The man's very facial expression reflects the country he had defied and built. In retrospect Vanessa is able to understand the importance of the free pioneering spirit to her own nature: "I had feared and fought the old man, yet he proclaimed himself in my veins."

Like Hagar Shipley, Vanessa realizes that in this environment there is so little for the imagination, for the spirit. Such an attitude is completely opposite to Stead's, whose prairie is the very repository of things spiritual. Now the sudden verticality in Vanessa's description of Manawaka serves as a reminder of an emotional vacuum: "At the furthest point of the town the C.P.R. station stood, respectably painted in the gloomy maroon colour known as Railway Red, paradoxically neat in the midst of the decrepit buildings around it. Above and beyond the station rose the peaked roofs of the grain elevators, solid and ugly but the closest thing there were to towers here" (p. 168).

Her desires are the same as those implied by her disappointment with the prosaic pioneering of Grandfather Connor. Vanessa yearns to see something rise above the flat emptiness, looks for some surprise and adventure, the turrets of a castle perhaps, in the grinding dullness of Manawaka life. The ultimate response is ambiguous. Manawaka, gloomy and decaying, nevertheless fostered in its pioneers, and passed on to its children, a determined respect for man and the dignity of human life. What Wallace Stegner feels for Whitemud, Margaret Laurence feels for Manawaka: "Let it be, at least for a good long while, a seedbed, as good a place to be a boy and as unsatisfying a place to be a man as one could well imagine."[16]

The prairie settings of McCourt, van der Mark and Laurence draw on the wasteland motif. The prairie has become in Eliot's terms

> A heap of broken images, where the sun beats,
> And the dead tree gives no shelter, the cricket no relief,
> And the dry stone no sound of water.

The absolute sterility and life-denying quality of the prairie wasteland anticipates, and blends with, the bewilderment and alienation prevalent in the post-Hitler, nuclear era. In attempting to depict the universal meaninglessness posited by existentialism, the Western Canadian writer found an obvious metaphor in the prairie landscape. The logic of the metaphor is confirmed by the setting of Beckett's *Waiting for Godot*, a stage bare except for a single tree, which buds more as taunt than as promise.

The bleaker prairie novels evoke a similar desperate blankness, as in the

---

[16]*Wolf Willow*, p. 306.
[17]Patricia Blondal, *A Candle to Light the Sun* (Toronto: McClelland and Stewart, 1960), p. 10.

tortuous pages of Patricia Blondal's *A Candle to Light the Sun* (1960). Blondal tells the story of the agonized lives within the monotony of the small prairie town. She depends heavily on the Depression landscape for her mood: "How thin we were upon the land. 1936. How untouching we were, with all the miles between us, the thin fine soil in the air between us. How thin the land made us, parching our lips, stretching fine the bones to unmuscled waiting. How it paid us out, whose fathers had made the land thin. Our sins stood thick upon the thinness of our worth, thick between us and the low red sun."[17] The exposed man comes face to face with the existential paradox—he is utterly alone and shrinking into insignificance; yet his sins stand out, reminder of his failings and his personal responsibility for his fate.

David Newman is agonized by this sense of insignificance and failure:

> Whatever man had built was lost against a horizon so vast no house or pathetic valley could hold the eyes. Eyes and heart, like the two live lines of steel that braced all together, must follow the sweep west, forever traveling over immensity, proportionately nothing.
>
> Roots? Who could be rooted in such vastness? Mouse Bluffs is a journey (p. 227).

When David's search ends with the death of Gavin Ross and the confirmation of Roselee's love, the essential nothingness remains, for he is but "freed... to loss," and even his mourning must be sheltered from the wind which threatens to "tear it to tatters against the great sky." This frighteningly immense dust-bowl landscape is a still more dominant factor in George Ryga's novels.

Snit, the narrator of *Hungry Hills* (1963), lives in the parched Alberta foothills. He is a bastard child, orphaned by his father's suicide and the fundamentalist community's decree that neither his aunt nor his mother is fit to care for him. When he runs away from the orphanage, Snit, finding the city to be "one huge cement ant-hill,"[18] soon decides that the dry country is a preferable environment. Stark grey, with a constant hot and dusty wind, the hills have a "desperate climate which parched both the soil and the heart of man." The land demands everything a man has, leaving no room for human relationships: "You tolerated your neighbours and your family, but you could never love them. For love was sacrifice, and you sacrificed all when you were born to the hills" (pp. 18-19). In a sense, then, the novel is about starvation—physical, certainly, but also emotional and intellectual. Snit looks for some sort of meaning in a world devoid of beauty, where men are without sympathy and end "broken on the earth like pieces of rotten wood by the cowardly greed of these hungry hills." Those things which might have been meaningful, which should have been a part of what "home" meant—"stones by the roadside, broken fences,

---

[18]George Ryga, *Hungry Hills* (Toronto: Longmans, 1963), p. 52.

cattle losing tufts of winter fur, a man limping with weariness, or a bunch of weed blown in a ball across a field''—are, like the "heap of broken images," withered, decaying and devoid of significance.

Though his search is usually unconscious and is abandoned for a time in the seamy world of bootlegged homebrew, Snit, merely by telling his story, is discovering the meaning of his life. Aunt Matilda recognizes the fundamental necessity of self-expression: "'We never learned to talk, Snit—never learned how to defend ourselves, or explain how it feels to be us.'" Snit's narrative fills the need, explaining "how it feels" with depressing accuracy.

When Snit tries to end his participation in the contraband whiskey business his partner, Johnny Swift, taunts him ceaselessly. In Snit's mind Johnny's torture is mingled with the heat and dust of the parched hills, an expression of the agony of life with one's fellow men and with the land: "And still behind me I heard Johnny. He began whistling. . . . It was a senseless, small sort of thing I could have ignored. . . . Yet now it was a part of the heat and dust of the road. A part of the sun-scorched hills and dead grass around me. Even a part of the thirst which hurt my throat so I couldn't swallow the pasty saliva in my mouth" (p. 154).

Man is a tortured creature, bound to a wasted earth and a burning sun. Even his affection for the earth, like Snit's perverse attraction to these hills, is quite unacknowledged: "This wasn't farming; this wasn't even living. It was penal servitude to the blasted hills and desert-making sun; yet men clung to the soil like flies to a cadaver and wouldn't let go" (p. 161). The earth is dead and man is a mean and desperate parasite on the body. Moisture, when it finally comes, is, ironically, in the form of hail, stripping the earth bare and prompting Snit's despairing question: "'What's this all mean?'" Snit's is the agony of existential man, convinced that his own actions are meaningless yet, paradoxically, aware that he is the product of the choices he makes.

Still, to the man of the land there is a glimmer of hope: "It was a depressing scene, and yet there was a feeling of exhilaration in the air, for the ground had been watered after many dry seasons, and the scent of moist earth was sweet." There is, however, little cause to believe that things are going to improve. The novel ends essentially unresolved with Snit's own recognition of the need for self-expression: "'We gotta cry a lot if we gonna live.'" Despair may be inevitable, but Snit senses the need for a cry of rage; man must lash out against his starvation and try to embrace his world no matter how bleak the prospect.

Ballad of a Stone-picker (1966), Ryga's second novel, has a setting and tone similar to *Hungry Hills*. It is again told in the first person, with a narrative technique recalling the dramatic monologue, in which the reader is occasionally made aware of the unspeaking magazine reporter to whom the story is told. With virtually nothing in the way of conventional plot *Ballad of a Stone-picker* can be described as a novel of self-therapy. The suicide of Jim, the narrator's brother, as the novel's title makes clear, is only incidental to the attempt of the stone-picker to define the character and limits of his own life.

As in *Hungry Hills* the narrator insists on the importance of the land to his story. As the novel opens, he indicates to the reporter that were it not raining, the land itself could tell the whole story better than he:

> On a clear day I would take you up Windy Hill.
> From there you could see five miles in every direction. You would see all there is to see in one day of our countryside. Tomorrow you would be gone and it would be enough.[19]

Beauty is rare in a grey and severe land where stones have to be picked by hand to make any form of agriculture possible. Walt, one of the stone-pickers who appears briefly in the novel, sums up the land: "'Kid—you don't live here. It's a damned graveyard, that's what it is. The place of the blasted and dead back in the pines! Will you look at the bloody country? Grey, an' thirsty with heat. Same's the farmers I've seen here.'" (pp. 92-93).

In this blighted and withered wasteland man is not only doomed to death but he is also dead in life, for imagination and love and courage, the essentials of vitality, are dead. Yet not even this desolation can break man's ancient bond to the earth and its produce: "People born generations to earth know about seed, water and sun without being told. They can suffer the kind of pain that sends a city-bred man to suicide, and they come out of it a little more bent and wrinkled, but still doing the things that give food and shelter to themselves and their children" (pp. 123-124). The simplicity of this commitment is appealing, but its essential emptiness and passivity make it inadequate.

To the narrator-balladeer the challenge is to express his own life, so much of which has been formed by his solitary intrusion in the wasteland and by his struggle to till the earth: "I've stood for hours out there in the field, the wind blowing all around me, drying the soil and sapping the water out of my flesh. I've felt it all, but could never tell others how it felt" (p. 124). In the end the stone-picker does tell, with the simple fluidity befitting the ballad, how his life felt.

His final insight is precipitated by his father's death and burial. The fields are "ashes," the "trees parched and wilted," the sun is a "red heat," and the house "listing and scaley." This is the wasteland where "nobody tore themselves from the world beyond mine to come to me." This is the wasteland where no one lives or loves. The love of Nancy Burla and the beauty of Elizabeth Junco's dance are both beyond it. Building his father's casket and digging his father's grave, the stone-picker discovers the existential reality, that his life consists of physical strife and the efforts of his own hands and body. His unremarkable experience is given universality by the quiet sincerity of his story.

---

[19]Ryga, *Ballad of a Stone-picker* (Toronto: Macmillan, 1966), pp. 5-6.

The stone-picker's life is stone-picking, real to him simply because it is his own, no matter how much it may have seemed to others, and even to himself, but "wasted shadows on a landscape that had never been painted." But even this description of his life is, in a sense, inadequate. In effect the contours of a vacuous existence have been painted by the stone-picker himself, not visually but verbally. Although in the completeness of his solitude the stone-picker senses that he is not so unlike his brother Jim, he turns toward life, to what he can do best, and picks up the shovel to fill in his own father's grave.

For Gabrielle Roy, as for Ryga, the curiosity to know oneself can in part be satisfied by knowing one's place. Particularly in *La Route d'Altamont* (1966) she recognizes man's distinctive position in the prairie: "D'où venait chez les enfants de par chez nous, en ce temps-là, le goût de se haut percher? (Notre pays était plat comme la main, sec et sans obstacles.) Était-ce pour voir loin dans la plaine unie?. . . Ou plus loin encore, dans une sorte d'avenir?"[20] The prairie child on stilts is emphasizing his verticality, insisting, as it were, on his own existence. His landscape of great spaces is also a landscape of time, suggesting man's ancient desire to know the future. Moving toward that future is travelling through life: "Car, dans cette immobilité de la plaine, on peut avoir l'impression d'être entraîné en une sorte de traversée d'un infini pays monotone toujours pareil à lui-méme." The image of prairie as sea is repeatedly invoked. Although Roy presents the details of the prairie with loving precision, the landscape is completely universalized.

Hers is a landscape of time and of the mind, a landscape through which all men travel because it is the landscape of life:

> Cette absence de secret, c'était sans doute ce qui me ravissait le plus dans la plaine, ce noble visage à découvert ou, si l'on veut, tout l'infini en lui reflété, lui-même plus secret que tout autre. Je ne concevais pas, entre moi et ce rappel de l'énigme entière, ni collines, ni accident passager contre lequel êut pu buter mon regard. Il me semblait qu'êut été contrarié diminué, l'appel imprecis mais puissant que mon être en recevait vers mille possibilités du destin (pp. 191-92).

Life's seemingly frank and open proposition is ultimately an enigma. The writer's task, the effort to know oneself, to pursue these "mille possibilités de destin," is a difficult, perhaps unending one. One of its key elements, Christine recognizes, is "cette vulnérabilité extrême." Visually, physically, one is dramatically aware of this vulnerability on the prairie. It proves essential to whatever measure of self-understanding Christine achieves, to her understanding of the utter isolation and ultimate personal responsibility of the artistic vocation.

With the growth of large cities on the prairies, the setting of fiction inevitably

---

[20]Gabrielle Roy, *La Route d'Altamont* (Montréal: Editions HMH, 1966), p. 62.

shifts from the rural to the urban. The modern city is large and cosmopolitan, in itself a total environment for the artist. For example, John Marlyn's Winnipeg, the setting for his novel *Under the Ribs of Death* (1957), is a restricted, inward-looking community. The reader is scarcely aware that this microcosm of the wide urban world is a prairie city. The background is totally cityscape from the "endless grey expanse of mouldering ruin"[21] in the North End, to the "palaces, great and stately, surrounded by their own private parks and gardens" which make up River Heights. Similarly, while the city in the first section of Jack Ludwig's *Above Ground* (1968) is presumably inspired by the author's native Winnipeg, it could be any cold northern city. The timeless space of the prairie, the "familiar earth slanty with windruffled wheat" where "grain elevators were land lighthouses,"[22] is a resonant image but quite unconnected to the location of Ludwig's city.

But *Under the Ribs of Death* and *Above Ground* are exceptions. Remarkably, most of the urban prairie novels continue to show intense consciousness of the distinctive prairie geography. The emphasis, of course, varies. In Wiseman's *The Sacrifice* or Kreisel's *The Betrayal* the prairie is a minor concern. In Peter's *Take Hands at Winter*, Hunter's *Erebus*, and others, it is a metaphor of substantial importance.

Canadian historian W.L. Morton, attributing his indifference to urban literature to his rural Manitoba upbringing, might be commenting unconsciously on the prairie writer's neglect of the urban setting: "A cityscape, after all, is man made and to that extent humanized. But how to humanize what was not human to begin with? . . . In all but accidents—which may be important and con-soling—any city is within like any other city. They know neither the revolution of the seasons nor the relevance of time and place, but live contained and self-impelled lives."[23] Apparently the prairie artist is compelled by the same sort of sentiment to recognize the massive presence of the prairie.

For the urban writer, the compulsion is only slightly diminished; his typical novel is remarkably sensitive to the natural surroundings out of which the city has grown. The image of man exposed remains basic. Vertical man is no longer primarily exposed to the physical violence of existence, but to the frightening knowledge of his own condition. He is isolated in an empty world. The landscape in which he must exist is vacant of meaning. Since the city is an extension of man, it shares the same situation. Like Roy Daniells's Winnipeg it is "lost in a level land of endless acres."[24] The city's towering marks of human achievement ultimately conceal the same total emptiness that the prairie itself conveys.

Adele Wiseman regards "the stubborn monotony of landscape and the no-

---

[21]John Marlyn, *Under the Ribs of Death* (Toronto: McClelland and Stewart, 1964), p. 17.
[22]Jack Ludwig, *Above Ground* (Boston: Little, Brown, 1968), p. 230.
[23]W.L. Morton, "Seeing an Unliterary Landscape," *Mosaic*, III (Spring 1970), 7.
[24]Roy Daniells, "Farewell to Winnipeg," *Mosaic*, III (Spring 1970), 216.

nonsense climate'' with mocking affection in an article occasioned by Manitoba's centennial: "Here you hang in the sky with only the soles of your feet glued to earth, flies on the ceiling of the universe. Breadth and depth of sky, uncompromising stretch of prairie, leading on like the endless dream, the dream of being a writer someday, of taking the maximum risk, of discovering whether, if you go far enough, sky and sod will meet and be reconciled.''[25]

Wiseman's sense of being exposed and insignificant, yet lured by the freedom of space, is only slightly reflected in her first novel, *The Sacrifice* (1956). The Winnipeg setting is used to give a sense of place, and occasionally to reinforce the themes of the novel. Abraham is a Ukrainian Jew who comes with his wife, Sarah, and sole surviving son, Isaac, to start a new life in a new land. Isaac sees the city as an intrusion in the prairie: "The city rose about him, planted on an undulating countryside that seemed to have spilled over from the ridge of dark hills in the western distance. The life that he remembered wavered uncertainly forward to meet the life that he seemed just about to live.''[26] In a sense the wavering past, the ancient heritage of the Jewish people and this family's terrifying experience in Europe, is identified with the undulating countryside. The city planted uncomfortably on the countryside seems to represent the experiences and experimentation of a new land and a modern time which inevitably clash with the centuries-old traditions: "To Isaac the land seemed like a great arrested movement, petrified in time, like his memories, and the city crawled about its surface in a counterpoint of life." Something of the conflict of generations, which is the main theme of the novel, is captured in this image. For Isaac and his wife Ruth, and, in turn, their son Moses, the traditions of religious and family life to which Abraham clings so tenaciously seem static relics of the past. Their attempt to temper past tradition with the vitality of a contemporary approach is the source of the novel's conflicts. At the end of the novel the gap between past and present is bridged as the boy Moses discovers the true humanity of his grandfather and the urgent need to understand and forgive. From the mountain which overlooks the city, ancient tradition and the vital processes of day-to-day living are seen to harmonize. Humanity and life, Moses senses, must be trusted even in death's darkest days.

A similarly limited use of the prairie occurs in Henry Kreisel's second novel, *The Betrayal* (1964). More definitely than Wiseman, Kreisel has shown an interest in the prairie metaphor in Canadian writing. In his paper, "The Prairie: A State of Mind,''[27] Kreisel recalls his own short story, "The Broken Globe,'' in which he explores the rift between an old farmer and his son on the primitive question of the earth's motion. The story is Kreisel's recognition of the centrality

---

[25]Adele Wiseman, "A Pithy Statement," *Mosaic*, III (Spring 1970), 102.
[26]Wiseman, *The Sacrifice* (Toronto: Macmillan, 1968), p. 12.
[27]Henry Kreisel, "The Prairie: A State of Mind," *Contexts of Canadian Criticism*, ed. E. Mandel (Chicago: University of Chicago Press, 1971), pp. 254-66.

of landscape in the prairie mind, a testament to the simplicity and unvarying faith of the farmer's belief, based as it is on long observation of the monumental vastness of the prairie:

> With a gesture of great dignity and power he lifted his arm and stood pointing into the distance, at the flat land and the low-hanging sky.
> "Look," he said, very slowly and very quietly, "she is flat, and she stands still."
> It was impossible not to feel a kind of admiration for the old man. There was something heroic about him.[28]

But the prairie metaphor, so central in "The Broken Globe," is only occasional in *The Betrayal*. Mark Lerner, history professor and the novel's narrator, suggests the significance of the northern prairie city as the meeting place for Stappler, the betrayed, and Held, the alleged traitor: "I thought of these two men meeting suddenly, in the desert, alone. For so, he [Stappler] had told me, he had always imagined it. And so in a way it had happened. For they met here, in this northern city, in the middle of a pitiless winter, with the indifferent moon gazing down from the cold, clear sky, thousands of miles from the place where the original tragedy had played itself out."[29]

The landscape is appropriate to a confrontation in which the central figures and essential issues stand in bold relief. The cold, indifferent and remote landscape reflects the lives these two men have lived since the betrayal, lives in which human relationships were undesirable if not impossible. Here both men, as Stappler observes about himself, are " 'utterly alone' " and forced to encounter themselves. But their self-examination has no satisfactory resolution. Joseph Held escapes guilt through suicide, while Stappler flees to weigh further his personal responsibility. Perhaps, ultimately, man is no traitor but only victim, victim of irrational circumstances in an absurd world.

In the novel's postscript Stappler returns briefly to Lerner. His view of Edmonton from the plane, isolated in the prairie night, sums up the novel: " 'Suddenly, you know, out of an immense darkness there comes a great circle of light. God how marvellous! But frightening, too. Because the darkness is so vast and the circle of light so small' " (p. 211). The prairie void, the vast unknown, surrounds man whose knowledge is a pitifully small light in the darkness. Only in the Arctic landscape, even more featureless and empty than the prairie, does Stappler find relief from this terrifying insignificance, for " 'there is no movement by which you can measure time. Time has been abolished, has been swallowed up in space.' " The triumph of space is what Stappler was seeking; in a timeless world there is no memory and no past. Here he

[28]Kreisel, "The Broken Globe," *The Best American Short Stories 1966* (Boston: Houghton Mifflin, 1966), p. 165.
[29]Kreisel, *The Betrayal* (Toronto: McClelland and Stewart, 1964), pp. 102-103.

can live, moment by moment, in service to his fellow man, yet freed from the awesome burden of self. And here he dies in an obliterating avalanche.

Whereas Wiseman and Kreisel incidentally explore the metaphorical potential of place, Edward McCourt invests place with such moral significance that it becomes a dominant structural factor in his novels. According to R.G. Baldwin,

> McCourt proves himself what might be called a regional psychologist, for his concern is to probe the influence of a particular region upon its people. The prairie environment in his novels is never merely descriptive—an ornament or a piece of painting. Rather, it is for him the single most important element in the shaping of the people within its confines, and he therefore employs its physical feature as data in exploring the minds and souls of his characters.[30]

This relationship between the physical prairie and human psychology is as prominent in McCourt's novels of the university world as it is in his rural novels. In *The Wooden Sword* (1956) Steven Venner is an English professor at a prairie university, not unlike the University of Saskatchewan, where McCourt himself taught. The novel tells the story of Steven's recovery from despondency and impotence as he gradually acquires the courage to face his past and his future. As a psychological study, the novel's account of Steven's recovery is both predictable and simplistic, with a resolution that comes perilously close to sentimentality. As a metaphor for the spiritual vacuity of twentieth-century urban life, the novel's setting, however, is worth comment.

McCourt takes a standard comparison of the prairie landscape with the desert and makes it the basis of much of Steven's psychology. Having served in Africa during the Second World War, Steven is plagued by a dream about the desert. The dominant feature of this dream landscape is a "great black cloud"[31] which the dreamer knows he must penetrate but from which he always turns and flees. Even in waking hours the desert intrudes on Steven's thoughts; for him the desert landscape is quite distinct from the prairie:

> The prairie was like the desert in its flatness, its immensity, its colour at a time like this, but there was no real, no significant resemblance....
> No one understood him when he said the prairie was without life....
>   The desert was old. Old beyond memory and the records of men. Across its shifting sands from the first day of light caravans had moved, armies had marched. There men fought great battles and founded great cities and raised mighty temples to their gods (pp. 14-15).

The desert is romance and mystery and a sense of history. It represents the

---

[30]R.G. Baldwin, "Pattern in the Novels of Edward McCourt," *Queen's Quarterly*, LXVIII (Winter 1962), 577.
[31]McCourt, *The Wooden Sword* (Toronto: McClelland and Stewart, 1956), p. 7.

possibility of the fullness of life, colourful and vigorous, while the prairie is "a land without memory. . . . That was why he didn't like it. Nor would this land, in time to come, hold memories worth concealment. Here drab men lived drab lives, lives that knew nothing of the great extremes—conquest and abnegation, lust and asceticism, hatred and love. Here men lived only for security. They risked nothing except their souls, and on their souls they set no value" (p. 17). Clearly Steven can be identified with the sort of life which he despises. He, too, is living a drab, spiritually exhausted life, unable to be inspiring in his teaching, unable to communicate with his acquaintances and, most agonizingly, impotent in his love for his wife Ruth. The romanticizing of the desert is a way to escape this empty life, but it is also, as Steven's nightmares indicate, a way of forgetting something horrifying about the years spent in the desert.

Steven fears the void, the unknown, or simply death. In the colourless fall landscape, in the freezing over of the river, and especially in that ominous black cloud of his dreams, the presence of death constantly confronts him. Strangely he recognizes quite clearly what he must do. Christ provides the example: "Christ knew a man had to stand alone. When He went into the wilderness He went alone. And at the end He learned what all men have to learn—a man must die alone" (p. 78). The problem, of course, is to find the courage to face one's isolation. The event that precipitates Steven's discovery of courage is worldly and commonplace. The challenge of Julian Fairchild, a young handsome new member of the English department, for Ruth's love brings Steven's resolve. He must not throw away his wooden sword (which, incidentally, resembles Christ's cross) but rather match his dream with the determined action which alone will give it validity. Steven plunges into the black cloud, acknowledging his past and what it contained. He recognizes that his own reckless heroism cannot negate the horror of war and death. His love affair with the mysterious Helen, previously blotted from his memory, comes to the fore as a realization that she is dead or gone, like her mythical namesake, a traitor both in love and war. Having discovered the emptiness at the core of his infatuation with Helen and the desert, Steven can return to his ordinary world with a new, vital awareness of its past and its possibilities. He is now determined to fight for his wife's love rather than wallow in despondency. Ruth's love and his teaching in a prairie university may not match the dimensions of his dream, but his determination to pursue that dream provides at least the possibility of realization.

In the urban novel, I have suggested, the prairie city occupies a similar position to that of man or his huddled sod hut in earlier novels. The city is as much an intrusion, and often as aware of the surrounding prairie, as were the first tentative farms. The image of the city as illogical, vertical intrusion is prominent in McCourt's second novel about the university, *The Fasting Friar* (1963). Walter Ackroyd, like Steven Venner, is an English professor, dispirited by his participation in the pettiness of university politics, the speciousness of university scholarship and the pretentiousness of university teachers. His loneliness is dramatized by the geography:

> The grey walls held all of life that had meaning and design. Beyond lay disorder, triviality, and a loneliness that was without logical origin. Except, perhaps, in the long reaches of Canadian plain that stretched without interruption from the border of the campus to a far-off horizon. Fear of open spaces—maybe that was what ailed him. This evening the fear, the loneliness were stronger, more oppressive than usual—he did not know why. He thought with regret of the great universities in the east which in times past had offered to open their doors to him. They did not stand in fortress-like isolation, beleaguered by sinister powers of which the prairie was the visible expression. They harmonised with their environment.[32]

The open spaces are frightening because they pose the possibility that what goes on within the fortress, either of the university or of Ackroyd's own life, is meaningless. Man, the university, the city itself, is terrified by the thought of a universe without design. Ackroyd's despair implies that human institutions will only harmonize with their environment through age or the incorporation of potential meaninglessness in their makeup. Ackroyd, as he himself admits, has consciously " 'cultivated indifferences' " in order to avoid contact with other people. He is an isolated man, agonized by a feeling of being at the edge of "nothingness." Ackroyd represents all men involved in a "pathetic search for joy in a world where no joy dwelt."

Marion Ettinger, the wife of a fellow faculty member, offers the only possibility of true joy. Ackroyd, however, is a long time realizing that the profound delights he can share with Marion are more important to them both than the niceties of social convention and the nastiness of narrow minds, before which they feel " 'so unprotected.' " The desire for freedom and joy is forgotten in a bitter (and ironic) fight to protect Paul Ettinger's academic freedom. When he returns alone to the ravine where he had found such comfort with Marion, the change from spring to summer seems to symbolize Ackroyd's own change of heart: "There was no life here, and no magic. Only a sense brooding and profound of the transience of all things lovely. . . . He was right to hate this great desolation where nothing lived but death" (p. 162).

The changed character of the one-time retreat indicates the tentative nature of the fortress, the impossibility of avoiding confrontation with desolation. But even having felt Marion's trusting love, Ackroyd remains in terror of the infinite plain: "The great empty sky now darkening into night, dotted with remote frozen stars, and the infinite reach of plain still visible below, depressed and

---

[32]McCourt, *The Fasting Friar* (Toronto: McClelland and Stewart, 1963), p. 11.

frightened him." Only a last-minute impulse makes him realize that he cannot leave the town without Marion. He abruptly and finally rejects the role of fasting friar for the "exaltation of the spirit and the wild almost unbearable ecstasy of physical love" which he can share with Marion. His decision is a breaking out from his walls and a thrust towards the complex joy which defines and makes life meaningful in the face of encroaching emptiness.

The growth of exultant extra-marital love amid bewildering prairie emptiness is also the theme of John Peter's second novel, *Take Hands at Winter* (1967). As the young Englishman, David Gilpin, discovers his way in love he also discovers a land and a country. As an artist, Gilpin senses the possibilities of the landscape: "The whole effect was so blank, so bare of living creatures, that it could have represented almost anything: peace, sterility, or cataleptic anguish."[33] But as a vulnerable man David is increasingly staggered by the prairie's immensity: "In all directions, nothing but space and sky. Because of the flatness the horizon was close, giving a curious double sensation of confinement and release. . . . After Surrey and Oxford it all seemed infinite, inconceivable, mile after mile of stupefying space" (p. 54). The key words of this description—nothing, space, flatness, infinite, inconceivable, stupefying—summarize the bewildering, meaningless world of Canadian prairie fiction during the past two decades. David repeatedly encounters the suggestion that life in such a world has created a nation of neurotics, perplexed alike by space and climate.

David's recognition of the utter emptiness of his relationship with the seductive Kirsten stimulates the hope of an escape from a world of stultifying convention and meaningless process. Having shared with Margaret Dacre the agony of losing a new-born child and the joy of acting together in the theatre, David acquires the strength to rescue her when her world begins to crumble. In the meaningless limbo of the prairie's "stupefying space" David and Margaret's newly-discovered love is an assertion of man's presence, a celebration of the human and vital. The fruition of a love based on deep mutual respect ends in a "perfect suspension in space," beyond time. The discovery of love is the discovery of a country, not so much of a political entity as of a region of the mind and soul. Margaret finally responds to David in a voice "gently Canadian," evincing a human element in an awesome, empty land, the quiet voice of love in the "enormous Canadian silence."

Neurosis is succeeded by insanity in Robert Hunter's first novel, *Erebus* (1968). Hunter sees the modern city as Erebus, a tormented, unreal underworld. His narrator works in a slaughterhouse, microcosm of a deperate universe: "At no point along the line is there any hope for the animals. The slaughterhouse is as escape-proof as life. Death is the only way out, or occasionally complete madness."[34] The world of *Erebus* is mad, "*all* the tensions are out, running

---

[33]John Peter, *Take Hands at Winter* (Garden City: Doubleday, 1967), p. 3.
[34]Robert Hunter, *Erebus* (Toronto: McClelland and Stewart, 1968), p. 48.

crazy: racial, social, ideological, political, religious, philosophical, even *sexual*.'' For such a world the prairie city provides a grotesquely appropriate image:

> Depression scrapes away the urban consciousness, letting the fear of nature emerge like escaping gas. You are reminded of the bleak and vast plains that ring the city. You are reminded of the smallness of the city in all this bulk of raw, murderous prairie. Like a great germ culture, the prairie eats out the heart of the continent, freezing at its northern extremes into tundra and lichen, rotting in the south into swamps; in the east it bangs up against the solid wall of forest; in the west it gnashes against the Rockies. In the middle, stranded like a corpuscle, is the city—a horrifying microscopic clot of humanity. With a single twitch, the prairie could snuff us out. The steel, the iron, the stone—it could be crushed to powder. It takes a moment like this, when the fear of the prairie touches me, for the city's vulnerability to register. I am filled with pity for these edifices. The pity, of course, is really self-pity (pp. 120-21).

From the bizarre and horrible scene emerges the basic image of man in the prairie, threatened with instant extermination or doomed to slowly rot and decay. Man's exposure has its most extreme consequences here, when fear is replaced by insane horror and defiance abdicates to passive self-pity.

In "a vast quiet world of horizons," the narrator comments, "we are lonely vertical objects." This singular figure, experiencing an abrupt existential awareness, finds that the only reality is the surrounding void: "Land has come to an end. Ahead is only a pale mist and a wide sky of stars. To go forward is to go into space, over the edge of the world" (p. 21). But, beyond the void is the semi-paradisical Island, which balances the seething ugliness of the city. On The Island the narrator and his companion, Konrad, triumph over time, regaining the innocent freedom and peaceful silence of childhood.

Throughout the novel Konrad and the narrator are increasingly obsessed with the dream of repeating their trip to The Island. At last, from the hollow emptiness of a weird and terrifying existence, these two, Konrad now pathetically blind, yet filled with new awareness, set out to The Island. Strengthened by the possibilities and hopes of teaching young children at Konrad's school, they return to this place of beauty. Their recognition of responsibility and the impossibility of escape recalls Stein's advice: "In the destructive element immerse." The end of the novel is a beginning, a resolute determination to pursue the dream in spite of the "vast tormented universe" in which they must live. Wading out into the stormy lake, they roar lustily, a gesture of acceptance and approval, a way of defining their presence in the face of emptiness: "So we yell, as loud as we can. The wind dashes the shouts away. They sound feeble in the overall tumult. Now, taking a deep breath against the shock of the icy water, we move forward" (p. 255).

Most recently, Robert Kroetsch's novels seem to defy the existential despair characteristic of contemporary prairie fiction both rural and urban. Kroetsch's anti-heroes are painfully aware of their isolation in a meaningless world running to waste; but they escape their anguish, not in the conventional love affair of Walter Ackroyd, or David Gilpin, nor in the geographical shift of *Erebus*, but through sheer gusto. Kroetsch's prairie men are the inheritors of the stone-picker's simple determination to endure and of Hagar Shipley's unregenerate, saucy humour, but they have an unquenchable exuberance which transcends both.

Johnnie Backstrom, the narrator and protagonist of *The Words of My Roaring* (1966), is, at thirty-three and six foot four, the giant of a man so typical of the prairie novel. Johnnie, the local undertaker, is running against Doctor Murdoch, the incumbent, for a seat in the Alberta legislature. He backs into a rash promise to bring the constituents rain before election day, a promise which in 1935 had particular appeal to drought-stricken electors. Johnnie was a prairie dreamer from the time he "saw all that distance out beyond; . . . that horizon so far away."[35] But the dream and Johnnie's ambition are constantly mocked by the parched, implacable land: "Hope was faltering. . . . The stinkweed was shriveled and small, clinging to life low on the shoulder of the road; even the thistles, Canada and sow, looked stunted. Stunted and mean. The wheat fields themselves seemed to be praying for water, stirring as they did dumbly before a small wind" (p. 181).

In a sense this is a familiar landscape, but Kroetsch's fresh vocabulary and irreverence give it a new complexion. The dry, sterile prairie is no longer simply an effective symbol of an unfulfilling world peopled by hollow men. The prairie has become a joke, a wonderful incongruity.

> All those damned dirt roads running nowhere in straight lines. . . . All those telephone poles with their burden of wire, trying to hold the horizons together.
>
> Or the sky. That was one thing I managed to shut out of my head. Nature can be so damned unnatural. That red Who-er of a sky trying to suck you up into its own cursed hollowness. I could give you a whole damned sermon on that sky. And every day and always the sun, it comes bulging out of the dawn, stunting those few little plants that have somehow overnight peckered up their leaves, their petals, their stems. What a blue-eyed bitch of a country this is (p. 59).

The landscape is bewildering, almost nightmarish: determinedly straight roads leading nowhere; modern communications futilely trying to bridge the great emptiness; the relentless sun torturing man with his impotence. Yet, when the

---

[35]Robert Kroetsch, *The Words of My Roaring* (Toronto: Macmillan, 1966), p. 160.

earth mistress can be recognized as whore and bitch and labelled so, then man is ready to transcend his bond to her. Certainly at moments Johnnie, by his rhetorical gusto or his elaborate dreams, can escape the ties to a brutal land. When he makes love to Helen Murdoch, the enthusiasm of their passion renders totally unimportant the "dry broken grass, and the dust" amidst which they lie.

For Kroetsch, as for Mitchell, the prairie is a landscape of elementals where the primary questions of existence become immediate. For Johnnie Backstrom the question is one of "beginnings and endings. The old confusion." Where and why was I born and why must things die? Johnny is ecstatic when rain finally comes, until his realization: "I had nothing to do with the rain." He is, like Tristram Shandy, merely the sport of small accidents. Control of one's destiny is ultimately illusory: "The dust was settling, I can tell you. But I felt that one hundred yards up ahead of that cloud that chased me, I'd be back in my drought" (p. 193). The climax of the novel, however, does not bring a sudden and permanent change in Johnnie Backstrom. In retrospect, this acknowledgement of his humanity and weakness takes its place with all the other jumbled insights into life which make up Johnnie's narrative. He now knows his exposure, like so many prairie men: "A man my size is a large target for the brute knuckles of existence. I was being pummeled." But he cannot forget his pride and ambition; he is still very weak in the face of temptation. The novel leaves him in a conundrum, perhaps to conclude that "chaos is the only order." Though Johnnie Backstrom is "forever condemned to grope," his natural ebullience transforms the groping into part of his essential vitality.

Like *The Words of My Roaring, The Studhorse Man* (1969) is a novel in which the serious and the touching are nicely balanced by comic zest. *The Studhorse Man* combines the boisterousness of Fielding and the lustiness of Sterne with the madhouse atmosphere of Ken Kesey. Told from within an insane asylum by the eighteen-year-old Demeter Proudfoot, the novel relates Hazard Lepage's travels throughout Alberta in search of the perfect mare to match with his noble stallion, Poseidon. The search for love and perfection is as much Hazard's and Demeter's as it is the stallion's. Hazard sacrifices all to his ultimate purpose, experiencing the worst that the brutal climate can do: "He had travelled bent and freezing against the snows of spring and now he was warm; rain squalls came with thunder to drive him across a treeless prairie and now he was dry; hailstorms knocked at his eyes and set the cannonballs of ice to leaping on the sun-packed roads; mud spattered him brown and gritty black; the wind drove dust into his flesh."[36]

The fantastic extremes of the prairie climate are evoked, yet negated, by the delighted confidence of Demeter's description. Hazard gives up the warmth

[36]Kroetsch, *The Studhorse Man* (Toronto: Macmillan, 1969), p. 58.

and dryness to risk all for the rash, unpredictable, and stubborn forces of sexual attraction: "His only means of livelihood was the white and black dink of that stallion." He is at the mercy not only of equine sexual whims but of his own almost insatiable sexual appetite. The consequence is not comforting—as he faces the elements alone, so in all things is he utterly alone: "He must eat alone, travel alone, work alone, suffer alone, laugh alone, bitch alone, bleed alone, piss alone, sing alone, dream alone— . . ."

Kroetsch's exuberant style is richly humorous, yet beneath the humour is one of the most forceful expressions of human solitude to be found in the Canadian prairie novel. The prairie again provides the image for the meaningless void which hovers at the edge of Hazard's experience. The prospect of a vacuum, of total emptiness, is too real and Hazard seeks escape: "Surely the glare of the sun on snow that had melted in the wheat fields, only to freeze again, was enough to make him seek comfort in the forest: the confrontation with mere space can be so appalling." Apparently, however, the emptiness wins out. Hazard's dream is ended by the stallion in which he had placed total faith. Poseidon's sexual energy is ultimately inverted and commercialized at a Pregnant Mare Urine farm. Man's desire to satisfy his lust ends in sterile oblivion. Or does it? Even near death Hazard has one last glimmer of sexual vitality, impregnating Martha, and leaving behind a beautiful heiress. The answer must lie with the narrator who observes that the world beyond the walls of the institution is as great a madhouse as that within. The "confrontation with mere space," the outlook on a world devoid of expression or purpose leaves man terrified and neurotic.

In *The Studhorse Man* Demeter Proudfoot is quite insane. Yet Demeter's enthusiastic expression of the human quandary points to the artist as the source of some order. If this is the case the order is discovered, not as a replacement for the bewildering world, but from within the welter of paradox and inconclusiveness, a vigorous affirmation of life: "The very process of recurrence is what enables us to learn, to improve, to correct past errors, to understand the present, to guide the generations that are to come. Yet it is precisely this same characteristic of life that makes life unendurable. Men of more experience than I have lamented at the repetitious nature of the ultimate creative act itself" (p. 124).

The knowledge of oneself is in great part acquired from the knowledge of one's place. "The prairie taught me identity by exposing me"[37] affirms Wallace Stegner in acknowledging the influence of landscape. The precise nature of such identity is inevitably difficult to define. It emerges, however, in all its complexity as part of the experience of reading George Ryga, Margaret Laurence, Edward McCourt, Robert Hunter and Gabrielle Roy—these recent writers who represent, collectively, a maturity of interpretation in Canadian prairie fiction. Yet is is particularly appropriate to conclude with Robert Kroetsch, for his

[37]Stegner, *Wolf Willow*, p. 22.

fiction is at once a culmination and an indication of new directions. In the best tradition of Ross and Mitchell, Kroetsch discovers a symbolic richness in an empty vastness which has so often defied the imagination. But further, Kroetsch articulates new comprehension of the prairie landscape, both embracing the destructive nullity of his environment and defying it by a comic ebullience which celebrates man and life. "How do we fit our time and our place?"[38] is the question Kroetsch poses to himself. His fiction has the conviction of the "simple necessity" which he recognizes will dictate his answer.

[38]Kroetsch, "A Conversation with Margaret Laurence," *Creation* (Toronto: New Press, 1970), p. 63.

Epilogue

The pulse of our flesh
beats at your ear-drums
as we caper ungainly
singing out of tune
but singing
after a lonely and menaced
apprenticeship of silence.

PETER STEVENS, "After This Message"

For all its variety, both of quality and theme, the unity of Canadian prairie fiction, if not readily apparent, is, I believe, radical and compelling. Most of its authors show an unusual interest in the physical landscape; their approach to the relationship between man and landscape is usually a variant of the primitive geometric contrast between vertical and horizontal. Prairie man, we have seen, may feel insignificant or immensely self-confident; he may feel free or inescapably trapped; he may be deeply religious or a rebel against all authority; his imagination may be stifled or stimulated. In each case, however, his nature or outlook will be linked to his curiously abrupt position in a vast and uninterrupted landscape. Each of the works discussed is a mosaic of these variations, emphasizing some over others, but often implying most of them.

Mrs. Bentley's one-time thought "that only a great artist could ever paint the prairie, the vacancy and stillness of it, the bare essentials of a landscape, sky and earth"[1] points to a basic problem of the prairie writer. How is he to interpret a landscape that is without sounds and devoid of anything concrete to catch the eye or stimulate the imagination? How does he express the barest elemental constituents which make up his landscape? The artist is faced with the dilemma of man in a world that is hostile, indifferent or, at worst, utterly meaningless. In a sense, of course, this is simply to reiterate that the prairie artist is dealing with universal themes. Yet, by his constantly returning to the physical landscape itself to express the human experience, he is presenting them in a distinctive way. In the best of the Canadian prairie writers, this achievement of universal expression through a consideration of the particular situation of man on the wide land is marked by an enduring sensitivity and power.

Nowhere, perhaps, can the artist's view of man in the prairie be so pithily and suggestively summarized as in a recent article by Buckminster Fuller which makes absolutely no reference to the prairie. From his observation that babies live horizontally for many months before they can stand vertically, he notes

---

[1]Ross, *As For Me and My House*, p. 59.

the basic geometric contrast: "Vertical is objective. Horizontal is subjective, yielding. In extreme, the vertical characterizes life and the horizontal characterizes death."[2] Fuller reminds us that "children learn from birth onward that no one force operating in their lives is so constant, unforgiving and relentless as gravity. Verticality opposes gravity." The inherent parallels between such theorizing and prairie fiction are reinforced when Fuller goes on to explain man's conduct on the sea (the metaphor so often applied to the prairie landscape) by his dramatic awareness of "the multi-fathomed, lethally suffocating depths." The prairie writer, I am sure, is particularly sensitive to these distinctions. They may operate in his unconscious, but they do not limit him—if, in the extreme, the horizontal represents death, it may equally evoke the eternal and infinite.

In a broad sense, however, those authors given major attention in this study demonstrate an increasingly mature willingness to examine the basic opposition to which Fuller gives expression. Although in Stead's generally sanguine view of man's position in the prairie there is little sense of this contrast, it is a strong factor in Grove and the writers who followed him. Grove looks particularly at the physical forces in nature which inevitably dictate the return of the vertical and vital to the horizontal. In the pages of Sinclair Ross the prairie man must deal with other than literal death, with the absence of emotional, intellectual and cultural vitality within his life. Mrs. Bentley yearns in vain for the vertical, the vigorous and positive, in Philip and in Horizon. For W.O. Mitchell, man, from the vantage point of his tentative verticality, contemplates the vast horizontal world and the certainty of death which it, in part, represents. In more recent writers such contemplation becomes the cause of acute anxiety as the possibility of total obliteration and complete absence of meaning, imaged in the horizontal landscape, becomes increasingly immediate.

The continuing interest in the landscape among writers as diverse as John Peter and George Ryga, as eccentric as Robert Hunter, or as ribald as Robert Kroetsch, confirms that Canadian prairie writers find a common denominator in the physical environment. In the midst of "vacancy and stillness" man searches for his significance, seeking to know himself and his landscape. The literary artist, however tentative and inconclusive his vision, provides a sense of that significance. Whatever uncertainty there is, seems, for fictions set on the prairie, to be not inappropriate. The prairie landscape so often proves to be defiantly irreducible—the flat cannot be made flatter, nor the infinite less mysterious. As is usually the case with all forms of art, the cause for excitement lies not in absolute success but in the dimensions 'of the attempt. The prairie writer is, as Peter Stevens describes him,

> singing out of tune
> but singing

[2]R. Buckminster Fuller, "Vertical is to Live—Horizontal is to Die," *American Scholar*, XXXIX (Winter 1969-70), 27.

after a lonely and menaced
apprenticeship of silence.[3]

Unlike the melancholy utterance of the Kirghiz herdsmen, the new song is not a distillation of the landscape but an assertion in its face; while it may still lack harmony, there is in the midst of the prairie silence a voice distinctive and rich in meaning. The prairie writer, and certainly his reader, can now concur with Wallace Stegner's ambiguous assessment of his prairie home: "I may not know who I am, but I know where I am from."[4]

[3]Stevens, *Nothing But Spoons.*
[4]Stegner, *Wolf Willow*, p. 23.

SELECTED BIBLIOGRAPHY

Listed here are the most significant primary sources upon which this study is based, and a selection of the most relevant, or useful, of the secondary sources.

PRIMARY SOURCES:

Beynon, Frances. *Aleta Day*. London: Daniel, 1919.

Bindloss, Harold. *Ranching for Sylvia*. New York: A.L. Burt, 1913.

Bowering, George. *Rocky Mountain Foot: A Lyric, A Memoir*. Toronto: McClelland and Stewart, 1968.

Eggleston, Wilfrid. *The High Plains*. Toronto: Macmillan, 1938.

Forer, Mort. *The Humback*. Toronto: McClelland and Stewart, 1969.

Fraser, William Alexander. *Bulldog Carney*. Toronto: McClelland and Stewart, 1919.

Gill, Rev. Edward Anthony Wharton. *Love in Manitoba*. Toronto: Musson, 1912.

Gordon, Rev. Charles William. (Ralph Connor, pseud.). *Black Rock: A Tale of the Selkirks*. Toronto: Westminster, 1898.

_____ *The Sky Pilot*. Toronto: Westminster, 1905.

Grayson, Ethel Kirk. *Willow Smoke*. New York: Harold Vinal, 1928.

Grove, Frederick Philip. "Apologia pro Vita et Opere Sua." *Canadian Forum*, XI (August 1930), 420-22.

_____ "Democracy and Education." *University of Toronto Quarterly*, XII (July 1943), 389-402.

_____ *Fruits of the Earth*. Introduction by M.G. Parks. Toronto: McClelland and Stewart, New Canadian Library No. 49, 1965.

_____ *In Search of Myself*. Toronto: Macmillan, 1946.

_____ "In Search of Myself." *University of Toronto Quarterly*, X (October 1940), 60-67.

_____ *It Needs To Be Said*. Toronto: Macmillan, 1929.

_____ *Our Daily Bread*. New York: Macmillan, 1928.

_____ *Over Prairie Trails*. Introduction by Malcolm Ross. Toronto: McClelland and Stewart, New Canadian Library No. 1, 1957.

_____ "The Plight of Canadian Fiction? A Reply." *University of Toronto Quarterly*, VII (July 1938), 451-67.

_____ "A Postscript to *A Search For America*." *Queen's Quarterly*, XLIX (Autumn 1942), 197-213.

_____ *A Search For America*. Ottawa: Graphic, 1927.

_____ *Settlers of the Marsh*. Introduction by Thomas Saunders. Toronto: McClelland and Stewart, New Canadian Library No. 50, 1966.

_____ *Tales from the Margin: The Selected Stories of Frederick Philip Grove*. Edited by Desmond Pacey. Toronto: McGraw-Hill Ryerson, 1971.

_____ *The Turn of the Year*. Toronto: McClelland and Stewart, 1923.

_____ *The Yoke of Life*. Toronto: Macmillan, 1930.

Hiebert, Paul. "The Comic Spirit at Forty Below Zero." *Mosaic,* III (Spring 1970), 58-68.

Hiemstra, Mary. *Gully Farm*. Toronto: McClelland and Stewart, Canadian Best Seller Library, 1966.

Hunter, Robert. *Erebus*. Toronto: McClelland and Stewart, 1968.

Kreisel, Henry. *The Betrayal*. Toronto: McClelland and Stewart, 1964.

_____ "The Broken Globe," in Martha Foley and David Burnett, eds., *The Best American Short Stories 1966*. Boston: Houghton Mifflin, 1966.

Kroetsch, Robert. *The Studhorse Man*. Toronto: Macmillan, 1969.

_____ *The Words of My Roaring*. Toronto: Macmillan, 1966.

Laurence, Margaret. *A Bird in the House*. Toronto: McClelland and Stewart, 1970.

_____ *The Fire Dwellers*. Toronto: McClelland and Stewart, 1969.

_____ *A Jest of God*. Toronto: McClelland and Stewart, 1966.

_____ "Sources." *Mosaic*, III (Spring 1970), 80-84.

_____ *The Stone Angel*. Toronto: McClelland and Stewart, 1964.

Lewis, Sinclair. *Main Street: The Story of Carol Kennicott*. New York: Grosset and Dunlap, 1920.

Livesay, Dorothy. "A Prairie Sampler." *Mosaic*, III (Spring 1970), 85-92.

Ludwig, Jack Barry. *Above Ground*. Boston: Little, Brown, 1968.

_____ "You Always Go Home Again." *Mosaic*, III (Spring 1970), 107-111.

McClung, Nellie Letitia (Mooney). *The Black Creek Stopping House and Other Stories*. Toronto: William Briggs, 1912.

_____ *Clearing in the West*. Toronto: Thomas Allen, 1935.

_____ *Sowing Seeds in Danny*. New York: Doubleday, 1908.

_____ *The Stream Runs Fast: My Own Story*. Toronto: Thomas Allen, 1965.

McCourt, Edward Alexander. *Fasting Friar*. Toronto: McClelland and Stewart, 1963.

_____ *Home is the Stranger*. Toronto: Macmillan, 1950.

_____ *Music at the Close*. Introduction by Allan Bevan. Toronto: McClelland and Stewart, New Canadian Library No. 52, 1966.

_____ *Saskatchewan*. Toronto: Macmillan, 1968.

_____ *Walk Through the Valley*. Toronto: McClelland and Stewart, 1959.

_____ *The Wooden Sword*. Toronto: McClelland and Stewart, 1956.

McDougall, E. Jean (Jane Rolyat, pseud.). *The Lily of Fort Garry*. London: Dent, 1930.

_____ *Wilderness Walls*. London: Dent, 1933.

Maclean, John. *The Warden of the Plains and Other Stories of Life in the Canadian North-West*. Illustrated by J E. Laughlin. Toronto: William Briggs, 1896.

Marlyn, John. *Under the Ribs of Death*. Introduction by Eli Mandel. Toronto: McClelland and Stewart, New Canadian Library No. 41, 1964.

Mitchell, William Ormond. *Jake and the Kid*. Toronto: Macmillan, 1961.

_____ *The Kite*. Toronto: Macmillan, 1962.

_____ *Who Has Seen the Wind*. Toronto: Macmillan, 1947.

Newlove, John. *Black Night Window*. Toronto: McClelland and Stewart, 1968.

_____ *Moving In Alone*. Toronto: Contact Press, 1965.

Niven, Frederick. *The Flying Years*. London: Collins, 1935.

_____ *Mine Inheritance*. London: Collins, 1940.

_____ *The Transplanted*. Toronto: Collins, 1944.

Ostenso, Martha. *In a Far Land*. New York: Seltzer, 1924.

_____ *Wild Geese*. New York: Grosset and Dunlap, 1925.

_____ *Wild Geese*. Introduction by Carlyle King. Toronto: McClelland and Stewart, New Canadian Library No. 18, 1961.

Parker, Gilbert. *Pierre and His People: Tales of the Far North*. London: Methuen, 1892.

Parsons, Nell W. *The Curlew Cried: A Love Story of the Canadian Prairie*. Seattle: Frank McCaffrey, 1947.

Peter, John. *Take Hands at Winter*. Garden City: Doubleday, 1967.

Ross, Sinclair. *As For Me and My House*. Introduction by Roy Daniells. Toronto: McClelland and Stewart, New Canadian Library No. 4, 1957.

_____ "A Day with Pegasus." *Queen's Quarterly*, XLV (Summer 1938), 141-56.

_____ *The Lamp at Noon and Other Stories*. Introduction by Margaret Laurence. Toronto: McClelland and Stewart, New Canadian Library No. 62, 1968.

_____ "On Looking Back." *Mosaic*, III (Spring 1970), 93-94.

_____ "Saturday Night." *Queen's Quarterly*, LVIII (Autumn 1951), 387-400.

_____ *The Well*. Toronto: Macmillan, 1958.

Roy, Gabrielle. *La Route d'Altamont*. Montréal: Editions HMH, 1966.

_____ *Rue Deschambault*. Montréal: Beauchemin, 1966.

_____ "Mon Heritage du Manitoba." *Mosaic*, III (Spring 1970), 69-79.

Ryga, George. *Ballad of a Stone-picker*. Toronto: Macmillan, 1966.

_____ *The Hungry Hills*. Toronto: Longmans, 1963.

Salverson, Laura G. *Confessions of an Immigrant's Daughter*. London: Faber, 1939.

_____ *The Dark Weaver*. Toronto: Ryerson, 1937.

_____ *The Viking Heart*. Toronto: McClelland and Stewart, 1923.

Saunders, Thomas. *Horizontal World*. Toronto: Ryerson, 1951.

——————— *Red River of the North and Other Poems of Manitoba*. Illustrations by George Swinton. Winnipeg: Peguis, 1969.

Stead, Robert J.C. *The Bail Jumper*. Toronto: William Briggs, 1914.

——————— *The Cowpuncher*. New York: Harper, 1918.

——————— *Dennison Grant*. Toronto: Musson, 1920.

——————— *The Empire Builders and Other Poems*. Toronto: William Briggs, 1908.

——————— *Grain*. Introduction by Thomas Saunders. Toronto: McClelland and Stewart, New Canadian Library No. 36, 1963.

——————— *The Homesteaders: A Novel of the Canadian West*. London: Unwin, 1916.

——————— *Neighbours*. Toronto: Hodder, 1922.

——————— *The Smoking Flax*. Toronto: McClelland and Stewart, 1924.

——————— *Songs of the Prairie*. New York: Platt and Peck, 1912.

Stegner, Wallace. *Wolf Willow: A History, a Story, and a Memory of the Last Plains Frontier*. New York: Viking Press, Compass Edition, 1966.

Stevens, Peter. *Nothing But Spoons*. Montreal: Delta Canada, 1969.

Stringer, A. J. *The Mud Lark*. Indianapolis: Bobbs-Merrill, 1931.

——————— *Prairie Stories*. New York: A.L. Burt, 1936. Incorporates *The Prairie Wife* (1915), *The Prairie Mother* (1920), and *The Prairie Child* (1922).

Tegart, W.A.S. *In the Face of the Winds*. Saskatoon: Modern Press, 1962.

Trotter, Beecham. *A Horseman and the West*. Toronto: Macmillan, 1925.

van der Mark, Christine. *Honey in the Rock*. Toronto: McClelland and Stewart, 1966.

Wiebe, Rudy, ed. *Stories from Western Canada*. Toronto: Macmillan, 1972.

Wiseman, Adele. "A Brief Anatomy of an Honest Attempt at a Pithy Statement about the Impact of the Manitoba Environment on my Development as an Artist." *Mosaic*, III (Spring 1970), 98-106.

——————— *The Sacrifice*. Toronto: Macmillan, Laurentian Library, 1968.

SECONDARY SOURCES:

Addison, Joseph. Number 412. *The Spectator*. Vol. III. Edited by Donald F. Bond. Oxford: The Clarendon Press, 1965.

Baldwin, R.G. "Pattern in the Novels of Edward McCourt." *Queen's Quarterly*, LXVIII (Winter 1962), 574-87.

Barclay, Patricia. "Regionalism and the Writer: A Talk with W.O. Mitchell." *Canadian Literature*, No. 14 (Autumn 1962), 53-56.

Bentley, Phyllis. *The English Regional Novel*. London: Allen and Unwin, 1941.

Berger, Carl. "The True North Strong and Free." *Nationalism in Canada*. Edited by Peter Russell. University League for Social Reform. Toronto: McGraw-Hill, 1966.

Bloore, Ronald L. "The Prairies: 'to assert man's presence.'" *Arts Canada,* XXVI (December 1969), 24-29.

Brooks, Cleanth. *William Faulkner: The Yoknapatawpha Country.* New Haven: Yale University Press, 1963.

Burnet, Jean. *Next-year Country: A Study of Rural Social Organization in Alberta.* Toronto: University of Toronto Press, 1951.

Cameron, Doris Margaret. "Puritanism in Canadian Prairie Fiction." Unpublished M.A. thesis, University of British Columbia, 1966.

Clark, Kenneth. *Landscape into Art.* Boston: Beacon Press, 1961.

Clough, Wilson O. *The Necessary Earth: Nature and Solitude in American Literature.* Austin: University of Texas Press, 1964.

Collin, W.E. *The White Savannahs.* Toronto: Macmillan, 1936.

Daniells, Roy. "Literature: Poetry and the Novel." *The Culture of Contemporary Canada.* Edited by Julian Park. Ithaca: Cornell University Press, 1957.

Eggleston, Wilfrid. "Canadian Geography and National Culture." *Canadian Geographical Journal,* XLIII (December 1951), 254-73.

_____ "Frederick Philip Grove." *Our Living Tradition: Seven Canadians.* Edited by Claude T. Bissell. Toronto: University of Toronto Press, 1957.

_____ *The Frontier and Canadian Letters.* Toronto: Ryerson, 1957.

Elder, A.T. "Western Panorama: Settings and Themes in Robert J.C. Stead." *Canadian Literature,* XVII (Summer 1963), 44-56.

Folsom, James K. *The American Western Novel.* New Haven: College and University Press, 1966.

Frye, Northrop. *The Bush Garden: Essays on the Canadian Imagination.* Toronto: Anansi, 1971.

Fuller, R. Buckminster. "Vertical is to Live—Horizontal is to Die." *American Scholar,* XXXIX (Winter 1969-1970), 27-47.

Fussell, Edwin. *Frontier: American Literature and the American West.* Princeton: Princeton University Press, 1965.

Graham, Neil. "Theme and Form in the Novels of Edward A. McCourt." Unpublished M.A. thesis, University of Windsor, 1968.

Greene, Donald. "Western Canadian Literature." *Western American Literature,* II (1968), 257-80.

Harris, Cole. "The Myth of the Land in Canadian Nationalism." *Nationalism in Canada.* Edited by Peter Russell. University League for Social Reform. Toronto: McGraw-Hill, 1966.

Jackel, Susan. "The House on the Prairies." *Canadian Literature,* No. 42 (Autumn 1969), 46-55.

Jones, D.G. *Butterfly on Rock: A Study of Themes and Images in Canadian Literature.* Toronto: University of Toronto Press, 1970.

Klinck, Carl F., general ed. *Literary History of Canada: Canadian Literature in English.* Toronto: University of Toronto Press, 1965.

Kline, Marcia B. *Beyond the Land Itself: Views of Nature in Canada and the United States*. Cambridge: Harvard University Press, 1970.

Kreisel, Henry. "The Prairie: A State of Mind." *Proceedings and Transactions of the Royal Society of Canada*. Fourth Series: Vol. VI, June, 1968. Ottawa: The Royal Society of Canada. Reprinted. *Contexts of Canadian Criticism*. Edited by Eli Mandel. Chicago: University of Chicago Press, 1971, pp. 254-66.

Lawrence, D.H. *Selected Literary Criticism*. Edited by Anthony Beal. Compass Books Edition. New York: Viking Press, 1966.

Lee, Robert Edson. *From West to East: Studies in the Literature of the American West*. Urbana: University of Illinois Press, 1966.

Liddell, Robert. *A Treatise on the Novel*. London: Jonathan Cape, 1947.

Lynen, John F. *The Pastoral Art of Robert Frost*. New Haven: Yale University Press, 1960.

McCourt, Edward A. *The Canadian West in Fiction*. Revised edition. Toronto: Ryerson, 1970. (Original edition published 1949).

McMullin, Stanley Edward. "The Promised Land Motif in the Works of Frederick Philip Grove." Unpublished M.A. thesis, Carleton University, 1968.

Marx, Leo. *The Machine in the Garden: Technology and the Pastoral Ideal in America*. New York: Oxford University Press, 1967.

Meyer, Roy W. *The Middle Western Farm Novel in the Twentieth Century*. Lincoln: University of Nebraska Press, 1965.

Miller, Perry. *Nature's Nation*. Cambridge: Harvard University Press, 1967.

Morton, W.L. *Manitoba: A History*. 2nd ed. Toronto: University of Toronto Press, 1967.

Nash, Roderick. *Wilderness and the American Mind*. New Haven: Yale University Press, 1967.

Nesbitt, Bruce H. "The Seasons: Grove's Unfinished Novel." *Canadian Literature*, No. 3 (Winter 1960), 17-22.

New, William H. "A Feeling of Completion: Aspects of W.O. Mitchell." *Canadian Literature*, No. 17 (Summer 1963), 22-33.

_____ "Sinclair Ross's Ambivalent World." *Canadian Literature*, No. 40 (Spring 1969), 26-32.

Pacey, Desmond. *Frederick Philip Grove*. Toronto: Ryerson, 1945.

Pizer, Donald. *Realism and Naturalism in Nineteenth-Century American Literature*. Carbondale: Southern Illinois University Press, 1966.

Read, S.E. "The Maze of Life: The Work of Margaret Laurence." *Canadian Literature*, No. 27 (Winter 1966), 5-14.

Rogers, Linda Jane. "Environment and the Quest Motif in Selected Works of Canadian Prairie Fiction." Unpublished M.A. thesis, University of British Columbia, 1970.

Ross, Malcolm, ed. *Our Sense of Identity*. Toronto: Ryerson, 1954.

Scholes, Robert, ed. *Approaches to the Novel: Materials for a Poetics*. San Francisco: Chandler, 1961.

Shepard, Paul. *Man in the Landscape: A Historic View of the Esthetics of Nature*. New York: Alfred A. Knopf, 1967.

Smith, Henry Nash. *Virgin Land*. Cambridge: Harvard University Press, 1950.

Spettigue, Douglas O. *Frederick Philip Grove*. Studies in Canadian Literature, Number 3. Toronto: Copp Clark, 1969.

_____ "Frederick Philip Grove in Manitoba." *Mosaic*, III (Spring 1970), 19-33.

_____ "The Grove Enigma Resolved." *Queen's Quarterly*, LXXIX (Spring 1972), 1-2.

Stephens, Donald. "Wind, Sun and Dust." *Canadian Literature*, No. 23 (Winter 1965), 17-24.

Stevick, Philip, ed. *The Theory of the Novel*. New York: The Free Press, 1967.

Story, Norah. *The Oxford Companion to Canadian History and Literature*. Toronto: Oxford University Press, 1967.

Tallman, Warren. "Wolf in the Snow: Part One, Four Windows on Two Landscapes." *Canadian Literature*, No. 5 (Summer 1970), 7-20.

_____ "Wolf in the Snow: Part Two, The House Repossessed." *Canadian Literature*, No. 6 (Autumn 1960), 41-48.

Warkentin, John, ed. *The Western Interior of Canada: A Record of Geographical Discovery 1612-1917*. The Carleton Library, Number 15. Toronto: McClelland and Stewart, 1964.

Warwick, Jack. *The Long Journey: Literary Themes of Franch Canada*. University of Toronto Romance Series, 12. Toronto: University of Toronto Press, 1968.

Watson, J. Wreford. "The Role of Illusion in North American Geography: A Note on the Geography of North American Settlement." *The Canadian Geographer/Le Géographe Canadien*, XIII (Spring 1969), 10-27.

Watt, Frank W. "Western Myth, the World of Ralph Connor." *Canadian Literature*, No. 1 (Summer 1959), 26-36.

_____ "Nationalism in Canadian Literature." *Nationalism in Canada*. Edited by Peter Russell. University League for Social Reform. Toronto: McGraw-Hill, 1966.

Welty, Eudora. "Place in Fiction." *Critical Approaches to Fiction*. Edited by Shiv K. Kumar and Keith McKean. New York: McGraw-Hill, 1968.

Wilson, Edmund. *O Canada, An American's Notes on Canadian Culture*. New York: Farrar, Straus and Giroux, 1965.

Woodcock, George, ed. *A Choice of Critics: Selections from Canadian Literature*. Toronto: Oxford University Press, 1966.

INDEX

Principal references are printed in boldface type.